With You by Bike

WITH YOU BY BIKE

One Couple's Life-Changing Journey around the World

By Katrina Rosen

RMB

For information on purchasing bulk quantities of this book, or to obtain media excerpts or
invite the author to speak at an event, please visit rmbooks.com and select the "Contact" tab.

RMB | Rocky Mountain Books Ltd.

rmbooks.com

@rmbooks

facebook.com/rmbooks

Cataloguing data available from Library and Archives Canada

ISBN 9781771603157 (paperback)

ISBN 9781771603164 (electronic)

Printed and bound in Canada by Houghton Boston

We would like to also take this opportunity to acknowledge the traditional territories upon
which we live and work. In Calgary, Alberta, we acknowledge the Niitsitapi (Blackfoot)
and the people of the Treaty 7 region in Southern Alberta, which includes the Siksika, the
Piikuni, the Kainai, the Tsuut'ina and the Stoney Nakoda First Nations, including Chiniki,
Bearpaw, and Wesley First Nations. The City of Calgary is also home to Métis Nation
of Alberta, Region III. In Victoria, British Columbia, we acknowledge the traditional
territories of the Lkwungen (Esquimalt, and Songhees), Malahat, Pacheedaht, Scia'new,
T'Sou-ke and W̱SÁNEĆ (Pauquachin, Tsartlip, Tsawout, Tseycum) peoples.

We acknowledge the financial support of the Government of Canada through the Canada
Book Fund and the Canada Council for the Arts, and of the province of British Columbia
through the British Columbia Arts Council and the Book Publishing Tax Credit.

For Mike

CONTENTS

AUTHOR'S NOTE

In order to live an inspiring, bright life, one must chase after dreams. Wake up, shed fear, make space, do whatever needs to be done to push hard to get out of that comfort zone.

It would have been much easier not to write this book. Never mind that – it would've been so much simpler if I hadn't lived this book! I could have hidden the first few chapters away, but then you wouldn't have the full story. I decided to be brave and put myself out there. So here's my disclaimer.

We all have our own paths; our own journeys and dark nights. I don't want to live with a pile of papers and regret never letting others read them, the same way I don't want to live regretting the choices I made. This was very therapeutic to write and, I hope, is an enjoyable read. I'd encourage anyone to give it a go and share your story with the world. How lucky am I to do so? And what an adventure we went on…

Here's to no regrets, accepting ourselves and all our flaws and living life to the fullest.

Lots of love,
Katrina

CHAPTER 1

HOME
Make or Break

Summer heat poured through the window, but I was shivering. Curled up at the end of our couch, I pulled my feet closer, hugging myself. My head was stuck, staring at a spot on our hardwood floor stained blue from a carpet we bought in Morocco together, years ago.

"Mike, do you want to bike around the world?" The words sounded ridiculous. Wrenched free from somewhere deep inside me. Now there they were.

I didn't look at my husband. I didn't know if he understood how serious my question was.

To leave everything and go cycling.

The idea hadn't been forming for long, but, once it started, I couldn't let it go. To take off with Mike and travel. To explore – each other and the world, wherever our wheels would take us. Hopefully, far, far away. To places we had never been, never even imagined. But now I was. I dreamt of long days of movement that would squash my problems with the spin of the tires. We could ride on gravel or dirt track, feel the crinkles and waves of the land before making camp whenever we felt done for the day. I wanted to watch the earth sink into the stars as we held deep conversations and steaming mugs of hot chocolate. No goal, no time limit.

For me, the idea wasn't far-fetched. I was an adventure athlete and was used to multi-day trips. It wasn't even far-fetched that the two of us could do it together. The only absurdity was the timing. The last time Mike and I had talked, really talked, was nine months earlier, when I had blurted out that I wanted a divorce.

But I had thought this bike trip through as well as I could and had concluded that it was the best decision for us. *The only decision for us.* This was the first time I'd asked Mike about it, and I wasn't sure if he'd heard me because he didn't reply.

"Mike, will you bike around the world with me?" I asked again, and this time I turned to look at him.

Mike sat at the other end of the couch, wearing a shirt I had brought home for him from one of my adventure races and his favourite blue surfer shorts we'd bought in Brazil nearly a decade earlier. His long legs stretched onto the ottoman he had upholstered, the rest of him relaxed into his worn spot on the couch. Stinky black socks were piled nearby, I noticed.

As he often was, he had been immersed in a television show, but now he reached for the remote and pressed pause. He leaned back more and brushed his hand across his forehead and through his hair. I wasn't used to that movement. His brown hair, which he had kept shaved for most of our 11 years together, now grew long, making him look a little more erratic than his steady self. With a tilt of his head in my direction, deep-set blue eyes quickly took me in, but, in that split second, I could see many thoughts were going through his head. Fair enough.

Mike and I had been together since we were 18. We had backpacked through Central and South America and travelled around Europe in a dizzying depth of love. I remember cuddling on single beds and in leaky tents, thinking there was no one else for me. It took him years to propose and I tried not to push him. Mike needs to be sure of decisions, but at the time I worried it would never happen. He asked when we were high upon a chairlift, our snowboards dangling from our boots as we soared up the snow-filled Rocky Mountains. I felt like I was floating in bliss. Although I thought he was crazy to take off our gloves in that frigid air, my heart raced with excitement. And then he slipped a diamond on my finger. A moment suspended in time, frozen in the peaks.

We married that summer and bought our first small house, only ten minutes away from where we grew up. When I was younger, and imagined what my marriage was going to be like, I envisioned we would do everything with each other, just like my parents. We'd share the same best friends, the same hobbies, the same world. Life would be simple and carefree as I cruised along with my soulmate.

For a while it was.

Yet, somewhere after the travel and the house purchase, we fell apart. My adventure racing took me further and further away while Mike stayed home. Or I'd come home late at night from an outdoor pursuit only to be out again by six in the morning to head to the gym. Mike worked, played golf or hockey, and hung out with his friends. He never asked me to go on a date or to stay home with him, and I'd given up on planning things. Mike proved to be incredibly supportive. He supported me in whatever I wanted to do, a new goal, a new race, as long as I didn't make him join me. So I didn't. And, eventually, I stopped asking him to come along. Every time I left, it was with his encouragement, but, every time I walked out the door, we grew further apart.

Drifting apart occurred so slowly that we didn't see it happening. Before we knew it, our relationship had become fragile. Damaged like forgotten house plants no one had watered: brittle, broken and nearly dead.

I loved Mike. My problem was I was not *in* love with Mike and, I'm sure if I pressured him to answer the question truthfully, he would say the same. I certainly didn't feel he was in love with me. We had become acquaintances instead of lovers.

I had tried to explain to Mike all that happened in an adventure race. What it feels like to ride a mountain bike so fast your eyes water and tears stream down your face, knuckles burning from controlling the handlebars and legs shaking from exertion. The thrill of being enveloped in a sea kayak for hours while the ocean creates turmoil around you. The panic of losing sight of teammates as swells go up and down and not having a single break for the better part of a day due to the constant fear of tipping over into freezing water.

Unfortunately, explaining my experiences to my husband was not the same as doing it together. I wanted him to be with me. I wanted to do things with him, but, before long, we ran out of things we enjoyed doing together. He was no longer the person I felt closest to.

Discovering that the reality of marriage did not live up to my fantasies came as a surprise. And the biggest shock – that a good relationship took work – disabled me. I was not enjoying our marriage. I did not want to change. I did not want my husband to have to change for me. Yet the distance had spread too far. *Something* needed to change.

Mike dropped his feet to the floor and finally spoke. "Well, we could certainly start…" His words trailed off, as they often did. I needed a few minutes to register that he'd agreed, had said yes. My eyes focused again on the stained hardwood. Mike slid close to me and took hold of my hand. He gave it a squeeze and I'm not sure how long we just sat there, but I became lost in thoughts, remembering when I'd smacked hard into my rock bottom.

It had been another weekend away without Mike. For hours, on the long drive home, tears rolled down my face. The reality of my situation flooded my vision. Peering through the windshield of the car that night was like trying to see while swimming at the bottom of an ocean without goggles. It was impossible.

I am in love with someone else.

When I finally slammed the car into park in the driveway, I cried harder. Weeping, I couldn't find the strength to even open the door. I never wanted it – I hadn't sought love out. I had fought against the feelings that developed for my co-worker, fellow adventure racer and, unfortunately, best friend. But there they were. I was in love with someone else. Mike already knew. Perhaps he knew it before I did.

Mike hadn't left me and I hadn't left him. For nine months, we were paralyzed in place. Waiting for something to happen without either of us knowing what that should be. *Should we move on together, or figure out how to move on apart?* But, on that drive, I realized I was sick of not being close to Mike, sick to my stomach that there was nothing we did together. We didn't even watch movies together anymore, and I couldn't remember the last time he'd asked me to come to his hockey game. I was disgusted that my marriage was failing. And so, so sad.

Mike wasn't home and I went to bed alone. Again. In the morning, the sadness had consumed me. It was a Sunday and I was about to head out ice climbing. My head was pounding, as though the axe I was going to smash into the wall of ice was pummelling me instead. I sat on the stool at our kitchen table. Mike poured me a cup of coffee and brought it to me in my "Life Is Good" mug. He took a tentative seat on the other stool and I had a sip of coffee. Then I threw off the cloak of sadness and exploded. "I cannot do this anymore! I can't! This isn't what our relationship should be like. I wanted you to be my *everything*, but you're not and you don't seem like you want to be."

I paused. I could hear the voice of a friend who celebrated 60 years with her husband: *You will fall in and out of love multiple times, but the secret to longevity is staying in it. Not giving up.*

"I think we're done." That last sentence came out so definitive. Boom.

Then I slumped, my burst of energy gone, nearly slipping off the stool and under the table. My shoulders shook and I had no control over them. I wished I felt numb, but instead I felt everything: pain, hurt, sadness, the emotion of being with someone for 11 years and then facing a goodbye.

"I think we should get a divorce." My words came out heavy, in a whisper between sobs. My entire body vibrated with heartbreak.

Mike's eyes widened, his mouth lay taut in a hard line. I had clearly upset him and caught him off guard. Nevertheless, his one-word answer shocked me.

"No."

"What do you mean, no? Why do you want to live like this?" In defeat, I threw my hands up in the air, taking in our newly renovated kitchen. New backsplash, mango-coloured walls and perfectly placed spotlights. The kitchen we had started together but Mike completed while I was away.

"You're not happy, I'm not happy. How long are we going to work on this marriage?" I asked. "How long until we call it quits? How long?"

We never fought. Mike has never seen the point in fighting. Even when I'm in the mood for an argument, he won't give me one. He is always calm. Beautifully and frustratingly calm. Mike's chest rose and fell with a big sigh. He stood in front of me and put his large hands on my shoulders to stop my trembling.

"Kat, we are going to work on this forever."

Mike's words clunked around my brain like an old bicycle bottom bracket. Functionally rotating yet in desperate need of maintenance. Coming out of my minor trance on the edge of the couch, I reached over to turn on the lamp, bringing light to the warm evening. I felt a bubble of hope. He said yes to the bike trip! But I also felt scared. Terrified. I needed to leave the city. I wanted to get as far away as possible. I wanted a new life, new friends, new adventures. Mostly I wanted a new us. But I didn't know what any of that would look like.

"You'll have to leave your job," I said. I raised my eyebrows, making the statement a question. He worked at an engineering company as a project manager with a great team of people. He loved his job.

"Okay," he said.

"And I want to go really soon. We can't think about this decision anymore. I believe it's time to go, and if we're going to do it, let's do it! What would we be waiting around for? We need to do this together." I paused, bringing my hands up to my head to rub my temples. Trying to rid myself of negative thoughts, like we couldn't pull this off.

"Maybe this is a drastic decision," I said.

"No, it's a good decision. We love to travel together." His eyes brightened a little. "Does this mean I get to buy my own bike?"

Some of the tension left my body as I laughed. I had my race bikes and, though Mike always supported me, he had never bought a bike of his own, contenting himself with my old bikes when I asked him to ride.

"Yes, you should totally have a new bike." I stood up, tapping his leg as I walked by into the kitchen to grab something to drink. As I opened the fridge door, Mike came up behind me and wrapped his arms around my waist. He pulled me close and pressed his chest against my back to snuggle his face into the crook of my neck. He rarely did this, but he knew I loved it because I had once told him it made me feel like a movie star.

He whispered in my ear, "It will be all right, you know."

It was my turn to say, "Okay."

The truth was, I wasn't convinced.

CHAPTER 2

MANITOBA

Switching Gears

"What are people going to think?" I asked my sister, Michelle, who was peering through the glass of her oven door.

"It doesn't matter. Seriously, stop worrying about what everyone else thinks. You are not everyone else." My younger sister is always direct and to the point. It's one of her qualities people are drawn to, but a risk if you don't want the truth. She doesn't waste time and energy in trying to be polite.

"You and Mike have your own relationship, and no one else can tell you how to do it. I know you didn't mean to hurt Mike, but crap happens." She turned and made sure I was looking at her. "Open your eyes, Kat, lots of people have problems and their own issues. Don't be so sensitive."

She pulled a cake out of the oven while I studied her. *How did she get all the kick-ass genes?* I thought. If I weren't so upset, I would have laughed. She made sense though. I'd always been vulnerable to what other people think. I scooped up my nieces and nephews' toys from a chair and sat down.

"Listen," Michelle said, as she placed the warm chocolate cake on the table. "Mike wants to stay with you for a reason. Mostly because he's incredible, but seriously, you are too. You're worth fighting for and Mike knows that." She took off her oversized oven mitts and pulled me up into a hug. "I'm going to miss you though."

"Now look who's sensitive!" I teased, grateful for her support.

My friend Eleasha was gentler in her approach but just as powerful. I called her on my cell and walked through the park near our house while we talked.

"Katrina, life is not simple. We change and we grow. The two of you have been a couple since you were 18! You were only babies then. Of course, you have become something different; you have been moving in different directions for years, but you have something special together too and you will remember what it is soon."

"But what if we don't?" I asked.

"It's not for nothing. You'll see. I've known you two since you began dating." It was true. She had. We had also met Eleasha in France when we were 21 years old, where she had seen first-hand how well Mike and I travel together. We'd been teaching ourselves to snowboard by spending the winter in Europe. After paying for a lift ticket, we were too broke for food, so Mike would make popcorn and open a can of fruit for dinner, and we'd enjoy long evenings playing cards. I remember spending days strolling through beautiful historic towns more in awe of each other than our surroundings. "You were so in love then," Eleasha said. "I believe in the two of you."

After that loaded question to Mike came out of my mouth, we decided to leave quickly, setting our departure date for September 15.

Many who wander take months, or even years, to plan. The excitement alone of planning a trip may be worth delaying the departure date. To spread maps across dining room tables, read books about distant lands, wrap tongues around the shapes of new languages and learn about different cultures far afield. The anticipation is part of the fun. It would be great to take the time to plan an extensive adventure, but I didn't think our relationship could afford the luxury of prolonging a drastic change. I reasoned the longer we stayed at home, the more we put ourselves in situations that moved us further apart. So September 15 it was.

The date made us commit. It gave us six weeks to get ready. Six weeks to finish a multitude of tasks we needed to complete before we could leave. Six weeks to find enough money. Six weeks to organize gear, and six weeks to decide where to go.

Six weeks to change the direction of our marriage.

First, we needed money. This, surprisingly, was easier to find than I first thought. When Mike and I had married, we bought ourselves a fixer-upper house for $69,000. Luckily, the housing market in Winnipeg, our home city, had gone up. We took out enough money from the mortgage to sustain us for a year on a minimal budget. We rented our home to a friend, cancelled our cable and phone contracts and secured travel insurance.

Second, we made an appointment with a doctor to get the shots we needed for travel. "So let me get this straight," the travel doctor said, studying the two of us sitting antsy in her office. "You would like to get immunizations, but you're not sure where in the world you're going?" She pulled down the mask covering her mouth to smile.

"Yes, well…I don't think we'll go to Africa," I said, looking over at Mike. "Unless, you want to go to Africa?"

"Not right away, so let's take that out. What shots do we need to travel in Asia?" Mike asked.

He offered his arm to the doctor, and we began a full round of immunizations, including polio, hepatitis A and B, tetanus and typhoid fever.

Third, we began to spend our evenings at a local bike shop with our friend and bike mechanic, Craig. I initially wanted to use the mountain bike I raced on, but Craig convinced us it would be difficult finding parts to maintain and fix a high-end bike in remote areas around the world. In the end, we chose simple, inexpensive, aluminum-frame, front-suspension, Trek 4500 hardtail mountain bikes that we could fix in most countries. Craig hand-built new wheel sets for both bikes, picking quality hubs and spokes, as well as stronger rims. Mike researched racks to fit on the front and back of our bikes to carry our panniers, since not all racks can attach onto bikes with suspension. We wanted bikes with front suspension to take pressure off our bodies when cruising over bumps and potholes by absorbing a lot of the impact within the bike, rather than within our arms, wrists and hands. Our new bikes were ready for gravel and backcountry roads.

Fourth, we quit our jobs. Mike's company threw him a party, wishing him well. Leaving my work was more complicated. For eight years, I had worked at an outdoor specialty store with my close friends. I considered it somewhat of an art to mold the perfect backpack, and I loved to assist our customers in getting ready for travel or adventures in the wilderness. Handing in my resignation letter to my best friend nearly broke me, the words in it filled with angst and pain.

But I had to pull myself together and use my training to create a list of everything Mike and I needed to take with us. The main difference between my customers and us was that most of them knew where they were going. How do you begin to prepare for an adventure when you have no idea what you're doing? We didn't know if we'd last a week on this bike tour, let alone a year. Adding more to complicate the decisions around gear was anticipating what environments we might encounter: frigid Canadian winter, humid Asian jungles, hot sweltering deserts, high Himalayan mountains or relaxing beaches? I wanted to be prepared for anything.

Although we didn't know where we were going, we did plan a training ride to test our bikes and gear. On the day of the ride, we loaded our panniers, hooked them onto the racks of our new bikes and rode north of the city. We were not used to the weight of the bags, so even with the slightest of movements, the front handlebars would swing into a full turn. My bike wobbled, *as unbalanced as my life*, I thought. At the edge of the city, a motorist drove by and a skinny punk hung his face out the window and yelled, "Off the road, assholes!"

I turned around to look at Mike but, in doing so, swerved my bike and hit the curb with my front right bag before bouncing back onto the road. Mike yelled to me (I could sense him grinning), "He just said, 'Have a good ride *'Souls'*!"

Yeah, right, I thought. What are we getting ourselves into?

All I could think about were the big ifs. What if this didn't work? What if this decision drove Mike and I further apart than we already were? What if we ended up being *more* disappointed in each other? Was I disillusioned to think the trip might make a difference? *Or here's a novel idea*, I told myself, *go to a therapist rather than using travelling as therapy.*

I stayed quiet, but negative thoughts filled my head for the next 30 kilometres. We stopped at the Half Moon restaurant in the town of Lockport. Mike went inside to order, and I walked to the river and collapsed on the bank.

I'm not afraid to leave, I thought to myself. But I was terrified about coming home. What would I be coming home to? I no longer had a job, our house was rented out, and, worse, I was afraid I'd lost a few friends after opening up to them. Coming home without really trying would be failure. I kept swallowing sobs that wanted to escape from the back of my throat so Mike wouldn't notice when he walked back.

The wind whipped up. Leaves flew off the poplar trees, swirling around me and landing in the river. A black-capped chickadee called out in song and the skin on my arms started to tingle. I noticed the water ripple, and I thought about the long journey it had already made from the far south. How the mighty river in front of me split the city in half and would now continue to flow north to Lake Winnipeg and Hudson Bay.

Take it, I whispered to the river. Take this heartache and give me some peace. The river seemed to respond and picked up my negative energy as the muddy waters swirled past. I imagined it leaving to the Far North, where the humpback whales slapped its surface.

Mike came back with our burgers and fries. I looked at him with a small smile and then stared back at the river.

"You're quiet," he said.

"I was feeling terrified, but I'm better for the moment," I told him. He didn't reply but munched his burger. I had to admit being outside in the country air gave me new breath. I gulped it down to my core and tried to hold it in my gut before it evaporated back into the environment. Nature always brought me back to myself.

The breeze stopped. The sun shone. It was a lovely afternoon in September.

We sat in our spandex, brand spanking new spandex for Mike, and talked about what we still had to organize before our departure date. Five weeks had flown by. There was one last week to finish chores and say goodbye to family and friends. We needed to box up and store all of our personal items. We would spend the last few days at my parents' house. The day before our departure, Mike would drop off our car at his uncle's property. He grinned and said he hoped the mounds of snow that would fall over the winter wouldn't ruin it.

I finished the last of my fries and stretched to get ready for the pedal back home. Mike was already on his bike, eager for the next leg of the training ride.

It was late at night by the time we finished all we needed to do. Our panniers were fully packed. Eight bags took up much of my parents' foyer, ready to be put on our bikes the next morning. A snake of nerves had coiled itself around my belly and kept flicking its slithering tongue to the base of my throat, making me feel sick.

I walked to the corner of my bedroom in my parents' house and reached up for a box on the shelf. It was the size of a shoebox, covered in striped green and white fabric, with a thick silk ribbon to tie the top snug.

I pressed "send" on my phone. *The last text*. I blinked hard. Silent tears rolled slowly down my cheeks with thoughts of all I was leaving behind. Admittedly, *whom* I was leaving behind.

I powered off my cellphone and put it inside the box. The phone bounced against my house keys, car keys and daytimer; items that had been so important only that morning but would not be needed in my new life tomorrow. I tied the ribbon on tight. Mike stirred beneath the blankets. He must have heard the beep from my last outgoing text message.

I let out a sigh and then asked, "Will you be my new best friend?"

"I already am," he mumbled sleepily.

I could say nothing in return. I could only hope I would become as dedicated and sure as he seemed. I had asked Mike to take this trip, yet I couldn't say I was ready for it. I was just ready to go. To escape. *Am I running away?* I asked myself. Maybe. *Are we running away?* Possibly. Whatever the answers to those questions, leaving felt like the only thing left to do.

CHAPTER 3

PRAIRIES

One Rotation at a Time

If you really wait until you are ready to go, you'll never go.
—AUTHOR UNKNOWN

Morning arrived. I shook with anticipation. I fidgeted. I sighed. I was impatient to leave. I drank a whole pot of coffee, which made me shake more. Our bikes leaned against the pillars holding up my parents' deck in the driveway. I thought my bike looked cool with its new, bright red panniers. We waited for friends to arrive to start the trip with us. Craig, our bike mechanic, was joining us for two days. Leigh, a paddling and adventure buddy, would keep us company for a week.

Lacking a plan, Mike and I had decided to leave from my parents' house in Winnipeg and bike east. I kissed and hugged my mom and let her hold me tight in her arms. She cried. I had been too ashamed to talk to her about my marriage. If she and my dad ever had any problems in their relationship, they certainly did a brilliant job of hiding it. They must have known that something was amiss with ours, but they gave us space. Beneath all the unspoken observations, I thought they were proud of us and supported our decision. Letting go of her, I felt like I was 15 again and leaving home for the first time.

It was time. We straddled our bikes.

My right leg pushed down for my first pedal stroke and I rolled away from the driveway. I turned back for a last glimpse of my mom and almost fell off the bike. I hadn't mastered riding with heavy bags hanging off the front wheel like antlers. Other than Craig, we were unaccustomed to the unwieldy panniers. We slowly cycled down the street I had grown up on. Cycling through my home city felt foreign. An older man, excited to see us, waved and asked where we were from. It was not common to see cycle tourists in the city. He didn't seem too impressed when I said Wolseley Avenue, just a few blocks away.

My emotions bounced around like my bike. I rode through the last stoplight at Winnipeg's perimeter and my stomach flip-flopped. I felt excitement and hope.

Just then a truck blasted by, nearly running us off the road, and my hope disintegrated again. Mike and I gave each other a panicked look. *An omen? What have I gotten us into?* I came too close to Leigh's back pannier and it hit my front-left pannier, pushing me into the curb as if it was hockey boards. I squeezed the handlebars so tight. *Pull it together Kat.* I began to talk to myself like I was in a race. *You can do this. You're tough. You're smart. You can figure out how to ride this bike.*

With an auspicious tailwind and flat land, we moved across the golden prairie of Manitoba. The wind blew adamantly from the west, a constant whisper of refreshing autumn air. Long grains of wheat tilted beside us, pointing the way. Low clouds darkened the background and a sunbeam highlighted the yellow grain like a spotlight, showing off its life and vitality.

Around and around our legs went. This was our chance. We were starting over on this earth. For a few minutes I stared at my front tire rotating, wondering where it was going to take us. I admired my bright red panniers again. My bike matched Mike's. His was larger to accommodate his long legs and was black with green writing. Mine was silver with red writing. Both splashed out the name Trek 4500.

The terrain changed as we came to the fault in the Canadian Shield. Prairies disappeared into pine trees, clear lakes, granite rock ridges and grey cliffs. Our bums shifted on our seats and we took breaks every hour. I kept my eyes open for black bears but met only deer and slow-moving turtles. In the late afternoon, I parked my bike on the side of the general store in Rennie, Manitoba.

"Where are you going?" the owner asked.

"Not sure." I smiled. "We're going somewhere."

"Well, good for you. Best to get out there and do it. You can camp in my backyard if you like." She motioned behind the store.

Was she the first of many who would welcome us into their lives? We put up our tents and Mike blew up his sleeping pad and collapsed inside our new home. After 130 kilometres, the day had been his longest ride ever.

I squirmed into my separate sleeping bag. Although we were content with our first day, a barrier still kept us from each other. We lay in the silence of unspoken words.

The sun rose and we pulled our bodies from the tent to begin breakfast and the process of packing up, something that would take hours until we developed a routine.

Craig began to teach Mike important riding skills and demonstrated the valuable technique of drafting. Drafting while cycling is when one person blocks the wind and others bike in a line behind their rear wheel.

"Even when there are only two cyclists, drafting relieves a lot of effort needed by the person at the back," Craig said as we rode in a line like ants. We crossed into the province of Ontario on a quiet cottage road and into lake country. The autumn sky was clear, and the sun made the lakes sparkle like tinsel.

"My bike feels extra bouncy!" Mike yelled.

"You have a flat!" I hollered from behind him. Our first flat of the trip. We stopped and squawked like baby robins, hoping Craig would do something about it.

"Well, you better learn how to do this. I doubt it'll be your last," Craig said to Mike. Craig took the panniers off the bike and removed the back wheel, then showed Mike the best way to check and change a flat tire. He looked along the outside of the tire for nails or objects sticking out of it. Then he took off the tire and rubbed his hand on the inside of the rubber to make sure no sharp objects had wiggled into the rubber and punctured the inner tube.

"Aha!" Craig said, as he discovered a piece of wire, which he removed with a pair of tweezers. He then showed us how to properly patch a tube.

"How do I pump the tire up to sixty-five psi *with this*?" Mike held up a small travel hand pump we purchased for the trip.

"Muscles," Craig smirked. "I think that's a good lesson for you to learn on your own."

Our bike-fixing skills were limited. But we could both now patch a tube and lube our chains. The rest, like our relationship, we figured we would learn as we travelled.

About 115 kilometres later, we veered north on a dirt road to Black Sturgeon Lake, where a teammate and friend Bruce, along with his wife, Val, were expecting us.

Bruce gave me a bear hug when we arrived.

I knew Bruce from adventure racing, a multi-sport event where teams race nonstop around the clock. Races can be a few hours long, 36 hours long, or, my favourite, week-long events. They typically involve mountain biking, trekking and paddling but can also require mountaineering and, my most disliked discipline, inline skating. Navigation and route finding are done only by map and compass to search for checkpoints. Bruce and I were part of a team of four, and, as a team, we got to know one another during long nights of talking to keep ourselves awake so we could constantly be moving. We became personally exposed; with little more than ten hours of sleep in seven days, no one can pretend to be someone they're not. There wasn't enough energy for faking happiness if sad, hurt or annoyed. We learned to rely on each other and that led to deep relationships. After travelling through the wilderness for a hundred hours, you get to know someone inside and out. Bruce knew the real me. Far more than my husband did, sadly.

"Well Kat, what would make a better story?" Bruce asked when his strong arms let go of me. It was one of my favourite sayings of our team while we raced. We used it whenever something was not going according to plan: when we were off course, lost, too tired or if we came upon tough terrain to navigate. As far as he understood, Mike and I were off on a great adventure. There was no time to talk with Bruce about my concerns because minutes later our friend Dawn arrived from the city. In two and a half hours, she drove what had taken us two days to bike.

Dawn, one of my closest girlfriends and a co-worker, wrapped her arms around me and I nearly broke down in her embrace in the doorway. She whispered in my ear, "He wants me to give you a hug. This is from him."

Alex.

I took a deep breath, filling my lungs until my chest swelled. My training partner, co-worker and best friend: Alex. But he had become more than that.

"And this is from all of us," Dawn said out loud, handing me a gift. I opened the box. It was a SPOT, a small device that, at the touch of a button, communicates via satellite your coordinates to predetermined email addresses. It can also be used in a case of emergency, notifying authorities in a desperate situation.

I reached out to hug Dawn again. "Thank you! I cannot tell you how much this means to me."

"All of us from the shop are on there. We'll receive the emails and will look each day to see where you are in the world," Dawn smiled, but her eyes were misty. "Alex will get the coordinates too. You can delete him if you want." (I didn't.) "Listen, I know you and Mike will try to be safe, but this makes us feel so much better. Just know we are watching out for you all of the time. Your parents will get the email too." She squeezed my hands.

A few hours later, Dawn gave us her best wishes and packed up Craig, leaving Leigh with us. We waved goodbye as they drove away in Dawn's truck.

Before we left the next morning, I stood in Bruce and Val's bedroom, staring at a large framed photo of the two of them in 1982. They have their arms holding one another with homemade leg gators wrapped around their calves. Thick wool sweaters hang down past their waists. Their huge smiles looked back at me as the two of them stood in front of the tallest mountain in the world – Mount Everest. I felt inspired. But I also felt sad. From the outside, and from this photograph, their relationship looked easy. I knew they liked being together. They had travelled the world together. They had a family. I wanted all of those things, but I didn't know if Mike and I would make it. I felt distant from him. I didn't know who "we" were.

I didn't want life to be so serious. Yet it was. And I was a serious mess. I'm normally happy and easy-going. But I was lost standing in their bedroom. I had been lost in a forest – numerous times, actually, and one time over an entire dark, scary night. But it never felt like this.

This time, I had no navigational equipment.

Mike, Leigh and I travelled in silence. We turned south off of the main highway for an even quieter road that wound its way through terrain that held more lakes than land.

Leigh could have been the outsider, the third wheel in our twosome, but, in actuality, he was more of a buffer than anything. With another rider, I felt I wasn't the only one responsible for Mike's happiness. I could live on a bike for years, but I didn't know if Mike would make it to the weekend. Frankly, I was relieved to have Leigh along for the first week, as I felt Mike and I were yet to face up to the awkward situation that our relationship was in – despite everything we had done to move ahead.

And yet here we were, embarking on the biggest expedition we would take. How to heal our wounds? Our hearts were still broken. And, each morning, it was all we could do to bandage them up, cover them in duct tape, or, better yet, Leukotape, which is waterproof and stretchable. And we kept moving, one rotation at a time. Every few days, I would peel back one of the Band-Aids and reassess our scars. It wasn't easy.

A few nights later, we camped behind a tiny church on a long country road. In the early morning, I shook ice crystals off the tent and dumped it upside down to bounce out bits of sticks and mud. I walked the tent across the field to lay it out in a patch of sun. I hoped the tent would dry, even a little bit, before I packed it into my pannier. The frost penetrated my bike shoes and I tiptoed back on frigid feet.

"Maybe we should have gone south." I said to Mike. It was late September. Canada was getting colder with every sunrise.

"It's not too late," Mike replied. "The US border is close. Isn't it only about half a day's ride away?" he asked, since I always had the maps. "We could head south," he continued. "I think it's getting too cold for me anyway. I'm not keen to bike in a parka and ski goggles, but I don't want to stop riding. What do you think?"

What did I think?

I was elated. He wanted to keep biking! I felt a tension I had been holding in my body release and my entire core warmed all the way down to my toes. It was as if the last week had been a test and I'd just found out I'd passed. He liked to ride. *With me.* Mike liked to bike with me!

I was thrilled to go south too, as I couldn't shake the feeling we were too close to home. We could have hitchhiked back by evening. I wanted to be further away.

"Let's go south," I smiled, and went to update Leigh with our new plan. Well, the beginnings of a plan anyway.

CHAPTER 4

NEVADA

Going Somewhere

"You're going to die," our friend Rob declared. "It's true! You aren't going to make it out of the city in that heat." Rob sauntered over to the window and pulled aside the thick blinds. Brilliant sun filled the room and sparkled off the studs decorating his ears. "You're going to burn to death in the desert. People in cars perish! How the heck are you guys going to pull it off on bikes when you don't even have a plan?" He rubbed his perfectly manicured beard.

"You want to leave this shit $30-hotel on the Las Vegas Strip, with the noise blasting from the street below and the smoke seeping in through the walls?" Rob kicked at the vent that grumbled out noisy air conditioning. "This, my dear, is going to be your heaven! You are going to want to be back here." He looked further down out the window. A smirk spread across his face and he let out a throaty laugh. "Yup, you're going to die!" he confirmed.

I sat cross-legged on the lumpy queen-size bed. Mike lay down beside me and maps of the area were spread out around us. *Why were we in Vegas?* I asked myself. It had been a quick decision to fly from Minneapolis in search of warmer weather and to join my sister Michelle and friends who were celebrating a thirtieth birthday. But now, after a few days at the pool and pretending to play poker, trepidation coursed through me about what might come next. How were we going to make it out of the desert?

"Thanks for the vote of confidence! I'm sure we'll be just fine," I told Rob. I leaned forward to take a closer look at the maps and the land surrounding Las Vegas. The Mojave Desert stretches west and spreads toward the hottest place in North America: Death Valley, California. To the east, the Mojave wraps around a large water reservoir called Lake Mead. When I couldn't find a road to go directly north, a force against my chest began to crush me. "You're right, we might die."

Mike rolled over and propped himself up on one elbow. "Well, I was unsuccessful at gambling, so we can't afford a Hummer. We're going to have to bike." He smiled. "Not that you would rather a Hummer," he added under his breath so only I heard him.

"I don't know, you two are pretty smart, but it just doesn't seem right to me," Rob said. "I think you're crazy, and if the heat in the desert isn't going to do it to you, then you'll get blown off the road by a maniac driver!" He shook his head. "Ha! You're nuts!"

I ignored our friend and stared at the maps, willing the appearance of a route that would escape the desert. I finally noticed a small black line, indicating a road that ran out of the city east to the Hoover Dam, along the north shore of Lake Mead and eventually to Utah.

"Aha! I found a solution," I said to Rob smugly.

We left mid-morning with the lights of Las Vegas dazzling in the bright day. Ladies walked down the strip in tight miniskirts and bikini tops, carrying margaritas in plastic glasses the size of a human leg. By the city outskirts, my mouth was already parched like the desert we rode toward. Our water bottles boiled in the hot sun. Rob's words churned through me: "You're going to die. You're going to die." Only an hour on the road and the heat was too much to handle.

Desert sand and cacti took over from skyscrapers. I drew in a hot deep breath and whinnied out the chaos of the city in one big exhale.

"Everything okay back there?" Mike asked.

"Yup, all good." I answered. *Was I good?* It was now just Mike and me. No more plans to meet other friends. We were alone.

Alone.

Mike was a husband I barely knew anymore. *Where will we even start? What are we going to talk about?* This was the most time we had spent together since we were married. It wasn't that we hadn't wanted to spend time with each other, we just forgot how. Mike had not pushed for any time together, which was something that had upset me. It was always me asking to do things – but to be fair, they were usually the things I wanted to do. I had offered to go golfing once a year. He liked that. He paddled with me once a year too. That was a deal we had made. Another deal that did not make a relationship. Part of the problem may have been that Mike is generally content. Annoyingly content. I wanted him to strive for more and he wanted me to strive for less. Not that he asked.

That's how I ended up being with Alex all of the time. We had the same interests and were both driven to try ridiculous adventures. For years, actually, this seemed like the perfect arrangement. Alex was married as well and, because we'd been friends since before he met his wife, we never thought it was wrong to spend so much time together.

Long before this bike trip, Alex and I had gone on a paddling trip in the Whiteshell, a Precambrian Shield provincial park dotted with lakes near our home in Manitoba. Our canoe had sailed toward the end of Caddy Lake while stars illuminated the sky and reflected in the water. We paddled through a tunnel and into the next bay as the moon rose. Every dip of my paddle in the calm water filled my spirit with energy and I was thankful. Thankful for the glorious night. Thankful for my husband, who didn't mind when I did these adventures without him. And I was thankful to be on an overnight paddling trip in the back of the canoe with Alex, the same person who had taught me how to hold and maneuver a paddle, how to climb and how to navigate in the first place.

Later, Alex steered the canoe through a small rapid. Stars had begun to fade and early morning light filtered through the mist. Cattails waved softly in the soggy marsh. Red-winged blackbirds ruffled their shoulders and sang songs. Their musical trill caught in the spruce trees and echoed across the lake.

"This is pretty awesome," Alex had said from the stern of the boat.

"Yes. It's incredible," I responded. "Thank you."

"For what?"

"For hanging out with me all the time. For being my training partner and my closest friend."

"You got it girl," he replied, happily. We had paddled for 17 hours. Eventually, we pulled the canoe up to a rock island and laid down on a soft patch of moss. The sky was bright blue and, as I gazed into it, I thought to myself, *this is such a romantic place. I'll have to make Mike come here with me one day.*

Make Mike come here. That's how I thought of it.

And now here I was, with all the time in the world, with my quiet husband in an empty stretch of land.

Mike never brought up Alex. Not since I told him. He never asked questions or demanded anything from me. He didn't have to say anything, though, because after 11 and a half years, even when we were no longer close, I could practically read his thoughts. He was upset, disappointed in me, angry, frustrated and mad. But not ready to give up on us.

Mike is content being quiet. Hours can pass and he doesn't need to speak. But that doesn't mean he doesn't like conversation. And it's not as if he can't be loud too. During a hockey game, he hollers at the other team or at the referees nonstop. And he loves to socialize. Give him a few beers with his friend, Steve, and they will entertain (or clear out) a social bonfire with their racket. Me, on the other hand, I love to talk. A lot. I enjoy verbally dissecting every situation, vocalizing every thought. I don't hold back.

Yet, riding along, alone with my husband, I couldn't. What I wanted to say was, "I'm terrified this bike trip won't work. I want to go home." Then, in the next moment, "I never want to go home. I'm not sure how to be married. I miss someone that isn't you. And how, seriously, are we going to fill in all of this time together?"

Apparently, it began with *The Blues Brothers*.

"How have you not seen *The Blues Brothers*? It's been my favourite movie forever!" Mike told me.

"I don't know. I know you've mentioned it, but I don't even know what it's about."

"Well, get ready, because I'm going to tell you." And, so, for the next hour, he described the storyline with vivid detail, including images and sayings. We biked beside each other while I listened. The side of the road was wide and the traffic light.

"We've got a full tank of gas, half a pack of cigarettes, it's dark out and we're wearing sunglasses," Mike quoted from the movie. His voice filled the empty void. And this became our new way to communicate. I began to learn more about him through the stories he told, and he learned more about me. Stories that were not our own but had become a part of us. Filtered through the spokes of our wheels, we seemed to have enough movies and books in our memories to never run out of things to talk about.

The next day, after exploring the Hoover Dam and swimming multiple times in the reservoir, Mike became interested in our own water situation.

"So, tomorrow, we plan to ride around the lake, right?"

"Yes."

"But we can't go down to the lake to get water because the road is too far away, so I've been thinking we should buy a bag of ice from the marina and ask to store it in our camping neighbour's cooler. That way, in the morning, we can stuff ice cubes into our water bottles and into the hole at the top of our ten-litre water bag."

"That's a brilliant idea," I said. Mostly, I admired that Mike was beginning to take initiative. I knew being in the outdoors and travelling by bike was something I was more comfortable with. To this point, I'd been making the majority of the decisions and handling the logistics. Sure, the trip had been my idea and I was thrilled he had agreed, but that didn't mean I wanted to make all the decisions or not have his input. I watched him walk over to the closest RV, and I saw he was beginning to be a *part* of this journey, rather than just along for the ride.

That night, Mike recommended we not use the outer fly on our tent. We melted into our mats and gazed longingly upwards. The mesh screen allowed for an infinite view of the Mojave Desert sky filled with stars. It was a three-man tent, which gave us enough room inside to negotiate around each other. I felt Mike slide an inch closer to me. It dawned on me as I watched a falling star that this new beginning to our relationship would happen slowly. But it might just happen.

Back on the bikes the next morning, sleepy rolls of sand stretched sadistically into the desert. The heat intensified as the day wore on, and we began to ration our water. Mike's idea of ice was a good one, but the ice didn't last long. It melted within a couple of hours and our ice bag transformed into boiling hot water. We had gone from too cold in Canada to too hot in the southern states. We were exhausted when we finally pitched the tent by the lakeshore.

For our final push into the town of Overton, Nevada, we woke up at 3:30 a.m. to avoid the intense midday heat. We camped on the shores of Lake Mead once again, but this time it was an uphill slog back to the north road. For years, I had wanted to share the pleasure of night riding with Mike, but he hadn't been interested. Now he said yes when I suggested the early start. The birds were still asleep and vehicles were absent.

Our headlamps revealed a path and the moon bathed us in soft light. The surroundings were decorated with multiple shades of black and grey that looked like a palette of colours: dark black, light black, dark grey, smoky grey, soft grey. Our view was limited yet seemed limitless. The cloak of darkness made sounds clearer, more instant. I could hear Mike's chain ring rolling over the teeth, clunking softly when he changed gears. He could hear the ting of my spokes; ting, ting as my wheel turned. Mike's headlamp was slightly crooked on his helmet and shone a bit to the left. My lips curved upwards as I watched his shadow. He was the one I used to think about every time I biked, paddled or trekked all night. Now I was no longer only thinking about him. *He was here.* Darkness revealed that beauty: our own. When your vision is free from distractions, you can zone in on what really matters and begin to see things that often go unnoticed. Breath was heard: his and mine. Stillness was felt.

After a few hours, the desert started to stir. Towers of sandstone glittered as they strived to reach the dimming stars. Once the desert awoke, we stopped to put on sunscreen.

Mike glanced at his watch on his left wrist. "It's 7:00 a.m. I can't believe we're putting on sunscreen already."

Gone was our serene peacefulness of the night. We knew there would be no water along the road for 80 kilometres. Very few vehicles had passed and I was getting a lonely panicked feeling. I became anxious to ride faster. I was certain it was because I didn't understand the desert. I know people who love the desert: the beauty, the sleepiness, the tranquil crumpled landscape with reds, pale yellows, bright orange rocks, coarse sand, cacti and shrubs.

We were in an area named the Bowl of Fire, and all I could see once the sun was high was that it was empty. It was too hot, there was no water and we'd be in a desperate situation if either of us had any mechanical issues.

Gone were the lakes and forests where I could follow a compass needle and my instincts. Gone was the land where I could hike for days on no path, brushing branches and twigs from my face. That's the land I'm comfortable in. Where others may feel claustrophobic in dense bush, I feel free. But, here, I had all this open space and it made me small and insignificant. If I wasn't careful, the heat would pull all the moisture from my body and I'd lie starving in my skin on the side of the road like the expired snake we'd just rode past.

I reached down for my water bottle. The thin polyethylene melded into my palm and I gulped back mouthfuls of hot, plastic-flavoured tea. I moved my bike in front of Mike's and pushed harder on my pedals, wishing he'd speed up. I didn't want to tell Mike my fears because he seemed content, as per usual. It was so hot that three pens exploded in my handlebar bag, staining it permanently. Our food melted into pudding. We hid behind a roadside sign to take advantage of a patch of shade for lunch. We were alone.

I missed Alex.

After four days of riding in the desert, we rolled into Overton and headed to the local grocery store to pick up cold drinks and 59-cent burritos.

"So what do you do for fun on a Friday night?" I asked a large man in a plaid shirt standing in the not-so-fast "fast checkout" line.

"High school football!" He pushed his worn ball cap back on his head and scrunched up his face. "Now what else would there be? You two should really get yourselves over to the game. It's our team, Moapa Valley Pirates, versus our rival, Boulder City." He looked down at our food basket and stuck his hand in and pushed around our groceries. "No sense on fillin' yourselves on dem burritos either, plenty of food down at the game," he chuckled.

Before game time, we biked in the dark to the football stadium. A massive glow in the distance illuminated the desert.

"No way! Could that be a high school game?" Mike exclaimed. Sure enough, over two thousand people were in attendance, with hundreds more lining the outside fence with lawn chairs, hibachis and beer. We locked up our bikes and stood in the procession of people buying tickets for the game.

"You're not from around here, are you?" squinted the woman in the booth.

"No, we're not, but we heard about the game."

"Well, dears, you just go on in and make sure you cheer for the Pirates. There's no charge for you."

I stuffed my face with a greasy hot dog. The home team scored a touchdown. A cannon exploded over the uprights and two sets of cheerleaders ran out onto the field, their tiny gold skirts bouncing in the wind. They jumped, twirled and yelled, throwing batons and each other, responding to the emotion of the crowd. The cheerleaders ran into the end zone to create a pyramid while the kicker vied for the extra point. "This is a high school game?" I asked aloud.

"Welcome to America!" Mike yelled.

"Go big or go home!" I loved it.

Leaving Overton, we found ourselves caught on a section of a major interstate highway. I searched the maps but couldn't find a back road. The I-15 bisects the United States from Montana to San Diego. On the shoulder of the interstate, we felt vulnerable being so close to gigantic 18-wheelers, RVs and drivers heading from Las Vegas. Simultaneously, we both got flat tires and pulled off to the side of the highway. The desert roadside lay littered with debris and thorn bushes. It was a precarious setting, and we couldn't find the cause of our flats. We each put in new tubes and ventured back onto the psychotic freeway. The heat and blaring noise lit our brains on fire. Our skin scalded with blasts of hot air from passing monster vehicles.

My head hurt. When we were in nature and on quiet roads, it was easier to fall into this pattern of cycling. But, on a busy highway, I wanted to quit and go home. The physical endurance of cycling generally made my emotions evaporate, but along this blasted stretch of highway, my doubts resurfaced. *Who am I to think that going on a long bike ride is going to fix our marriage?*

"A rest stop ahead!" I yelled to Mike, and we pulled into a gravel pit to take a break. We hid our faces from a dust devil that whipped itself across the desert. When we looked back up, another cyclist was coming in from the other side of the pull out. This was the first cycle tourist we had seen on our trip. I became excited to share stories, hear where he came from and where he was going, what kind of gear he used and how he was enjoying himself. But, as he came closer, I found myself inching toward Mike.

A duffle bag rested precariously on top of his front handlebars and he struggled to control his bike. A two-litre Coke bottle was taped to his top tube. He was extremely skinny, with jagged tattoos etched onto his arms, shown off from his grey, dirty tank top. He had no helmet, and his hair was slicked back with grease.

His voice pierced through the commotion of the highway as he waved a massive pipe wrench in the air. "You are NOT ALLOWED on this highway! I WANT OFF, I don't know how to get off! The cops are after me, man. They'll catch us and we'll all get fined BIG TIME." His body shook. Saliva spewed out of his mouth and evaporated before it hit the dry sand.

Us? What did he mean US? I didn't say anything but wondered, why is he yelling? Why does he have a heavy-duty wrench on him? I tried to remember some self-defence moves.

"There's no other option but to ride this stretch of highway," Mike said. "A back road goes around Lake Mead and you can get yourself onto that in about 15 miles, but until then you have to be on the interstate." Mike stood tall and positioned himself in front of me. Strong and manly. (Well, as manly as a man can look in tight bike shorts. I appreciated his protective position, even though I'm not a small person.)

"They're gonna put us in jail!" the other man yelled, then looked us over, at our bicycles, at our gear. His eyes went as round as saucers at the appearance of our bright panniers. "So, man, you two are, like, really biking. You're really goin' somewhere," he gushed. "*Me*, now I'm doin' this because I have to, not because I want to. Yup, gotta get to Vegas by tomorrow or else."

I looked at his gear, or rather lack of gear, and the very large weapon. I didn't even know what could possibly be fixed on a bike with that tool. His jeans had slices in his pant legs where they must have caught in the rusty chain of his bike. I thought of the heat and the desert we had just cycled through and how many days it had taken us to do it. *Is he going to do it all in one day?*

"So you two have really nice bikes," he said. I stared him down and inched even closer to Mike. "Yeah, this bike here, I found it outside a 7-11 in Salt Lake. Somebody just left it there."

"Somebody just left it there?" I kicked myself for speaking up.

"Yes, well, do you need to look at the map again? You should be all good," Mike said after I'd opened my big mouth. "We've had no issues being on this highway. Be careful in the desert and fill up on lots of water. Good luck in Vegas. We have to get going because we're expected in the town of Mesquite tonight." The two of us jumped on our bikes and ramped them up to speed.

We then relaxed into the serenity of the humane and even relatively welcomed interstate.

We were in Mesquite for only two minutes when Mike had another flat. I was already bothered – not about the flat, those were just hiccups in what was now our everyday life – but the cigarette smoke, alcohol stench and the constant noise of bleeping VLTs wafting from the casinos urged me right out of town again.

"Mike, there's a coffee shop back down the street. I'm going to go grab one."

"Sure, I need to buy some new tubes, then I'll meet you back here."

I opened the door to the coffee shop. The air conditioning, sweet smell of fragrant coffee and gentle atmosphere pulled me further inside. I collapsed onto a large, soft leather chair in the corner.

"Ahhh," a deep breath came out from my body as I pleaded my negativity to escape. Cool air lingered on my hot skin like a caress and I melted further into the chair. Now that I was on my own, the emotions I tried to conceal when I was with Mike came out of hiding. Tears threatened to escape, but I wouldn't cry anymore. I had cried too much before we left on this trip. I was tired of crying.

I was with Mike all the time. Twenty-four hours a day. Yet I felt lonely. *How could I be lonely?* People were everywhere, on the streets, in the campgrounds. We met them, but any new relationships were fleeting, landing like a butterfly then gone again, leaving only remnants of personal touch. I missed home. I missed the constant chatter with friends, my sister and my customers at work. *I missed Alex.*

I kept these thoughts to myself. I was sure the last thing Mike wanted to hear was that I missed the very person who had split my heart from him in the first place and continued to cause the rift between us.

We had been on the road three weeks. I wondered when thoughts of Alex would fade. I had been going through the motions of cycling and travelling, but now I understood how a junkie must feel at the beginning of recovery. An addiction I didn't feed but still craved. *When will my mourning period be up? When will I have biked enough?*

I felt alone, like I stood in the shallows as waves and waves of emotion crashed into me. It was exhausting fighting against those feelings all the time while pushing my pedals up hills and across the desert. I was ready to be done with this emotional baggage, ready to pack up and leave this beach once and for all.

I closed my eyes, fighting back tears, and sighed loudly. *Be more gentle, Kat,* I told myself. *The healing will take time.* But I had a hard time listening to that side of my brain. I was in a rush. Patience is not a strong trait of mine.

"Hi." A soft voice made me open my eyes and I found a beautiful woman, with long, naturally grey hair, looking at me with compassion in her green eyes.

"I couldn't help but notice you. I'm Donna." She swooshed her thick hair aside so as not to sit on it as she took a seat across from me. I pulled myself up and wiped my nose on my napkin. If she saw I was upset, she ignored it and began a conversation that would go on for 40 minutes.

Her words were tender and thoughtful, even as she asked me the usual things like where was I from, what was I doing, where was I going. I could tell she loved to travel. I also felt like she wasn't in a rush. She wanted to hear my stories and tell me her own. She looked to be in her early 50s, the same age as my mother, and with that I felt comforted just seated across from her in that cozy coffee shop.

Her soul reached out and grabbed mine and fed it all it starved for. Without saying so, she told me I would heal. It would take time, but I would recover. *Be patient!* her presence screamed at me.

I'll try, I promised, wordlessly.

Uplifted, I went back to Mike.

"I met someone," I told him.

"That's good. I figured you had, you always do. Were they nice?"

"Stunning," I said. "Her name is Donna and she has the longest hair." I decided to admit to Mike that I was sad going into the coffee shop. "Since meeting that guy on the highway, I've felt really homesick." I looked up to Mike from where I perched on the curb sipping coffee. He had separated the wheel from the frame and pulled the tube away from the rim. He slid the tube through his palms to locate the cause of his multiple flats that day. The shoulders of the interstate were sprinkled with metal strands left from semi-truck-tire explosions. They were a pain for us cyclists.

"I'm sorry I'm homesick." I was. It must have been hard for Mike to watch me be sad, or to feel my unease. Even though I didn't talk about the details with him, I'm sure he knew why, and for whom, I was homesick.

"It's okay, Kat. You're going through a lot right now."

"Donna is really lovely. She invited us for dinner tonight. There's a sushi place right beside the coffee shop."

"That sounds great," Mike said, as sweat poured in big drops down his temples. How fortunate am I to have such an easy-going husband, who doesn't mind that I run into a cool coffee shop "for a minute" and leave him to fix the bikes, I thought.

"Yes! Look at this!" Mike proudly held up the tweezers so I could see the tiny piece of metal he found in his tire.

That evening, for three straight hours, Donna, Mike and I conversed about world travel, favourite books and what it meant to have everything one needs. I realized how incredible it was for us to be able to go on this bike trip. *Here we are, travelling and living out of four panniers each.* I could tell through Donna's eyes how lucky she thought the two of us were to be able to explore, to have no time limit, no plan.

I went to bed lighter. When I woke, my head was no longer bogged down. Instead, I felt rejuvenated and cared for. The roadblocks I felt yesterday moved aside. I was excited again to see where this road would take us. We met Donna for early coffee and she gave each of us a homemade knitted toque and, because she had learned how much I loved to read, five books. One of the books was a travel bible. Maybe she was trying to save me, trying to put me back together, I thought. I certainly felt less broken.

CHAPTER 5

ZION
Angels Landing

I changed gears. Lower and lower. Small ring in the front, big cog in the back and steadied my cadence. We were on the Old Highway 91 through northwestern Arizona and into southwestern Utah. It was my turn to tell Mike about a book: *The Notebook* by Nicholas Sparks. We rode beside each other and talked easily. There was no one else on the road for hours and hours, and I appreciated the continuous rhythmic rotation of our pedals on the empty back road. The land stretched toward the hot sun, dotted with the occasional knotted Joshua tree. In the afternoon, I fixed my second flat tire of the trip under the prickly umbrella of one, thankful for its offering of shade. My arms were a burnt crimson, but I enjoyed the heat, overwhelming as it was.

The desert no longer terrified me like it did on those first days. I started to slow down. *Life is not a race anymore*, I reminded myself. Instead, Mike became the teacher, the coach, showing me how to bike for pure enjoyment, rather than for training, a race or even a destination. I could have biked at breakneck speed, but after a few solitary experiments, I realized it never made Mike go any faster. He was not in a rush and I preferred to have his company. Mike liked to take a break every hour, which at first was hard for me, and I kept asking when he was ready to leave. I must have driven him crazy, but again, it did not rush him. It took a while until I began to appreciate the time to just be on our own. The time to listen to the land, the birds and the wind, without even our chains or tires making noise to interrupt them. When Mike was on the bike, he moved at a constant pace. It wasn't fast, but it wasn't slow either. I followed his lead and tried to emulate his easiness with life.

We pedalled four hours uphill before we crested the pass in the Beaver Dam Mountains. The bikes eased over the top. This is where I left Mike behind. I let go of all restraint and tucked low over the handlebars, allowing my wheels to spin as fast as they could downhill. My bike computer reached 60 kilometres an hour. Pretty good, considering the heavy panniers. I didn't mind that Mike wasn't fast on the downhills. I found it amusing how he was a speed demon when snowboarding but always used his brakes on the bike. I stopped at the bottom to wait with a huge smile on my face.

"That was fun!" Mike said when he arrived.

We crossed over the state line and into St. George, Utah, where we found a campground with a pool and hot tub.

"What do you mean you can't find your bathing suit?" I asked, staring at the huge mess in the tent.

"Well, that's not all. I can't find my entire clothes bag," Mike said, after scattering the entire contents of his panniers.

"How do you lose your clothes bag? Wouldn't you have noticed the weight difference?"

"Apparently not." He shrugged. We used a pay phone and, after a few calls, Mike found out his bag was left three days earlier in Overton, Nevada.

Three days! Apparently, he hadn't changed his clothes in three days either.

I was mostly amused. My panniers were organized, whereas Mike's were scattered. He treated them like a 2-year-old treats a toy box – one that got dumped in the middle of the room (for us, the tent) and flung around. Then everything (except this time it wasn't everything) was thrown back in, but he was never sure into which pannier. We made ourselves comfortable in the campground, as it would be a few days before his clothes were shipped to us.

With all Mike's clothes once again heaped into his panniers, we headed toward Zion National Park. In the late afternoon, nature called and I abandoned my bike, sinking into deep sand as I moved far enough off the road. The gurgling of a stream (not mine) excited me.

"Hey hon, come check this out!" I yelled. "There's a river here and I think it'll be an amazing place to camp."

I instantly stripped off my clothes and waded into the water, letting the cool stream rush past my knees and wash the dust and heat from my body. Mike, avoiding the cold water, set up our tent beneath the cover of a large cottonwood tree.

We were settling into a quiet night of playing cards, when we heard the rumble of a big engine and tires squishing into the sand. A door slammed shut.

"Hey bikers, you guys home? Want to come for whisky?" two boys called out. We did and introduced ourselves to Ken and Sam. I guessed they were in their mid-20s. We learned they were from Colorado and prided themselves on being rock-climbing bums.

"We raft guide for a few months of the year and take the other months off to climb and play," Sam said.

"It's a good life," Ken added. "Unless you want health insurance." Health insurance turned out to be their only worry. They both seemed to love life. I was under the impression they did their best to live the lifestyle that provided them with happiness and fulfillment. I was sure they had little money, but they were very generous.

We passed their whisky between us as our conversation circled around different perceptions of extreme sports. "You're crazy, man," Ken said to Mike when Mike admitted to loving scuba diving. "Scuba diving is a psychotic sport. You're down there in the deep depths of the ocean and a big fricken' shark is coming at you, but whoa, man, you gotta go slow. Can't go up too fast because your head might explode!" Ken's voice was long-drawn-out like a surfer, and he played with the straggling beard hairs trying to escape from his young face.

"Yeah, but you're dangling off a quarter-inch rope hanging ridiculously high in the air and you have to poop in a tube and tie yourself into a rope so you can sleep. You're the crazy ones!" said Mike. "I'm sticking to scuba diving. Now pass me the whisky."

We stared into the fire and laughed. When I looked up, it was nice to see Mike's face lit up from the glow of the flames. I caught his eye and he winked. Sometimes, even though we had been a couple for many years, I felt like we were brand new. There was a shyness between us. And a spark. Definitely a spark.

We went from overheating in the desert, to rivers, immense sandstone cliffs and cold, frosty mornings. Organic apple farms spread across the valley and we helped ourselves to the fruit. Cliffs of red rock reached up from the back of the orchards and I envisioned myself in a scene from the Roadrunner cartoon.

In the town of Springdale, Utah, just outside Zion National Park, touring bikes were propped against the wall of a coffee shop and we went in, eager to meet their owners. A woman sat at a table near the window and I knew instantly she was one of the cyclists. She wore a thin Lycra jersey and tight cycling shorts. Her hair was blonde, scooped into a ponytail pulled back from her gorgeous face and blue eyes. She looked like she should be sporting a bikini with a surfboard tucked under her arm. Instead, a bike helmet hung from her hand and she was about to venture out into the sleet, her slim frame a sure sign she was going to freeze that day.

"My name's Stacy," she said. "I'm cycling from California to raise awareness for a greener world." Stacy sat straight, her shoulders pulled back in perfect alignment. She looked tough and confident, yet winced as she took a bite of her peanut butter sandwich. "I've eaten so many peanut butter sandwiches the last couple of months," she explained.

"Why don't you change it up?" I asked. "Put more excitement into your meals?"

"Because it's cheap! At the most my friend and I survive on three dollars a day, and our budget would be a lot more than that if we splurged on food," she said, confidently. I felt a pang of guilt. Mike and I had stuffed ourselves with omelettes and French toast for breakfast and afternoon meals of steak stir fries and rich pastas. Eating on a budget we were not. Stacy's friend went to the condiments counter to help himself to packages of peanut butter, soup crackers and salt packets. For meals later on, he told us.

"In a hundred days of cycling through the States, we've only paid for camping once," Stacy confessed. I felt another pang of guilt.

"Really? That's interesting because in Canada I'm content to pull over and camp on the side of the road anywhere, and we did. But in the States, I'm not comfortable. It makes me nervous, and we've only done it once," I said.

"Why is that?" piped up Stacy's friend, while he spooned honey onto what looked like old bread.

"Guns."

They erupted with laughter. "Whatever! You watch way too much TV and Hollywood movies!"

"Signs on large properties in Canada read 'No Trespassing. Violators will be Prosecuted.' The signs in the US read 'No Trespassing. Violators will be SHOT!'" I tried to make my point.

"Well, don't camp there, but try other places," Stacy advised. I agreed that Mike and I should stop paying for camping every night. Although the price was minimal, it did cut into our budget.

I wished we could have convinced Stacy to stay an extra day, but she was on a mission and we had our own journey. Mike and I watched them roll away with their tiny back panniers and light, fast bikes. I could see Stacy shivering. She turned around on her bike to wave and yelled, "Go bush!" reminding me of our vow to free camp. Mike and I waved goodbye until they were out of sight, then we held hands and walked back to our bikes.

"In the near future, we'll have to work on our bravado and stop worrying about night bandits shooting us and begin to free camp," I said to Mike.

"Yeah, I just sleep anyway."

"I know! That's the problem!" I teased him.

We followed the river and set up our tent on the very edge of Zion National Park, with a plan to stay one night.

On our first morning in Zion, I opened the tent to cream-coloured escarpments, and pink, orange and red sandstone cliffs extending toward the heavens. It was the middle of October. The sky turned bright blue and the sun lit up the top of the peaks. It was the kind of day that made you want to chase time, experience everything before snow stayed.

We followed, by foot, the Virgin River up one of its tributaries into a slot canyon called the Narrows. It was fitting, since the canyon soon narrowed and the rock faces rose for hundreds of metres above us. Mike found hiking sticks and we used them to hop from smooth river rocks to boulders. Eventually, the bone-chilling water overtook the rocks, but we continued to push through. We wore our waterproof socks, which were about as waterproof as wearing old Subway sandwich plastic bags. Our feet froze.

Even so, my heart was on fire.

Hiking, one foot in front of the other. I watched Mike do the same. He placed his hiking stick, then walked toward it. He made it look easy. We were making progress and I realized how happy I was. I could breathe deeper; my heart beat stronger. That day, the freezing water froze my fears. Being there in the canyon with Mike felt right. I knew we had made the right decision to leave home together.

When we turned around, a bald eagle drifted high above in the sky as blue and clear as crystals. It looked down through that split in the earth and I'm sure saw us finding our way, pushing deep water on our path back to warmth. Even without direct sunlight, the hues of the expansive, smooth cliffs on each side glowed like stained glass windows in a cathedral. We walked on. The river constantly carved the chasm deeper, acting like sandpaper against the canyon floor, until it emptied into a valley full of Fremont cottonwood trees about to dress in gold.

Creation and change enveloped us. We could see it in the leaves. We could smell it in the air and feel it on our skin. The nights were cold and we wore all of our clothes around the campfire while we played games of cards. We chose between three: ten-card fish, war and rummy. Whatever we played, Mike usually won. He loved to win. The smoke mingled in our nostrils as we gazed up into the inky sky between turns. We planned to leave the next morning.

I awoke to the patter of snow falling on the tent. We had zipped our sleeping bags together for the first time. *It's warmer this way*, I told myself. I slid on my pants and fleece jacket while still beneath the blanket of down. When we were both ready, I reached for the zipper toggle on the door and slowly pulled it open. Each tooth separated one by one. There was sand already stuck in the zipper. From the desert, from the beach, from the red dust of the campground. I didn't care. It heightened the sound of the zipper. The noise was like a symphony, playing out our sacrifices, choices, awards. I knew, on the other side of the door, there were possibilities. There was the promise of adventure.

Before, when I used to open my tent, I would memorize the surroundings. I would hold onto the vision of the wind caught in trees, of whether the tent was pegged down into mud, sand or tied to rocks, I would catch the call of the birds waking; all so I could recall images for Mike when I went back home. Unfortunately, I seldom told him once I returned. More often than not, we didn't give each other the time the stories needed.

But now Mike was here. He clambered out first. I watched him unfold on the other side, then at his shadow against the nylon wall as he stretched upwards. He turned back until he stood in front of the open door. Now he reached to pull me out. Every morning, I went with him, he came with me. I grabbed ahold of his hand and noticed how mine just slipped into it. His fingers are longer, wider and wrap around mine naturally.

He wore his new toque. It was sky-blue, the colour of his eyes. His eyes are gentle, yet deep-set, framed by long eyelashes and intense brown eyebrows. I realized I hadn't *really* looked at him in quite some time and I found myself staring. His smile was wide; it lifted his cheeks, which in turn scrunched the sides of his eyes in a look of delight. His teeth are near perfect, with full lips and a thin, easy-to-miss scar that runs down his bottom lip. At nearly six feet, Mike is taller than I am by four inches. I put an arm around his waist and noticed how the biking was already making him thin.

The snow was light but large. We both lifted our heads up to the sky, stuck out our tongues and caught big, fat, perfect snowflakes.

"Do you want to stay another night?" Mike asked. My head nodded up and down in my new toque. It was the colour of a merlot, the same shade as the wet cliffs beside us. I didn't want to leave. Each day in Zion, I connected more to my true self and more with Mike. I could feel myself begin to affix to this earth. Waves of turmoil that had surged inside of me calmed, like the placid waters of a lake in the early mornings. With not a ripple to wreck the serenity, I could finally see myself in its reflection. Hiking and existing in Zion had cleansed me. I had found my sensei, my Buddha, or my God that lived in the cliffs around us. I was finding *me*. I was at peace for the first time in years.

The sun came out, the snow melted. Mike waved over new arrivals to share our site and the $18 fee. Once other campers departed, Mike walked the grounds to scrounge leftover wood so we could have a roaring fire every night. We might as well have been free camping on the side of the road, though, because there were no showers and we didn't bathe for a week. My head was greasy and slicked back in a buttery bun. Mike didn't seem to notice – when I caught his eyes landing on me, he looked at me the same way he did when he first fell in love with me.

The next morning, I stood near to where Mike was making a pile of firewood with a new brochure of the park in my hands.

"There's a hike called Angels Landing. With the sky clear this morning, it looks like today will be a great day for it."

"Sounds great," Mike said. "So we're staying another night?"

"Well, you were collecting more firewood." We both couldn't tear ourselves away from Zion. There was an embrace that was healing us. We grabbed our backpacks and began to hike up Angels Landing. It started modestly, but soon we climbed switchbacks right up a steep canyon wall. In the last kilometre, the ledge narrowed to barely anything. I steadied myself as consequential drop-offs fell 500 metres from both sides. We were exposed, scrambling for footing, yet Mike looked secure and confident moving along the spine. I followed him right up the guts of the rock formation, right through the heart.

Once at the top, we paused. The river ran far below, a strip of greenery flanked its edge. A young raven circled and cried out. We gazed far off into the distance, down the valley, up other peaks and into canyons. The cliffs, in astounding colours of reds, oranges and creams, soared up to the blue sky. *Where angels must live*, I realized.

Mike wrapped his arm around me.

"Check out that climber," he said, pointing to a speck in the distance. I smiled. I surprised myself by turning beneath his arm and reaching up to kiss him. Our lips lingered and I tasted how sweet he is. *This man has an amazing heart*, I thought. We may continue to struggle, but each day seemed easier as we grew closer and closer to each other. From that high up, on the top of Angels Landing, not only could I see this amazing view but I could also see our future.

On our last night in Zion, after our campfire, I lay on my quarter-inch mat, softened by the sand beneath the tent, while my head rested on Mike's chest. My mind drifted to the present, to living now, and I began to accept what

Mike and I had been through in our relationship, and the drive to work on it began to emerge.

I sat up and took out my journal. Made from the hide of a bison, the dark-brown leather was supple in my hands. I had dreamt of all the stories, adventures and love that would eventually fill its pages, but up until now I had not been able to write. I had taken the beautiful journal out many times to touch and hold it, but I never had the courage to write any words. I was afraid to break down and record what really happened between Mike and me: the heartache, the loss, the disappointment. So I wouldn't or, rather, couldn't write. But, as I began to thaw, my journal began. I wrote:

> Our days in Zion grew into each other as if they were a fresh field of pasque flowers. We only stayed a week, but we lived a month, a year, in those days. It was a place we had not heard of before our arrival, yet it clutched us, hugged us and nourished us until we felt loved enough to move on.

"Zion" is a word that describes a place of peace, refuge or sanctuary – a place where humanity connects with God. I didn't know this at the time, but we both felt it.

CHAPTER 6

UTAH
Learning Lessons

I dripped sweat. Breath hammered in my chest. My legs strained against the pedals, pushing and pulling. After hours of hard work, I crested the top of Boulder Mountain. Mike, already on the peak, had his bike lying in the snow beside a sign that read 9,600 feet. He cheered me on, taking photos as I came over the top. I glanced behind me. The night before, we had celebrated one month on the road, watching the sunset from the door of our tent on an escarpment in Grand Staircase-Escalante National Monument.

"You look great!" Mike clicked the shutter on our camera, bringing me back to the moment. "Okay, let's take one together near this sign!" He ran ahead to prop the camera on a wet rock, set the timer and ran back to me in time for the picture to be taken.

I wanted to drop my bike in the pile of snow and curl up into a fetal position for the rest of the night while Mike fed me hot spoonfuls of oatmeal. Instead, I straddled my frame and hunched over the handlebars for the shot.

"Look at you!" I said, exhausted. Mike had made it to the top minutes ahead of me and didn't seem to be breathing hard. "Good job, but from now on, you're carrying your fair share of the weight."

When we left home, Mike was a novice cyclist and I was stronger, so it made sense that I rode a heavier bike. I carried the extra water and hefty items like our laptop and batteries. My panniers easily outweighed his and now I wanted to give some of it up.

From the summit of Boulder Mountain, our bikes flew downward. Snow and hail stung our faces and stuck to our sunglasses. The mountain's aspen trees quivered in the wind. Bright gold leaves tore away from their branches and swirled in the cold air.

An hour later, at our free camp (free because the campground was closed now that it was October and cold), Mike gathered firewood, while I shivered and changed into my warmest dry clothing. Once dressed, I stood useless with my hands curled into fists inside my fleece mitts and stuffed into the pockets of my synthetic jacket until Mike made a large bonfire. In a slit between my neck warmer and toque, I watched Mike prime and then start the stove. He put butter into the pan and dropped in pieces of bread. When it finished sizzling, he held out the fried peanut butter and banana sandwich for me.

I stuffed the hot sandwich into my mouth, smearing peanut butter all over my mitts. It instantly soothed my tired, sore, cold and hungry body.

"Oh my gosh, this is delicious!"

"I'm glad you like this gourmet meal. Just another Mike Rosen special," he said, winking at me.

Mike continued to grin while my eyes took him in. He wore his red puffball jacket and his bronze tan was warm in contrast with his blue toque and shining blue eyes. His lips were weathered. Rough stubble grew on his face and he looked like a true wilderness man – a sexy wilderness man. One I knew washed only in creeks and water we heated in our pot. A smile came to my cracked lips as I realized he enjoyed this: he liked bike touring and being in the outdoors. And, now, he was taking care of me.

I felt comforted that Mike and I had returned to a rhythm of travelling we had honed over many trips together in the past. This type of travel isn't for everyone. The lack of routine, lack of sleep turning into exhaustion, eating food that doesn't come out of a fridge, the growing distance from home. It breaks people down. Some people hate it, yet others like myself, and now Mike, relished it.

In the confines of our cozy tent, we spread out the contents of our panniers. We divided our clothes, computer, camera gadgets, pots, kitchen set and tool kits into equal piles.

"So this is the reward I get for getting into shape?" He laughed and held up the heavy tool kit bag to stuff into his pannier.

"Nope…you also get me," I smiled, and pushed him over for a kiss.

The next day we spent in a town at the bottom of Boulder Mountain, called Torrey, where cottonwood trees lined the streets and dogs ran free. We took the afternoon to wash our tent and gear and did laundry in a real washing machine. It was our first wash in a month. After a huge grocery shop, we went to sleep in our spotless tent.

I fidgeted with my sleeping mat, blowing it up so it would provide the exact amount of comfort, smoothing out my sheet and sleeping bag. I slid in and closed my eyes. But I knew it wouldn't be that simple.

Sleep never came easy.

Even though Mike and I were getting along and becoming closer, my nightly dreams featured Alex. I hated them. I opened my eyes, pushed the sleeping bag away, sat up, slipped my sandals on and went back outside.

Breathe, Kat. I stood under the ceiling of stars and willed my subconscious to be stronger. Why did Alex still have to be with me? *Go away.* I took in a deep breath and wished for the nights to be different, for the dreams to disappear. I felt so out of control, as if it wasn't me in my body.

I remembered a conversation I'd had with a customer named Larry a few years earlier. We were at a small lake and I was helping him test out different kayaks.

"How long have you two been a couple?" he motioned to Alex, who was showing someone how to hold a kayak paddle.

"Huh?" I asked. "We're not a couple, we're just best friends."

"It's not right," Larry said.

"What do you mean?" I looked up from the kayak I had readied for him.

"It's not right that a woman and man should be that close. You're married to someone else?" he asked. I nodded.

"You should stop being friends. It never ends well otherwise."

I pushed Larry off and secretly wished he would flip over into the goose-poo-infested lake. *I'm not alienating half the population just because Larry thinks it's not right to be friends with the opposite sex. That's the most ridiculous thing I ever heard.* I stomped off to tell Alex; he always listened to my complaints and would make me feel better.

Alex and I had been best friends for ten years. I never expected that after such a long friendship, I would fall in love. But I did. We worked together. We trained together. I never felt alone. He knew when I was grumpy, happy or just being silly. He knew how to make fun of me. I felt he cherished me. I felt as important to him in his life as he was in mine. But we were only friends. We were always meant to just be friends.

I took in another deep breath and went back in the tent. I wrote, read and eventually succumbed to exhaustion. Uninvited, the shadow in me came out to play. My dreams that night were heated, filled with images of Alex walking away from me, telling me I'd never see him again, that he was no longer my friend. I tossed and turned and fought against my visions.

In the morning, fierce growling and yapping woke us. Mike jumped out of the tent to scare a pack of dogs away from our food bag that we'd hung – too low, we learned – in a tree. Gobs of blood and scraps of dog skin covered our punctured nylon food bags. The mutts had chewed and slobbered on 60 dollars worth of burritos, lunch meat, cheese, eggs and wraps. A large investment in our week's worth of food – all gone. It was an expensive lesson: hang food high.

The state of Utah would teach us many lessons in self-preservation: The importance of enough water to make it to the next river or town. Wearing sunscreen. How to quickly patch tubes. That the empty desert is *really* empty. It's a place where the temperature changed constantly. On busy roads, we learned the importance of the rear-view mirrors attached to our handlebars. Unfortunately, my mirror broke south of the town of Green River, right before the busiest road toward Moab. I stayed directly behind Mike's wheel while he kept an eye on traffic.

"Car! It's coming fast!" Mike yelled and we dove into the ditch.

"That was close. We could've been hit!" I exclaimed, pulling myself out from the thorn bushes. "What's up with this road?" I asked. This was the third time in as many hours that we'd biked into the ditch. Riding into Moab was the worst: there was no shoulder and cars wouldn't move over and sped by ridiculously fast. We picked up our bikes and looked for pesky goatheads, a thorn that could easily flatten our tires. I hesitated to get back on the road. *Maybe the horrible traffic was a sign we shouldn't go to Moab?*

I had been to Moab and Arches National Park before with Alex on a mountain bike trip. I was nervous to go back because, to be honest, I was pretty sick of thinking about Alex. Like the cars, a constant stream of emotions raced by. I often didn't know which one to grasp onto: heartache, not being worthy, sadness. Although, I *did know* I was scared to feel lonely in Moab when Mike was with me.

Get back on the bike, Kat. I had to. It was important to face my feelings. I couldn't run away from every place Alex and I had been. Plus, I wanted to share the area with Mike. I knew how important it was for us to create our own Moab experience.

The road stayed busy as the scenery changed from monotonous desert to brilliant walls of red rock. Towering formations in front of snowy mountaintops. Memories of that holiday with Alex were tucked away behind the upper hills of Slickrock, and in a canyon where we had found a waterfall and jumped into a deep refreshing pool.

I spotted a mountain bike trail. Mike and I took it and we bounced our way into Moab on a single track. We were on the main street when a cycle tourist called us over.

"Hey, are you guys here long?"

"We don't really have a plan," Mike told him. "You?"

"Oh, a few days anyways. I'm staying with a Warmshowers host."

"What's Warmshowers?" I asked.

"You haven't heard of it?" The cyclist was in his early 20s and was eager to tell us about two websites that would soon change the course of our tour. "Warmshowers is a website dedicated to cycle tourists and people willing to host us. The other, Couchsurfing, is similar but for any type of traveller. Both websites have maps of the world where we can pinpoint a place to check if there are local members. Hosts sometimes just meet up for coffee, but they often act as a tour guide or provide a bed. There's no charge, merely a shared love of travelling."

"That sounds awesome! Thanks for telling us," Mike said, and invited the young cyclist to meet us for dinner. Mike and I found a familiar (to me) campsite with free Wi-Fi and signed up for the Warmshowers website. We immediately wrote to Pat, a member in Moab.

Pat was quick to reply. He, along with his friend Luke, invited us for a hike the next day in Arches National Park. We were picked up in a white car dusted with red sand. I slid in beside Mike in the back. We drove over the Colorado River and up a road where I remembered camping with Alex. I choked back the memory. I knew I was still grieving. It was as if I was a tire full of air slowly bleeding out everything I needed to process. I wasn't sure if Mike knew what I was thinking, but, as I stared out the window, I felt his hand grab mine and bring me back inside the car. Thankful, I smiled at him.

We parked in a spot I had never been and began to hike. We soon came to a bright orange wall covered in petroglyphs.

"The Anasazi used to live here," Luke began. "They left petroglyphs that are believed to be around 700 years old. Notice how this one is etched and pecked into the rock instead of painted. See the hunter with a bow and arrow directing it at this deer." I followed Luke's gaze. With his eyes, we were able to see much more than we would have on our own. We slid through a slot canyon, extending our hands above our heads to push our bodies through narrow openings in the rock. We hiked to a high point to see the Dark Angel: a 45-metre-tall, free-standing, sandstone pillar. It was illuminated bright orange against the searing blue sky. Finally, we visited one of the most famous arches: Delicate Arch. I had seen it before: a long strip of sandstone that hangs like a rainbow in the desert. The sun was beginning to set, and Mike's body was silhouetted in the fading light. I couldn't help but think how we were our own delicate arch. If there had been any more pressure applied on either side of our relationship, we would have broken. I understood we were still delicate, but we were also becoming something new, something beautiful.

We left Moab a few days later and I let Mike break the wind. He sure was getting strong! We continued up into the La Sal Mountains toward the border of Colorado. That night we found a great place to hide. Free camp! *Stacy would be proud*, I thought to myself as I burrowed into my sleeping bag to write in my journal. Mike was already snoring while I kept an ear open for attackers. At the last shop we'd stopped at, the sweet old woman warned us about the megafauna in the area. "Watch out for yer bears tonight."

"Bears? What bears?" I asked.

"Well, the bears in the bush, doll. Ya know, big brown ones. They are here, yes they are. Why just the other day Ol' Johnny from down the road chased one away. Scared him good, he did."

I fumbled for Mike's wrist and illuminated his watch without waking him. Mine had died a few days earlier and I had yet to find a battery. 7:30 p.m. *Great*, I thought, *12 more hours until the sun comes up. When did I become such a chicken?*

As if I needed something else to keep me from sleeping. Nights in the tent were long. It was October, so the sun set around 6:00 p.m. and rose at 8:00 a.m. Mike was in his element because he loved to sleep for 14 hours. I only needed about six, so I practised yoga, read, wrote and started a blog documenting our trip. (We had two batteries for our laptop that provided 11 hours of power before needing a recharge.) Occasionally, I woke Mike if I became excited about a certain piece of writing or to have a conversation. I had tried to limit myself to carrying three books at a time, but people kept enabling my obsession and my collection kept growing.

I distracted myself; anything to not miss Alex.

It was probably in a tent when my feelings had deepened for Alex. I had tried to dismiss them, until I no longer could. Eventually, I told him how I felt. It was messy and complicated and we couldn't go back to only being friends. Losing him was like mourning the death of a loved one. I knew Alex was still healthy and well, but I had to live with the realization I was no longer a part of his life.

That was when I sunk into a dark hole. Everything in my life went dark during the year before this bike trip. I would go to sleep with a heavy heart, feeling completely debilitated. Waking up, each day was no longer shiny and new but the same shambles. I felt locked in a cellar with no way out. I could see out a window but didn't know how to get there. Exercising, time with my friends or family, talking about it … *nothing* made my depression go away.

Prior to this, I hadn't understood depression. I was generally a happy, enthusiastic person. I ignorantly associated depression with people who did not try hard enough to be happy.

Then depression happened to me.

People started saying I looked and acted differently. My smile no longer "shined," they said. I had "no life left in me," they mused. I laid blame on the diet I was on. Most people didn't ask any more questions. Friends who knew of my conflicted feelings between Alex and Mike quickly got tired of it. *Go to sleep, Kat.*

Mike rolled over, his sleeping bag rustled and his hand reached out to rub my thigh. His eyes stayed closed.

"You're still awake? Everything okay?" he mumbled.

"Yes, I'm good," I answered. And I was. It had been a long time since I'd given myself so much personal time. I processed a lot in those dark, quiet hours.

CHAPTER 7

COLORADO
Seduced by Summits

Water dripped from cracks in the rock, creating tiny streams. Small patches of grass began to show and then large evergreen trees towered beside us. We had left the desert behind.

"I think this is Colorado!" I said happily to Mike. "I'll make us a celebratory breakfast. How about egg muffins and dark roast coffee?"

"Sounds great!" Mike replied, already sprawled out on the thorn-free ground. For the first time in a long time, we weren't concerned about cactus thorns and spiky goatheads stabbing into our bums. Throughout Utah we had sat on square pieces of foam we'd found on the side of the road. I started the stove and began to fry eggs and ham. I brushed my hand over the shrubbery beside me. Some gold, some red. I was thrilled to be in Colorado.

Twenty kilometres past the border of Colorado, at the edge of Paradox Valley, we met two road cyclists. Joel and Steve were beginning a training ride up the hill we had just descended.

"Where you two off to?" Joel asked us.

"Not sure where we're headed to today but thrilled to be in Colorado," I said.

"Do you think you can make it to Norwood? It's about 60 miles further and you're more than welcome to stay with my family if you do," invited Joel.

"He has a hot tub and there's a community fundraiser party tonight with a huge buffet!" Steve added.

We immediately agreed and pedalled fast past ranch after ranch. Horses, cattle, sheep and herds of deer stared at us as we rode by. As we crested another hill, snow-capped mountains rose in the distance. A light wind pushed us toward them and my heart began to soar. The peaks seduced me with a promise of adventure and exploration; but mostly, I felt they would calm me.

Still an hour's ride from Norwood, Joel and Steve pulled up beside us in their truck. "Throw your panniers in the back. You can bike, but it'll be nice to go unloaded," Joel encouraged.

As they drove away with our gear, I said, "You do realize we've known them for a total of two minutes and we just handed over everything we have."

"It's nice being lighter," Mike said, unworried as usual.

Joel stood at the end of his driveway, holding hands with his beautiful 16-month-old daughter. We followed them into their home, and Joel introduced us to his wife, Jessica. Our panniers were waiting for us in a separate suite attached to a greenhouse. Everything looked and smelled clean. Afternoon sun pierced the windows and spun sparkles of sunlight over the bed. A bed! It would be the first bed we'd slept on in weeks. After washing our filthy bodies, we were whisked away to the event in town.

It seemed as if the entire town had come together to raise money for a family whose son needed numerous surgeries. We donated and then stuffed ourselves silly, while entertained by a phenomenal band. Mike and I met many wonderful, small-town Coloradans. I kept trying to find a kid to dance with me since Mike doesn't really dance. Years ago, when we backpacked down Central and South America, I wanted to take a salsa class. With him, of course. He refused and it became our only argument of that five-month trip. I danced with the instructor and now accepted I'd be without him on the dance floor. Mike watched me from the side of the room. My legs were so sore from biking that it was more of a hypnotic sway than dancing.

I woke rested the next morning. The bed was heaven in contrast to the mat I'd been sleeping on in the tent. But the best part of the night was I hadn't had terrible dreams! I awoke guilt-free. My head lay on Mike's chest while I watched the gradual light through the window. I wasn't naive enough to think it would last, but having a break in the night was incredible.

The road hugged a cliff, casting us in a shadow. Without direct sunlight, it must have been below zero degrees, and the thrill of a huge downhill was lost in the fact that we were freezing. Even with our warmest clothes and our hands and faces covered, we stopped often to shake feeling back into our arms and legs.

"The shadows in the switchbacks are freezing!" Mike yelled as we flew downhill.

"Winter is coming. I'm so glad we have a place to stay tonight and don't have to look for a camp," I yelled back. Joel and Jessica had called ahead to their friends in Telluride, to ask them to host us for a couple of nights.

"Where would you like to bike to next?" Mike asked.

"To Ouray, Colorado."

"No, I mean, like you said, winter is coming, we should probably start thinking about where to go. If we're going to head south in the States or fly elsewhere." Mike pulled up beside me and we relished the quiet road, riding alongside one another.

"Oh my gosh, I have no idea. I haven't really thought about it," I answered truthfully.

Mike held his right hand behind his back, attempting to warm it out of the wind. When the chill dissipated, he brought it in front of his mouth and blew hot air into his palm. Then he grabbed his handlebar and did the same thing with his left hand. "We should decide soon," he said.

We followed the tea-coloured San Miguel River – the first time we had seen so much water in a month. We pulled over to wash our hands and faces. We topped up our already full water bottles just because we could.

The last ten kilometres to Telluride seemed to take forever. We were exhausted from biking uphill in a short distance. We moved at a snail's pace, but we enjoyed it so much we hardly cared. The mountains reached above us and swept down to the road. The air was fresh, filled with moisture and life. Snow had fallen on the top of the peaks, and it glittered in the midday sun.

We arrived in Telluride at one in the afternoon on a Sunday. The small town met my high expectations of Colorado: big mountains, white water, great bookstores and healthy groceries. It being Sunday, I knew Mike would be thinking about home. For the last nine years, he and a group of friends had gathered around our TV to watch football. They ate pizza, drank beer and had guy time. I knew he missed it.

"Why don't we find a bar and go watch the game?" I suggested.

"Really?"

"Of course. It'll be fun."

At the bar, we sat down at a small round table. It took my eyes a few minutes to adjust to the dim light, even though TVs hung from every corner showing the game. I liked watching sports, but I would have rather seen Telluride. I shifted to look out the window. A large planter and curtain blocked the view, but I knew what was out there: mountains and more awesome mountains. I turned back to stare at Mike. His eyes lit up as his team ran for a touchdown.

"Yes!" he yelled and jumped out of his seat in excitement.

Relationships are about compromise, I told myself. I should have figured that one out a long time ago. We ordered nachos and I submitted to enjoying a lazy afternoon watching football.

Joel's friends hosted us for two nights. We spent part of our day in a bookstore cafe flipping through world atlases and reading Lonely Planet books. I opened a hardcover book and slid my hand across the pictures and words about Thailand. Beautiful silks, temples and Buddhist statues stared out at me.

"Kat, look at this one." Mike held out a book on Tibet, another place I felt drawn to from reading about Everest and Himalayan adventures. Barren landscapes, captivating mountains and people with windswept cheeks came to mind. My mouth watered with thoughts of dishes like pad Thai, yak butter tea, dumplings and pho. I went back to the beginning of the alphabet on the travel shelf and reached for a photo album of Australia. Kangaroos, koalas and big hairy spiders were featured. I imagined the sounds pulsating from a didgeridoo. I salivated with thoughts of eating fish and chips on a hot sunny beach after an afternoon spent surfing. *How could we decide?* There were countless places to visit and foods to sample.

We left the bookstore having made no decisions. Still, there was a feeling of liberty of having nowhere to go. We walked down the main street of Telluride, where we didn't have to be anywhere but where we were and where we wanted to be. We were learning to appreciate the freedom of waiting until we were ready before we continued on.

The next day, we pedalled seemingly straight up, pushing every relentless metre of the climb. To say my leg hurt was an understatement. The muscles in my left hamstring and calf were clenched like an angry fist. It was not unusual for my leg to get sore during a day of riding, but the pain no longer went away overnight. In the late afternoon, we made it to the other side of the mountains and rode through another valley.

"Kat, look!" Mike pointed to a sign that read, "Orvis Hot Springs." We didn't need to discuss it. We turned down the driveway. We were given a place to set up our tent and 24-hour access to the springs. A cobblestone path led the way to the first pool.

"Everyone's naked," Mike said. I was undressed in, oh, about one second. Mike took some more convincing, but he eventually slid in beside me. *Why is he shy?* I wondered. The pool was shallow and we sat on the bottom and relaxed our heads on the edge. Mike fell asleep while I thought about why he wasn't trying to make love to me. I reached for the robe beside me and opened up a romance book I had found in the reception area. For two days, Mike and I wore only a towel or a robe when we were outside the tent. The multiple pools of varying depths and temperatures relieved the pressure on my leg. The cheesy Harlequin romance gave my brain a rest from overanalyzing everything.

The pools were hot, but outside the temperatures steadily dropped. We woke up to frozen water bottles. With my leg feeling better, we finished the ride into the town of Ouray.

A month earlier, while walking back to our campsite in Zion National Park, we had met a rock climber named Jason. Sinewy muscles strained against his shirt and a rope hung from his shoulders while we talked. When he found out Mike and I didn't know where we were headed next, he recommended we ride to Colorado and his hometown Ouray.

Still, I think Jason's wife, Lisa, was surprised when we showed up at their front door. Their house sat on the outskirts of the mountain town and looked like a cozy country cottage. Lisa dashed our hopes of camping when she motioned to their backyard. My mood sank as soon as I saw the large hill butted up against their house. Their yard might be a good place for a waterslide but little else. *Where are we going to go?* I wondered. We'd already cycled past the locked gate at the campground near town. Camping season was obviously over.

"I'm sorry about the camping, but you're more than welcome to make yourselves at home," Lisa said. "Actually, you have great timing because our renter just moved out, so there's lots of space." I perked up. Lisa invited us to follow her through the doorway off the garage. "You two can stay in here. There's a room in the back, the toaster oven works and the stove and shower are good to go. I'll bring you both fresh towels. We have a workout tomorrow morning with our trainer, would you like to come?" Lisa asked.

I love you, I thought.

With that, we were home. Their trainer, Jeff, ran a CrossFit gym. We did push-ups, dips, pull-ups on rings and more squats than I care to remember. Exercising muscles other than the ones we'd been using for cycling for two months felt amazing. We promised to come back the next day.

But the next morning I couldn't move. Everything hurt. I had exercised more than my body could handle. It was no longer used to it. Under the bedcovers, I fought with myself for hours before it was time to go. *You have never missed a workout. You have to go.* My other side countered: *You should rest. You're working out muscles you don't need right now. Stay in bed! It's supposed to be a rest day anyways.* For years, I had gotten up early to train before work. I tossed. I turned. Lounging in bed was foreign to me. *I need to relax,* I told myself. *Hanging out with Mike in the morning is a good thing.*

As I made peace with being restful, I realized the trip was about more than renewing our marriage. It was about a new way of life and focusing on being happy in the moment. I submitted. I settled in the comfy bed, wrapping my arms around Mike.

Later that afternoon, I sat having a tea with Lisa, right before she and Jason were to leave on a climbing trip. "It's Halloween tonight and you and Mike should head to Main Street," Lisa said. "I have to show you something." She bounded up the stairs. My legs were not ready for stairs. I caught up to her at the top where she stood in front of a huge box overflowing with colourful fabrics. "This is our costume box. Find yourself something to wear and have fun!" She gave me a quick hug, ran back down the stairs and disappeared.

Mike and I dug through the box and picked a costume. Leaves blew in the wind and fell in little piles outside the door. The sun had begun to set, tucking itself in for the night behind one of the mountains. Once on the main street, we locked the bikes outside a chocolate and coffee shop and went in to change.

"Happy Halloween!" The staff greeted us. The music was loud and they were dancing behind the counter. I changed into a bright, green, red and white clown costume. The matching jester hat and bells jingled as I walked out to the shop's impromptu dance floor. "Cute," Mike winked at me and headed behind the closed doors to put on his costume.

The shop erupted with laughter as Mike waddled out wearing a sumo wrestler costume. It was massive, with a big belly, "man breasts" that jiggled as he walked and a black thong. We had to push him through the doors to leave, which caused more howling.

The kids of Ouray trick-or-treat up and down the main street, and all the shops and restaurants stay open late to hand out candy. Mike and I had bought a big bag of chocolates and suckers to give away. Adults took photos of Mike and kids ran from both ends of the street to gawk at him. Children wouldn't stop staring, even as I tried to hand them candy. I gave up and handed Mike the bag. His normal reserved nature hid beneath his costume.

Jeff, the trainer, spotted us while I sheepishly munched on a Halloween treat. I expected he was going to reprimand me. My own trainer would've been disappointed had I skipped a workout. But Jeff said nothing, surely noticing how sore I was when I dropped a sucker on the ground and could barely bend over to pick it up. I quickly changed the subject from CrossFit and made Mike dance in his Halloween costume. He slapped his thighs and pumped his legs up and down. I doubled over in laughter. My sore abs complained, which had me wriggle more in a hilarity of pain.

Mike and I spent six days in the little apartment. It is one of my favourite parts about travelling: finding special places that begin to feel like home. We worked out with Jeff in the mornings, hiked during the days, recovered in the chocolate and coffee shop, cooked dinners and researched possible travel locations at night. We spent hours discussing where we should go next while soaking in Ouray's hot springs. Soon the stiffness in my body from CrossFit subsided and I was able to get out of bed on my own.

On our last full day in Ouray, I rode into town alone. Restored Victorian houses built directly into the rock on the side of mountains held lit candles in the windows. Old mines, high in the cliffs above where I cycled, had their mouths wide open, as if gulping for fresh air. The bubbling of the Uncompahgre River soothed me. Trees, draped in thick moss, hung near to the road like an old man's shaggy beard. I had the road all to myself.

I bought a coffee at the chocolate shop before I walked down Main Street to use a pay phone to call my ex–best friend. I walked slowly and my stomach churned. The phone was cold when I held it to my ear. I typed in the numbers and waited for his voice. *Forget it, Kat,* I told myself as I slammed the phone back on its hook.

I leaned against the side of the booth to think about what I really wanted. Half of me didn't want to talk to Alex. The other half of me did. I stared up and down the street. It was pretty rare for me to be alone. In the two months Mike and I had been biking, we were always together, and I didn't know when the next chance to phone Alex would come.

He answered, "Hey girl." I waited for the sound of his voice to cut through my heart. I waited to crumble down to the ground. I waited for tears to come.

Silence.

"Hi," I said. I didn't fall apart. I missed him, but I realized I was doing just fine without him. In fact, I wanted to tell him I was pretty awesome, actually. Alex knew Mike was a good guy. He knew me leaving was the right thing for us to do.

The phone call was short. We didn't talk about it, but I could tell he missed me too. We agreed to not be in contact anymore. For the sake of our marriages.

Goodbye Alex.

I got on my bike and pedalled back to Mike. I was sad, but I also felt a lot lighter. I realized I felt like myself. I rode beneath the mines again, with their wide gaping mouths open as if in awe. And then I heard a cheer come out from the depths of me like I was winning a race, as if I had accomplished the impossible. I was glad I had made the phone call. Nothing was left hanging. Now it was time for me to concentrate on my personal repair. I noted I didn't think about Alex *all* of the time anymore. I looked forward to the day when he was no longer in my dreams and when his spot would be taken up by new best friend: my husband.

On the way back to Mike, I was totally present, riding in the most beautiful mountain scenery on this wonderful day. A grin covered my face. But, as well, I smiled from within. The depression that had lurked beneath the surface and poisoned my system had finally received the medicine it needed to go away. *Goodbye.*

Riding out of Ouray, the mountains glowed in the soft morning sun. The wind kissed the tops of white-barked aspens. Their golden leaves cascaded down on us like rice blessing Mike and me on our wedding day. For the first time, I felt as if I was moving toward something, instead of pounding on the pedals to run away. I looked at Mike and my face lit up. It was a new beginning.

"Do you get the same feeling I do while moving through this part of Colorado?" I asked Mike. A sensation in my stomach and heart had taken hold. "It makes me feel alive, like I'm in the exact spot I should be." I had enjoyed travelling through the deserts of Nevada and Utah, but I never felt the connection or the urge to stay forever. "These mountains. They're different," I explained. "I want to stay."

"Kat, you know I'd still be in my parents' basement if you never came along," Mike said. It was an old joke he's said for years. "But I understand. I love it here too."

"What would you like in a new home?" I asked. We had decided we would not be moving back to Winnipeg.

"Friends, a good job. You?"

"I've loved the smaller towns we've stayed in. The way people in the communities seem to take care of each other is incredible. I'd love to find a Canadian town with a great gym facility, friends, tourists, trails," I smiled. "And mountains!"

Big words for a prairie girl. We laughed.

And so began a conversation that would continue over the next year. What did we want to do with our lives?

Colorado never stopped being the most welcoming place. We biked out of the mountains and rolled downhill to the city of Montrose to Cristi's house, a match from the Warmshowers website.

In front of Cristi's home, I fell off my bike. Leaves had filled the drain and gave the illusion there was no curb. I hit the pavement and was laughing when a man pulled up. "You must be Katrina and Mike. Welcome to Montrose!" Gavin reached out a hand and I brushed mine off on my shorts before shaking his. "Cristi is my friend. She'll be back in a while, but I'll give you directions to an amazing coffee shop where you can wait for her." Gavin assured us he would see us later that night at a party.

After ordering coffees and snacks, the barista told us someone had called ahead and paid for our order. Mike and I were smiling, sitting outside with the pumpkins and admiring the fall colours when Cristi came by. She handed us a key. "Make yourselves at home," she said. "I have to get groceries after work so I'll be back around 5 p.m." This was the amazing thing we were learning on our trip: people were so trusting. They met us for a few minutes before handing over the keys to their house.

I awoke late the next morning. "Mike?" I leaned down and kissed him to coax him awake. We were meant to be on the road again. "I think you might want to take a look outside." Mike rolled over and opened the blinds above his head and instantly sat up to stare out the window. He let go of the blinds and they snapped back into place. He rubbed his face and let his hands run through his hair before opening the blinds again.

"Well, I guess it is November. I don't think *that* is too conducive to bike travel," he said. Over a foot of snow had fallen through the night. The ground was covered with a thick white blanket. It was still snowing. Falling and hugging the trees. *It's beautiful*, I thought.

"It's fine. We should still go. The snow will melt," I insisted.

"There's no way we're going to bike up the mountain passes. It'll be too dangerous," Mike said. I don't back down easily, so I grabbed my bike and pushed the snow away from the door to go for a ride. I like to be challenged. We could do this. My tires pushed at the top layers of flakes and melted the snow toward the pavement. I spun, slipped, skidded and was soon stuck. I was like Bambi on ice, limbs everywhere, spinning in circles.

We rented a vehicle.

I held Mike's hand as we drove through the mountains to stay with rock climbers Ken and Sam. Then to Warmshowers hosts in Boulder and later Denver. Mike bought two airline tickets and we boarded the plane to cross the Pacific Ocean. From the plane's window, I stared below as the terrain changed from mountains to desert. White to red. I spotted the Hoover Dam and the Colorado River below. *We've travelled so far*, I thought in wonder. Mike slept beside me. But he was there. We were together. I felt happy. And glad. Glad I'd asked him to take this trip. Happy he had said yes. Now we were flying somewhere new. Somewhere we could no longer just bike home.

CHAPTER 8

NEW ZEALAND
Fixing Leaks

The crazy thing about being married is two lives try to conform into one. Perhaps for some couples this happens naturally, but for others it's as foreign as landing in a new country with different laws, strange animals and driving on the wrong side of the road. Everything is upside down.

When the plane landed in Auckland, New Zealand, we had put an ocean between home and us. We had officially committed ourselves to travelling together. As we wrestled our cardboard bike boxes to an area designated for assembling bikes, I realized we were about to take on something bigger than we thought when we bought the tickets.

Although Mike and I never really fought, he did annoy me at times. Whenever I walked through the front door to find his shoes thrown haphazardly in the front entrance, ready to trip me up, or when his smelly socks were left abandoned at the end of the sofa. These small, careless things tested my patience – of which, admittedly, I had little. I'd make a snippy comment. Mike would only raise his eyebrows. Not that I was perfect. I knew it drove Mike nuts that I wouldn't remember to turn off the lights when I left the house, or when I turned the heat on in the middle of summer.

Those things were behind us now. Our home was reduced to what was packed in the cardboard boxes I helped drag out of the airport and along the pavement.

We opened the boxes and soon everything we owned was strewn across the pavement as if a tornado had dumped out the contents. *That is our lives,* I thought. I cringed as another couple arrived effortlessly carrying oversized black bags. I ran around like a hen collecting her chicks, amassing our gear into a pile. They casually unzipped their bags and pulled out bikes.

"Hi. Where are you two from?" I asked.

"Seattle. I'm Zach." His voice was soft and calm and he smiled as he spoke. His narrow face grew fuzzy sideburns and I noticed tattoos sneaking out from beneath his bike jersey on his right arm. I sensed they were each symbolic, holding important stories.

"I'm Elise," she said, reaching out her hand. Her grip was strong. She had the persona of independence and determination, yet her voice was kind. She didn't seem to judge the mess Mike and I had in front of us.

Zach pulled out a large wrench. I noticed the two of them had enough bike tools to set up their own shop. I found our comparatively tiny tool and began to assemble a rack onto my bike. I urged Mike on in my head, *Please speed up. Please let us have enough tools to put everything back together.* I didn't want to take longer to set up than Zach and Elise. I didn't want to show our lack of ability as a couple, demonstrating, even to strangers, that we were not perfect. Perhaps I wished I had already transformed in this trip, slowed down enough to not care about silly things like being faster, but, apparently, I'm competitive. I want to be part of a winning team. And I already felt we were losing.

As it turned out, I didn't have to send Mike telepathic signals, as his total disregard for any packing system whatsoever meant it went rather fast. According to Mike, everything just had to fit in the panniers, it didn't matter which one. This time, I kept quiet.

We biked with Zach and Elise into the middle of Auckland city before saying goodbye. Mike and I then spent three days with Warmshowers hosts.

"Since you don't have a plan anyway, you should spend your time on the South Island," our host Mitch said. "There's less traffic and great cycling routes." He explained how the South Island has only one million people, dramatic scenery and lots of free camping.

We bought tickets for an overnight bus to the bottom of the North Island, which would connect to the ferry for the South Island. Our last day in Auckland was spent preparing: finding new maps, gas for our stove, lighters and books. Once we finished our chores, we cycled back to the house to pick up our panniers so we could catch the bus, when Mike got a flat tire in front of a sushi shop (very convenient). We had patches on us but no tubes.

"I can't get the patch to stick," Mike said, after multiple attempts to adhere the patch.

"We passed a bike shop not too long ago, I'll go and buy a new tube," I said. I jumped on my bike and off I went. When I returned 30 minutes later, Mike was sitting on the curb with a mouthful of rice and salmon and a silly grin on his face.

"Patch finally held," he said. We cycled back to the bike shop to return the tube because we owned a few already. Five minutes *after* returning the tube, Mike got another flat. We were close to our host's home, so I left Mike on the curb and biked there to grab one of our own tubes.

In our bedroom, I opened Mike's four panniers. Bike parts were packed with clothes, toothpaste with repair kits, kitchenware with underwear.

I searched for the tubes, pulling out contents from the panniers, growing frustrated with Mike's disregard for simple organization. Even after spewing everything into piles, I couldn't find the tubes – but I did find Mike's blue shirt that he swore he had lost days earlier on the plane.

I cycled back to Mike downright irritated.

Mike didn't fight with me.

"Great! You found my blue shirt!" he exclaimed with enthusiasm. I went off in a huff to re-buy the tube from the bike shop.

We had cycled for barely five minutes through the town of Picton, on the South Island, when Mike had his 11th flat tire. He just stepped off his bike and shook his head.

"I think the punctures have to do with the rim-tape slipping," Mike replied once I sat down beside him. "I'll use our electrical tape and stretch it over the inside of the rim."

"Sounds good," I said, staring at the mess that had exploded on the curb. I realized every tool we had was spilling out of the panniers. We had to figure out how to repair his flat tire issue, and I had to figure out how to overlook his small annoyances as he seemed to disregard mine. I watched patiently as he made the repair.

It may have been that Mike noticed how annoyed I'd been at his lack of organization, or perhaps he realized he could be more efficient, but the next morning Mike took time to organize his panniers. The tarp, stove, pots and water filter were put in a pannier on my bike. One pannier each was dedicated to our sleeping pad, headlamp and sleeping bag. Another pannier each for clothes. Food was in one bag and the bike kit went in the last one. The tent was attached onto the back of Mike's rack.

I chose a secluded gravel road following the shoreline on the east side of the island. The road carried us upwards then dropped down to the ocean before venturing steeply back up. With each rise and fall, the South Pacific Ocean swelled and mountains rose in the distance. We shared the road with only sheep, cows and ostriches. We cycled continuously for hours but only covered 32 kilometres, collapsing in the tent by the time we made camp at White Bay.

"Kat, wake up! Something is outside!" Mike whispered and shook me into consciousness.

"Outside where?" I mumbled sleepily.

"Out there!" Mike reached for my shoulder while I struggled to find my way to the top of the sleeping bag, trying to decipher where I was. My brain, fogged with sleep, melded all of the nights in different locations together. The top of my head hit the cool air and I slowly emerged from the cocoon of down. My body responded with a shiver like I'd jumped into a bone-chilling lake. I could hear a buzzing pulsating around the tent. *Mosquitos?* I then made out the noise that had Mike anxious. Ice skates on a table. Tap dancers on a wooden balcony.

"Kat, go see what it is," said Mike, as he strived to push me out of the tent.

"No way, you woke up first! You go." I slapped a headlamp into Mike's hand. He wrapped the strap around his head and I heard the hum of the zipper teeth separating as he ventured outside.

But I was too curious to stay in the tent. *If Mike was going to be attacked by some brute, then I'd do my best to defend him,* I thought. I crouched low through the door and followed behind him to the commotion.

My toes squished into the wet earth and I bent down to pick up a rock. I was ready for attack.

"There it is – in the tree," said Mike. Something was after our food. We had hung our food bag up high – really high – ever since those dogs had attacked our food bags in Utah. But apparently not high enough for a tree-climbing animal the size of an overfed house cat that looked like a large rat. The beast's claws gleamed in the moonlight.

"What is it?" Mike asked.

"I don't know," I said. "Scare it away."

It was beside the food we needed to last two days until we reached the next town. The beast looked down, scrutinizing us, its large eyes darting between the food bags and us. Mike leapt for the bags. The animal ran off and we made our way back to the tent.

"I'm impressed you actually woke up before me," I said. We fell asleep again, only to wake to a crashing sound. It was the middle of the night and an hour since "the attack." This time, I jumped out of the tent to scare the animal away. I collected our pots and brought them in under the vestibule of the tent, but the animal kept returning, clawing our pots and panniers by poking its head into the vestibule. Finally, we pulled everything inside. The tent filled like a clown car: panniers, food bags, smelly shoes and us.

The morning brought a rare sound. Rain. We lay in the tent and listened to the sky release its grip. We listened to the low rumble of waves pounding the seafront. I could hear shells crest the shore and ting like a wind chime on a country patio. We listened to each other's breath. Light filtered through the tent and we watched as drop after drop fell on our tent then rolled down its sides like fingertips gently tracing a lover's body.

After cycling for two and a half months, this was the first time we had rain. I slid my rain pants over top of my tights, excited to finally be using the jacket I had carted around for ten weeks. Mike and I secured large rain hats onto our heads with the string tightened beneath our chins. I went outside to take in the fresh fragrance of wet grass and flowers, circling in place with my eyes closed and a simple smile on my face.

To make breakfast, we secured two corners of our tarp to our bikes, the other half to the same tree the creature had been in (but now was nowhere to be seen, thankfully).

"I want to figure out what that animal was," I said to Mike.

"Yes, what a crazy night," he replied. "So where are we going to today?"

"You could look at the map if you like. It's in my handlebar bag." Mike crouched beneath the tarp and moved awkwardly over to my bike, his hand brushed his hat back to let it hang from the string around his neck. The map was damp and it hung limp in his hands as he brought it over to where I sat, making coffee. It was Mike's first time looking at the map of New Zealand. He stared at it, locating the thin black line that had been our road from Picton. His finger traced along the line as it meandered north, then east and finally south, following the jagged outline of the coast. Not far from our small, wiggly black line was a large, bold red line running straight, north to south on the map.

"Kat, do you know there is another road here?" Mike asked me.

"Umm." I wasn't sure how to answer his question. *Of course, I knew there was another road*! A road that any cyclist who actually wanted to get anywhere would have chosen! It would have saved us a lot of time, but I had realized weeks ago this trip had little to do with getting anywhere and more to do with where we were. If we wanted to get somewhere, we would have had a plan. We would have had a goal, and a final destination perhaps. But that wasn't what this trip was about. More crucial than reaching a destination on a map was crossing borders in our relationship and, with every kilometre, leaving our past behind. It was not about where we had been or where we were going on paper. Our movement, slightly awkward as it was, was so much more than that.

The back road, or "gravel scenic tour," as I had dubbed it in my head, had provided valuable insights. We had worked together fixing Mike's wheel, tested our bikes and fitness to make sure we were ready for longer stints in remote terrain and stayed alone in the wilderness with unknown animals. The gravel scenic tour had given me confidence our wheels could go anywhere.

I laughed. "But it's been a great road. Are you going to look at the routes more now?" I asked.

"Maybe," said Mike. "How many scenic detours do you have in mind?"

"Lots," I replied.

We packed up. We were faster now that Mike was organized. Our tires squished into the slimy gravel road, spitting up stones and leaving tire tracks. Progress was slow and we worked for it, but the scenery was pretty: wet and crisp from the rain. The trees were bright green.

The road left the coast and turned inland until we came to the intersection of the main highway. As we halted at the stop sign, I looked to my right and spotted Richard from Colorado. We had met Richard on the plane trip over, but he had stayed on the flight to come directly to the South Island. He now sat beneath the awning of an old post office, staring down at a map, wearing the same beige pants and checkered shirt he'd worn on the aircraft. His bike lay beside him, with his dripping rain jacket slung over its handlebars. His bike shoes were ancient and held together by duct tape.

"Richard!"

"Hey! You came south?" He jumped up for a wet hug. We traded stories of our days on the road since we'd met. Mike and I recommended the back road and gave him pointers on where to camp. After an hour beneath the awning, snacking, talking and watching the rain come down, Mike and I got back on the bikes.

"Oh wait!" I stopped and yelled back to Richard through the deluge of the bursting clouds. "Richard! Don't hang your food in the trees!"

The next town was Blenheim. We parked our bikes outside a library and, dripping wet, went inside.

"Excuse me, we're trying to find out what animal we met camping. It tried to steal our food," I told the librarian.

"Oh, a possum bother ya, did it?" The librarian said in a quick Kiwi accent. "Ya, bloody pest they are. Ya know in Australia they're protected...Bloody Aussies don't know what's good for them!" We rushed behind her skinny frame, droplets splattering from our jackets, leaving a trail to the section of the library that had the possum books. She opened one to a picture of a possum. There it was, the beady eyes staring up at us from the page.

"Yes, you're right, the animal was a possum. It was a little aggressive." I told her.

"Ya, I reckon you must know you need to keep all the food inside your tent?" She quizzed me.

Good thing there are no bears here, I thought.

From Blenheim, we rode State Highway 1 beside Marlborough's most famous vineyards. In the afternoon, the wind changed, blasting from the coast across the fields and slamming up against Mike's load. The gale pushed him into the middle of the highway. Fortunately, no trucks were passing at that moment. Mike brought his bike to the side of the road and stopped.

"I'm done. I've never felt wind like this. It's too dangerous." He looked petrified.

A few years earlier, I'd experienced strong wind while racing through Patagonia, Chile. My teammates and I had to walk and push our bikes in a paceline, taking turns up front blocking the gale. I knew what wind could do, but this was a first for Mike. We took a break and ate peanut butter and banana sandwiches until Mike's nerves felt ready to cycle again.

"There's a house, let's go ask to camp." I turned off to the right. Mike stayed by the road, thinking one dirty wet cyclist was less intimidating than two.

I wasn't sure how it became my job to ask to camp. The ride up a stranger's lane is always nerve-racking. I was petrified of big dogs, guns or people who might be mad we were on their property.

"Please have no dogs, please have no dogs," I muttered to myself. I knocked on the glass and laughed so hard when a tiny pipsqueak of a pup bounded up to the door. Far from the ferocious monster I had imagined.

A couple in their early 50s opened the door. Olaf and Anna introduced themselves, said yes to letting us camp on their lawn, showed us where to set up and left us to settle in.

Setting up a tent in a windy rainstorm while exhausted and in the dark must be the ultimate compatibility test for some couples. But our tool for success was the tarp. We attached two of its corners to trees and the other two to our bikes. Olaf came out to invite us inside. I respectfully declined, pointing to the dinner we had started making. Dinner was pasta, garlic, mushrooms and olives, with hot chocolate and popcorn for dessert. I didn't look at Mike, but I'm sure he thought I was crazy.

The wind bellowed and collapsed the tarp. Then, just as quick, the nylon billowed up like a hot air balloon. We were dry and happy. I felt like a kid playing in a parachute.

"Are you sure you don't want to come in for a cuppa and a shower?" Anna stuck her head beneath our tarp to invite us in again.

"Yes, that'll be great," Mike answered quickly, before I could say otherwise. The hot shower, the conversation and "cuppa" with our hosts were also wonderful.

With the early morning sun, I unzipped our fly for fresh air. The little puppy sniffed at our screen. When I opened the door, he bounded inside, dancing on Mike's chest. After breakfast, we took a walk with Olaf.

"We used to have 4,500 sheep on this farm," Olaf said.

"And you don't now?" All I could see were rows and rows of grape vines gripping the soil.

"Nope. Three years ago we decided to make the change from keeping sheep to having a vineyard. Sheep farming is not as profitable anymore. At the peak in New Zealand history, there were 70 million sheep, now there are under 40 million. There are better returns for dairy farmers and keeping vineyards. Plus, I'd been sheep farming my whole life so it was time for a change." He opened up the door of a small rusted blue truck. "Jump on in. I'll give you a tour."

It seemed an incredible challenge to have changed such a large amount of land and use its soil for something else, but Olaf and Anna said they were happy. As we bounced along their property in the back of their truck, I smiled to myself: Mike and I weren't the only ones making major life changes.

Wind typically blasts cyclists from the wrong direction: a headwind, from the side, from an angle. But after we left Olaf and Anna's yard, the wind cooperated. A tailwind! Soon we spun along at a delightful speed. I would bet the wind was gusting nearly 80 kilometres an hour, whipping us from behind. It was like having a friend pushing us uphill. Rows of trees, planted for wind protection, leaned over and leaves flew through the air. Dust and gravel from the side of the road picked up and spun in circles around us. We came upon Lake Grassmere, a shallow saltwater lake off of the South Pacific Ocean protected by a layer of sand dunes. The warm wind lashed at the surface, sending salt into the air. It felt like the weight of our packs had been taken off our bikes or our legs had super strength. Until, all of a sudden, the wind changed and we were hit from the side.

"Whoa!" I shouted, my hands gripping the handlebars as the wind tore at my bike. I squeezed my legs against the seat to keep the frame upright. After another hour, my triceps screamed from clenching the bars, trying to keep the bike on the narrow strip of road. My muscles ached; a stabbing pain throbbed from my wrists to my shoulders.

We were on the main highway heading to Kaikoura. There were two opposing lanes of traffic and the wind kept pushing us into the wrong lane. I gripped my handlebars tighter as I tried to not get knocked over. My heart raced, but secretly I loved the challenge.

"I'm officially not enjoying myself!" I heard Mike yell from behind me. *Uh-oh.*

"All right, as soon as we can, let's pull off!" I shouted back.

Only there was nowhere to go. The ocean was to our left and a wall of rock was to our right. There was no shoulder to cycle on. Massive trucks blasted past with a complete disregard for our safety. Our balance would be thrown off, and we'd totter toward the side of the road – a steep cliff above the ocean. The fun and the challenge of the wind were replaced by the fear of becoming a hood ornament.

Eventually, the cliff to our left levelled off into a stretch of sand. Waves ran up to the beach in rhythmic strides. In the middle of the inlet, a restaurant named "The Store" became our respite.

"Sweet things, just tuck yourselves under the palms over there," said the owner, pointing toward the beach in a large gesture that included the entire beach and a cluster of cabbage trees.

We put up our tent as the sun set, turning the sand into a floor of gold. The ocean calmed to tranquil waters. The sky turned shades of red, pink and cinnamon as it melted into the earth. Mountains stood behind us like a shield. We felt rich, enjoying the finest of mansions and looking out on our vast acreage.

In the morning, once we left the beach cove, the terrain changed from the rugged coastal mountains to an open stretch of sand and fields, as if the land was tacked onto the edge of the mountains as some kind of afterthought. Farmers took advantage of the flats and we passed properties yielding grass, sheep and cattle on our way into the town of Kaikoura.

It was along this stretch of road when Mike began talking to the animals. We laid down our bikes near dozens of seals sunning on massive boulders between the sea and us.

"Ourh, ourh!" Mike yelled loudly and flapped his hands like flippers. The large grey seals opened up their mouths and exited a guttural threat so putrid that Mike briskly retraced his steps, his shoes clacking against the rocks back up to the road. I roared with laughter.

On our way out of Kaikoura, we swore, for our sanity and safety, we would not bike on the main highway anymore and took the first back road we found, called the Inland Kaikoura Road. A warm air front pushed the clouds from the island, and we were rewarded with a view of the rugged peaks surrounding us. The sun glared and sizzled our skin before we thought to put sunscreen on.

After gaining over 500 metres of elevation in 60 kilometres, we rolled onto a long bridge crossing a river. We stopped and looked over the railing at the long drop below.

"Look there," said Mike, pointing under the bridge. "That'll be a perfect place to camp."

Following a narrow trail through the trees, we made our way down to the clear braided river. I grabbed our laundry bag and Mike took the water filter and we walked the expansive river flat to where one of the thicker braids had deeper water. I washed our clothes downstream from where Mike filtered water. Mountains soared above.

All day and the next, my legs were tired. Every stroke was an effort. Mike was exhausted too. After five hours of pedalling, we came to the Waiau River. Flashing blue, gushing and cold. I hung off the edge and figured out an awkward way to filter water while I iced my calf in the cool river. We debated on spending the night, but we couldn't find a good hiding place for the tent. After five more kilometres, we cycled up to a house on a large property and asked to camp in the yard. Erica and Stefan, who had six kids, were happy to have us.

In the middle of taking the panniers off of the bike, Erica handed us each a cold beer. I'm not much of a beer drinker and I could see Mike's disappointment as I really enjoyed this one and downed my bottle without sharing a drop.

The kids took turns riding our bikes and, soon, the stars illuminated the night sky while we sat on the deck and talked about big dreams. The moon matched our moods: big and bright.

In the morning, snuggled inside our tent, I listened to light rain while writing on the laptop. Mike slept beside me.

I nudged him. "Want to take a day off?"

"Yes." He rolled over back to sleep. Convincing him to take a day off was always that easy.

After a day relaxing in hot springs, Mike and I wove our way along gravel roads toward the city of Christchurch like we were on a treasure hunt. Our route on the back roads was anything but direct. We took turns up front, pushing the headwind.

"Don't worry, it's all downhill from here," the owner of a shop informed us.

"I'm convinced these folks don't ever leave their towns," Mike joked as we pedalled uphill once again.

It didn't matter because we were learning how to exist with each other. Mike took longer breaks than I wanted, and I tried to be patient. Meanwhile, I was driving him to bike further than he wanted. I was more organized and willing to put up with bad weather, while Mike continued to show me how to slow down. He still left his stuff scattered sometimes, but after forgetting to bring his shoes under the vestibule one rainy night, he never forgot to tuck his shoes away again. I still forgot to turn off the light of my headlamp and I went through more batteries than I should have.

We camped beneath another bridge, managing to hide our tent in a small opening of the bushes with enough space to cook dinner. I pulled out my small mat from the tent to sit on while I watched Mike make popcorn. Making popcorn together was something we'd done often throughout our relationship. We loved having people over, watching movies and eating popcorn. We hadn't done enough of it in the last couple of years.

Mike opened the valve to the fuel from the canister. The fuel, fed through a line, created a pool in the cup at the bottom of the stove. He took the lighter, ignited the fuel and a black puff of smoke streamed out from the flame. The first time we filled our canister with gasoline was near Lake Mead, Nevada. At the marina, Mike had put the bottle beneath the hose and the fuel came out too hard and backlashed from the bottle into his eyes. He dove his head into the lake to save his eyesight and relieve the pain. We were a lot more cautious filling it up after that.

Mike listened patiently for the hiss that told him the fuel had vaporized and the stove was ready to turn on. It was something of an art and he was now able to get it right most days without having to relight the liquid fuel. Once lit, the stove roared like a jet plane.

Mike dug around our food bag, which still bore holes from the dog attack in Colorado. After finding the bag of kernels, he drizzled oil onto the frying pan and waited until it sizzled before he tested a kernel to see if it was hot enough. It was, so he covered the bottom with kernels and put the titanium pot on upside down so it worked like a lid. The kernels popped furiously. Shaking the pan back and forth, and holding onto it with the grippers, Mike listened for the moment the popping started to calm. He flipped it over so the popcorn was now in the pot. "Ta-da!" he said with a proud grin.

The river gurgled. Darkness surrounded us except what shone in our headlamps. I felt a tingle as if I yearned for Mike. I made note of how comfortable he was with living in the bush now.

The site reminded me of being a kid and playing in the forest with my sister and dad. We made stick brooms to brush the forest floor of our bush home and made beds out of moss. Everything felt cozy. I pulled out the SPOT and pressed the button that would send the email announcing our location. The SPOT blinked green, as if to say, "We're under the bridge, beside the river, hiding in the bushes, under the tarp, near the roosters. No need to worry. We're doing just fine."

In Christchurch, we rolled Mike's bike into a number of shops, trying to decipher the problem with his wheel and flat tires. Turned out the rim tape that protects the tube from the spoke nipples had been slipping, which caused heat friction holes in the tube. The electrical tape we'd put on it back in Picton had not worked for long. We bought new rim tape we hoped would solve the problem.

When it came time to leave Christchurch, Mike had another flat. *Here we go again*, I thought.

"Maybe you should buy a new bike," I joked. Even so, I found I had more patience than usual.

"It's just a nail, Kat!" Mike exclaimed. "Look at how fast I am at this now," he said as he expertly changed the tube.

From behind, someone shouted, "I know that Canadian!" I turned around to find Zach and Elise.

"So awesome to see you!" We hugged like long lost friends. While travelling, relationships are often swift and intense. Since we had met at the airport, we had begun emailing and reading each other's blogs. Mike and I couldn't leave now. We decided to stay to watch the Christchurch Christmas parade together.

After 5:00 p.m. we left the city. We had no concerns leaving a city late in the day in New Zealand. It felt safe, and even with no plans or destination, we found most people very welcoming. After a few hours of pedalling, we pulled into a property and asked to camp. We were invited in and I spent the evening cuddled into their couch, listening to Mike and two teenage boys talk about hockey. The next morning, I unzipped the tent to fresh, homemade muffins and a note of encouragement from the family. An amazing treat before heading up Arthur's Pass.

New Zealand's spine is the Southern Alps. This backbone is 500 kilometres in length from north to south and separates the east from the west. Arthur's Pass slips the traveller through the mountain range.

If we had done any planning before we started, we would have known prevailing wind comes from the west. It blew across the Tasman Sea, blasting the southern mountain range and gaining power through Arthur's Pass. The gale nailed us on the downward side in the Canterbury Plains. The wind howled and threatened to push us backwards as our jackets ballooned. Only with strength of will did we manage to keep the bikes going at a measly eight kilometres an hour.

Even at this ridiculously slow pace, we frightened sheep. As soon as they noticed us, the sheep turned away, presenting their furry bums. Lambs ran behind their moms, knocking out other baby sheep from hiding. There was lots of baaing (some of it Mike). We stopped to take pictures, but most of our photos are of sheep bums.

We disrupted grazing cattle too. Some stared, but often they chased us along the fenceline. Hooves pounding, dust billowing, heads twisting. Around a tight corner, we came upon cattle under the shade of a tree. The large animals toppled over each other to get away from us.

"No reaction when cars speed by, but the two of us on our bikes cause *udder* panic," Mike joked. (Probably not as funny for him when he had to explain it three times before I caught on.)

We woke the next day to a little less wind and a lot of rain. The clouds loomed heavy. At a thousand metres on our first pass, called Porters Pass, we found ourselves enveloped in them. I refrained from having my usual adventure race mindset where I picked one outfit and dealt with being too hot or too cold until it was convenient to change.

Put jacket on.

Take jacket off.

Put jacket on.

Take jacket off.

Mike preferred comfort over time loss.

Since the mountains lay smothered in a pillow of white, our eyes focused on the flora beside the road. Daisies grew in abundance and in patches across fields. Tall slender stalks with purple bulbs, called foxglove, brightened up the side of the road and tilted in the wind. Soft pink and dark purple lupins glittered in the soft rain. Perfect tiny yellow and violet wildflowers provided colour beside roaring waterfalls. Even common dandelions added to the rich beauty.

At Lake Pearson, we set up the tarp and began our familiar routine. We each had a piece of foam we used during the day to sit on. Now I laid mine at the front of my tent door. I stored two panniers on one side of the mat and two on the other. My shoes and sandals neatly placed in the middle so everything stayed dry beneath the fly. These small systems helped us feel comfortable, like we were at home each time we set up our tent. It didn't take long to put together our bedrooms anymore. We each had our own vestibule where we stored our belongings, and this made packing in the mornings easier, too, as we were no longer tripping over each other – especially in the rain.

By morning, the clouds had moved on and the sky was an uninterrupted blue. Majestic snow-covered peaks towered in front of us like an imposing castle. It appeared impenetrable, yet we followed the winding road, twisting our way up through the barrier until we found the gateway: Arthur's Pass. We crested the top and stopped to take in the view. The road fell away like a draw-bridge in either direction, the mountains gripped like handrails.

Mike stepped off his bike to check our brake pads. They were okay. I let him go ahead of me because he still braked more than me on the downhills. Just when I was starting to fly, I heard an explosion.

"You okay?" I asked, skidding to a stop.

"My back tube blew up again," Mike said as he flipped his bike upside down. "I'm not sure if the friction of braking on the downhill is causing enough heat to create a hole." We didn't know. I watched Mike calmly fix it and we continued on the decline until we found a place to camp in the bushes beside a waterfall. Mike pulled out a ridiculous amount of busted tubes from his panniers.

"I barely saved myself on that last hill. I did all I could to stay upright," Mike said.

"I'm glad you're okay," I said, and handed him a mug of tea, then shooed away a large, olive-green parrot. The kea briefly fluttered away, flaunting bright orange feathers beneath its wings. Then it came back. The keas pecked at our bikes with large, greyish-black beaks and, while we were focused on the tubes, one bit a huge chunk of foam out of Mike's helmet. The birds, once considered a nuisance to farmers because they attack the fat on the backs of sheep, are now protected. *What would the librarian have to say about that?* I wondered.

Then I watched as Mike got to work, having become quite proficient at repairing punctures. Strong patches were now blocking many of our leaks, in the tubes and in our relationship, I mused. I was glad for both.

CHAPTER 9

WEST COAST
Reading the Signs

For reasons unknown, I woke up on the wrong side of my sleeping pad. Our coffee filter was lost, perhaps donated to the coffee gods, perhaps in the mess of Mike's panniers. I roughly emptied one of his panniers. It wasn't there. I glared at Mike through the tent door, blaming him for not being organized.

"I'm sure we'll find it Kat," he said, unfazed by my exasperation.

"Is it so hard to put it back in the kitchen bag?" I huffed. Mike left my question unanswered. (It wasn't until much later I realized I should be happy he made me coffee in the first place rather than annoyed he did it wrong – according to my way of doing things.)

Near the town of Hokitika, on the West Coast of New Zealand, enticed by signs on the side of the road, we cycled up a gravel driveway to a produce stall. We dropped our bikes and walked through the door of an old tin shed.

"This one looks great!" Mike held up a crisp head of green lettuce. My mouth salivated from the excitement of fresh vegetables and we quickly filled our shopping bag.

"What do you want?" The words pierced the air behind us. Mike and I spun around to see a woman with frown lines and penetrating eyes.

"We'd like to purchase these vegetables, please," said Mike, handing her the bag. She took the bag from him like an eagle diving in for the kill.

"We only sell two heads of lettuce at a time, not one," she sneered.

"We're on our bikes and we'd really appreciate if we could buy these vegetables. We don't have any way of refrigeration," I explained. We didn't need two heads of lettuce.

"That's your problem, now, isn't it? Those are the rules." Her arm waved toward a piece of cardboard nailed to the side of the tin shed. A list of rules, scrawled out in scratchy writing read, "Only two heads of lettuce at a time." We sighed, bought the two heads of lettuce, and then continued to Hokitika, where we came upon a fish and chips shop.

"Mike, I'll run in and see if they have an outlet for the laptop," I said. I opened the glass doors to the diner. After plain lettuce, the delightful smell of grease and potatoes hit my nose. I scanned the small restaurant. All four booths were empty and three had an outlet. We ordered two large fish and chips and sank into the padded seats and pulled out our laptop, excited to be able to restore its power and work on our website. The doors swung open and four more customers walked in and soon after another five. A line formed from the old-style cash register, filling the small restaurant.

"Do you have your laptop plugged in?" Jostled from the intensity of my writing, I looked up into the midsection of a woman with her hands pushing into her hips. "What do ya two think you're doing?" She glared. Her eyes were filled with a piercing clarity. Her body whipped around, vibrating the table, making my coffee spill. "Did any of you give them permission to use our electricity?" She bellowed over the customers in line to the staff working the fryers. They bowed their heads and shook them, shrinking into their necks like turtles.

I realized we were in trouble. The customers in line had gone dead silent. Everyone stared. I couldn't tell if they took the side of the woman or pitied us. The entire restaurant was soundless but for shuffling of feet and heads hanging low.

Her hot breath expelled down my neck. "Now, what the hell! Do ya two reckon we're made of money?"

Mike spoke. "I'm sorry, we assumed we could use the outlet in our booth while we ate." My body slithered beneath the table to grab our cord. I closed the laptop and packed it away inside my pannier. My cheeks were red with embarrassment. I took a longing last look at the french fries and made my way to the door. Behind me, Mike stepped up to the front counter. "That ought to cover it," he said, placing two ten-cent pieces on the counter.

I should have known better. Every plug outlet in the country seemed to have a switch on it to shut the power completely off. My day was not going well. Once we arrived at a nearby campground, I laid down my bike and told Mike, "I'm going to go find an internet cafe where I can upload the website. I'm determined to upload it today." Writing about our trip and our relationship had been therapeutic for me. It made me happier, though the pleasure shrunk away with the frustration of trying to upload.

On Main Street, I found a video shop with a few computers. I put $2 into the machine to use the internet. Nothing happened. I turned the computer off and then on. Nothing happened. I hit the button on the screen to turn it on and then off. Nothing happened. I stood up and spoke to the girl behind the counter.

"Excuse me, I put money into the computer, but I can't get it to work," I said, trying to hold in my growing frustration with everything to do with the day.

"Did you read the sign?" She snapped her gum at the side of her mouth and explosions of saliva hit the desk. I turned to read the sign.

Use of the computers. $2 for 20 minutes.

If you need more help we cannot help you.

NO REFUNDS

Well, that summed up my morning and I burst into tears. I pushed the chair back under the desk as hard as I could to blow off some anger, but the chair, on wheels, only bounced in softly and then rolled back out.

AAAAHHHHHHHHH! *Seriously*! *Why is nothing going right today*? I packed my bag up. Tears flowed freely down my cheeks, even though I wiped them away every two seconds.

"It's not really that big of a deal," said the girl as she came over and handed my two dollars back.

It wasn't a big deal. She was right. But, in that moment, it felt like a big deal. I should have focused on the fact that I was lucky to be living the dream. *What's wrong with me?* I asked. *Great. Now I'm feeling bad that I'm having a bad day.* But not every moment while travelling is an amazing experience. Not every moment is worth leaving home, family and friends. It was times like this when I still felt distant from Mike; the times when I was an emotional wreck and used to having Alex to talk to.

I still missed Alex. I didn't think of him all the time, but he still came into my thoughts, especially when I was upset. He had always been there and would have known how to make me see I was acting like a spoiled brat. Some days I was so mad at Alex for not being around and frustrated I shouldn't reach out to him. *But why do I care? Why does he always have to enter my mind when I'm angry and grumpy?* I exited the door of the video shop, stamped my foot on the pavement and tried not to care.

"Pull it together, Kat," I mumbled to myself. I made my way to the public library, stubbornly hoping to find somewhere to continue to work on our website. I placed myself at an ancient, brown, collapsible table, after timidly inquiring if it was okay to sit there. I brushed away tears.

The shelves of books smelled of old paper. The history of the hardcovers calmed me and, for some reason, I thought of Stacy, the blonde girl we had met near Zion National Park. I wrote her an email.

Hey Stacy,

How are you doing!? Mike and I often wonder about you.

We are on the West Coast of New Zealand on a beautiful day and I'm in a grumpy mood. I miss home, I miss my mom, dad and my sister. I miss my coffee machine. I feel so bad for being grumpy because I'm here and I should be happy all of the time.

Do you ever have hard times? Mike never seems to have bad days, which makes me feel even more selfish.

Otherwise, things are great. We're loving the riding and NZ is free-camping paradise. You would be proud!

Your friend in travel,

Katrina

Venting made me feel better. In print, I could see how trivial my concerns were. I sighed and thought to myself I had little to complain about. *I need to change my attitude*, I told myself. I stared out the window at the open blue sky until I could remember how much I loved the freedom of travel. The ocean swelled, but it was not agitated.

An hour later, I flipped back to my email inbox. I already had a reply from Stacy.

Well hey there lady…I totally understand days of mood alterations far from your norm…I've actually had them more often lately and it's driving me insane to be honest. I've created an ideal life and am fortunate to be living my dream daily, but it's not always easy. My advice is to be gentle with yourself, you are allowed to be cranky…after all, it is a unique situation you are asking your body to endure…be kind, but more importantly just be (even if it's cycling with your cranky pants on, don't feel the need to be in the om-like state everyday…not even the Dalai Lama can do that…just sayin').

ok, get back to it…

be safe my friend ... tell Mike I say what up,

Stacy

I leaned back and rocked on the small chair in the library. *So this is what I'm going to do. I'm not going to be upset with myself for getting upset. I'm just going to be.* I walked back to the campground with a refreshed bounce in my step. I nearly started skipping when I realized I missed Mike. I was accustomed to being with him all hours of the day, so being away for five hours seemed like a long time.

I was reminded of when we were younger. We had been dating for a few years, and I'd saved enough money for a trip after a season of working at a women's shoe store. I saved until I could buy the backpack I wanted and the plane ticket I coveted, a ticket to Mexico. I was 20 years old and slept on beaches in a cheap kid's pop-up tent. I had no credit card or travel insurance, but I did have $13 a day to last six weeks. This was a time before email was common, and it took two weeks before I broke down and phoned Mike.

"Are you okay? Why haven't you called?" he asked. Because I'd been good. I'd been sipping margaritas and sailing on a new friend's yacht. I was having a blast. When I picked up the phone to call Mike, it was because I had my first bad day. Talking to Mike made me feel better. He was my emotional support and had been there when I needed him. From that day onward, I called often, using up much of my daily budget. (Too much – by the time I came home, I had lost 20 pounds from not eating enough.) We were young. And whatever version of love that was, we were in love.

I began to run. Mike was digging holes for new fence posts when I arrived back. A hammer was slung through the belt loop of his pants.

"I found work," he smiled, and wiped the sweat off his brow. I could totally picture Mike striking up a conversation with the men doing construction, asking to help. He missed what most consider the mundane part of living. He missed his job and he missed yardwork. (All of which endlessly amused me.) "The owner of the campground also owns a hotel. We've been given a suite for my hard work!"

Soon I stood in the kitchen of a historic hotel built in the 1860s. The shower ran warm and the pipes creaked and groaned. As Mike showered, I dug through my bags on the floor. Deep at the side of my pannier, I found the gift I had hidden from him for the last couple of weeks. I stood up to greet Mike on his way out of the shower holding open his early Christmas present.

"A towel! This is awesome, I never thought you would let me have a towel!" He wrapped the large, green, synthetic-wicking travel towel promptly around his body, cradling his arms inside like a young child coming in from a cold day on the beach. Our minimalist packing, or, as Mike would say, *my* minimalist packing, meant we only carried one very tiny towel we shared to dab ourselves dry. Mike was usually the second to use it, which was similar to drying off with a wet nappy. And, over the past few months, the towel had decreased in size as we chopped pieces off to clean our bikes.

"This is the best present ever!" he enthused.

"I bought myself one too."

"But I loved sharing one towel for the last three months," he said with a puppy dog look on his face.

"Liar." I laughed. I'm sure our neighbours on the other side of the thin walls heard us running around while he whipped me with his new towel. We settled down for a minute when my excitement from finding Garth Brooks's Christmas album on our laptop took over. I danced around in my towel, singing Christmas songs until we were interrupted by a knock on the door.

"Thanks so much for the help, can I take ya two out for dinner and drinks?" the owner of the campground and hotel asked. I looked over at Mike with a huge smile.

Over plates of sushi, I realized it's okay to have a bad day. It was completely normal, in fact. My emotions needed to be released so I could check in with myself. Yes, I still got sad, but I was doing well. Plus, the bad days really made me appreciate the great ones.

CHAPTER 10

QUEENSTOWN
These Are the Good Ol' Days

New Zealand's West Coast certainly lived up to its reputation of being rugged and sopping wet. Our tent was soggy and the sleeping bag weighed more each day. Even so, our spirits soared. Mike was becoming an expert camper, and I was thrilled to be living outside, no matter the weather.

"Hey Kat, look!" I turned my body toward Mike and caught a cold stream of water spraying from his water bottle onto my chest.

"Oh, it's on!" I grabbed my water bottle and retaliated.

For days it rained, the clouds danced a haka above our heads, moving, swirling, joining together and springing apart to provide views of New Zealand's highest peaks. We visited Franz Josef Glacier and Fox Glacier and drank the water that melted on its way to the sea.

We slipped south and inland to the town of Queenstown, where we were excited to meet Tyago, a Brazilian, who was on Warmshowers. His small house sat on top of a hill overlooking the town and Lake Wakatipu. Tibetan prayer flags hung outside the door, fluttering in the warm wind. The rich colours of cloth brightened the tiny blue and white home. We let ourselves in the front door and could see the entire house right away. Our first step brought us into the middle of the kitchen, which flowed into the living room, which doubled as the bedroom. Magazine clippings of travel and climbing decorated the walls. Crates overflowing with adventure books and CDs lay in the corner. A window took up the entire wall of the living room overlooking the electric blue lake. Mountains hugged the shore across the way, while paragliders floated in the soft breeze. It was perfection.

We were thankful Tyago was not there to witness the destruction of what happens when two completely drenched cyclists with dripping panniers invade a small place. He laughed when he arrived home from work. "No worries," he said. "I understand the mess. This is your home now too. I call it the Cosmic Cabin." With our laptop, he showed a video of himself cycling around Brazil. "See, I know what it's like to arrive somewhere wet and dirty."

I was intrigued by a remote road to an abandoned mining town near Queenstown, but when we went to ask questions at the local bike shop they didn't think we should ride it.

"It's too dangerous. The road is muddy and terrible and there's a lack of water," said the bike mechanic. "The only other people out there are rafting guides. And, trust me, you don't want to get pushed off."

"Sounds like my type of adventure!" I said. The mechanic gave me a dirty look. I shut up.

But once outside the shop, I convinced Mike we should try it. "If it's as bad as he says, then we can always turn around."

Mike just gave me one of his looks that said: *What are you getting me into?*

The mechanic was correct that our destination was remote. The town quickly slipped away as we rode up into the mountains. The muddy track squeezed into a canyon, and we barely managed to cling to the rock cliff on our right. On our left, the bright turquoise Shotover River raged far below. Rock towers rose above us. Waterfalls fell from large mouths in the mountain, sliding down tongues of complex terrain into the depths below. More than enough water for drinking ran down the cliffs.

Thousands of years earlier, a glacier had plowed through the canyon, dragging and depositing gold with it. The road, built in the late 1800s, was meant to be an access road for mining, but after years of rappelling down cliffs to pick away at hard schist rock to make the road, the biggest gold rush in New Zealand's history was already over. There was no more gold.

Only two vehicles passed us all day. At the end of the road, Mike and I pitched camp in the abandoned gold mining town of Skippers. We explored ruins dating from the 1860s, discovering an old school and homestead. After a meal of pasta, garlic, peppers, onions and hot Italian sausage, we played rummy. Mike won.

The wind began around midnight and ran into our tent with little resistance. Rain soon followed, a smattering at first, then a torrential pounding. Mike slept and I chased possums away from our vestibule. My sleeping pad had lost air again and stones poked at me under my side. In the morning, we stayed in the tent, hoping the rain would peter out, but by 9:30 a.m. it still raged on. We had already been taught on the West Coast that our tent was not a boat.

"We gotta get out of here," I said to Mike as I woke him, pulled on all my rain gear, quickly set up the tarp and made coffee. The rain created puddles and turned our camp into a mud pit. I imagined us slipping and sliding toward the cliff hazard. The potential for landslides on a day like this was high, as well as the likelihood of us having to push our bikes the entire way back to Queenstown.

"What's up? You're awfully quiet." Mike asked.

"I guess I'm concerned about this weather and the ride back through the canyon." I looked up at him, "Are you?"

He did not hesitate with his answer: "Nope." Then his bottom lip stuck out and his brow furrowed together. "Should I be?"

I slowly shook my head back and forth. I was being ridiculous. I wasn't even nervous for me, but I had felt the need to take care of Mike, as if I was his guide and he was my trusting client, rather than what he was – my partner.

The scenery had changed dramatically from the day before. With all the fresh water, tributaries eroded the rock and mud flowed into the river. Yesterday, the river had been bright and light, today a dark soulless stew boiled in the belly of the canyon. Mud stuck to our bikes like peanut butter to the roof of a mouth.

At times, we did not talk, each grinding away up the climb on the slick road. I rode right behind Mike, staring at his back wheel sinking into the mud. It created a dirty waterfall with each rotation. Our chains rasped due to the grit and sand caught in them, scraping and filing the teeth down on the chain rings. Mike had become more comfortable on gravel and rode closer to the cliff edge than I thought he should.

My vision blurred with each exhale. Everything was soaked. I balled my fingers into the palm of my hand and squished water from my gloves. Frigid air snuck through my wet layers of clothing, freezing my skin. My feet separated themselves from the rest of my body as I moved through stages of cold, freezing, pain, and then of not feeling them anymore. *When have I been this frozen before?* In a race in Utah, we had biked up the La Sal Mountains, freezing and pushing the final way in the middle of the largest flood of the century. At the peak, we couldn't find the checkpoint and Bruce, my teammate, lit emergency fire starters to try and warm our hands. Another time, in Patagonia, Chile, during a 12-day race, we were frozen for five of them, hiking through the mountains and lakes.

Mike's doing great, I thought to myself. *He couldn't possibly have been this cold before.* He still seemed positive and he confirmed this seconds later when he shouted through the downpour, "How ya doin' back there?"

I smiled, "Good, and you?"

"My feet are pretty cold, but I'm great."

Frozen. I could no longer change gears because I'd lost the strength in my thumbs. A few hours later, we began the downhill toward town. I went to squeeze my brakes. Nothing. I'd lost the power in my hands. Crap. I fought to get my strength back. I pumped the back brake and nothing happened. I dragged both feet behind me to try and slow down, digging into the soggy mud, squirrelling around the road like a toboggan on ice. I rolled out from the downhill and Mike came up beside me.

"Hey, what's going on?" he asked, concerned.

"Something is wrong with my brake. Even if I could get my hands warm enough to grip, I can't use it."

"Here," he said, as he reached out his hands and took mine in his. When he squeezed them, water drained to the ground. Mike took my gloves off and aggressively rubbed my hands with his. Just his touch made me feel better.

"Wave your arms around while I fix your brake," he said. He took my bike from me and looked it over for the problem.

I watched him take care of me and asked, "Have you ever been this cold before?"

"Oh yeah, don't you remember?" He looked up at me beneath his dripping helmet. "My feet were this cold when we hiked through that canyon in Zion, and my hands always freeze when I'm goalie in outdoor hockey." The corners of his lips rose as he kept working. It was an important lesson for me to realize that for too long I'd been thinking I had made him come on this trip and I was responsible for his happiness and safety.

I was done with thinking like that. He was here because he wanted to be here and he had the skills to be here. Mike had taken over all the bicycle maintenance needs at this point. He was someone I could trust and lean on when I needed help. Mike had as much of a voice in this trip as I did. I smiled and sighed with relief.

Tyago was asleep when we let ourselves into the Cosmic Cabin. "I bet you're happy to see us again," Mike announced our presence as I quietly shut the door behind us.

Tyago woke up and grinned, "I am! Welcome home. I rented the *Lord of the Rings* trilogy!" Dark waves of hair bounced up and down as he jumped out of bed. "We can watch it on your laptop tonight and you can see all of the places in New Zealand you've already cycled past." His thick Brazilian accent jumbled the words together in his excitement.

"Tyago, it feels as if we're coming home." I placed my bike shoes in the corner and Mike kicked his off randomly. The panniers exploded once again. Outside, the lawn was soon decorated with our wet tent, sleeping pads, sleeping bags and panniers. Mike went into town and came back with two new sets of brake pads. On the wet gravel road, we both wore through brand new pads.

A few days later, after a day of hiking, Mike and I walked back to the cabin to find our friend Richard, whom we'd met on the plane, sitting back against Tyago's steps, reading a book. He wore his worn dirty khakis with his plaid long-sleeved top tucked in. Straight hair was plastered in long strands around his face.

"Yay! I'm so glad you came!" I ran up to him for a hug.

"Thanks for inviting me," Richard said. I had sent him an email, inviting him to spend the Christmas holidays with us at Tyago's. Now there were four of us in the tiny cabin.

"Look at all these shoes!" Tyago laughed at the door after work and then pulled open the fridge. "My fridge has never been so full."

Richard made us dinner and licked his plate when he finished. No one mentioned it, but after a few days together, with him licking his plate after every meal, I asked him why.

"I hate waste. It's ridiculous," he told me. "I try not to buy things if I can find another way. There's usually another way. My clothes, bike, equipment and panniers are all previously owned." He pulled on the bottom of his plaid top to look at it. "Last summer, I never bought a single packaged item. It was tough in the beginning, especially with food. It took a lot of determination, but eventually a few stores worked with me so I could buy bulk items, fruits and vegetables without using their containers or bags."

We both sat back, lost in our own thoughts. Then Richard spoke softly, "There's too much waste in the world. I can only do what I can."

Richard may not have thought he made an impact, but he had me think about waste in ways I'd never thought of before. And it wasn't only environmental. For many, it's upgrade versus repair or reuse. I was within an inch of tossing my marriage away. Had I been searching for something new? More exciting? I looked at Mike now and was glad we had decided to "upcycle" our relationship.

Mike and I love being social, and it was perfect for us to be with others for the holidays. We all stayed up late in the evenings, chatting and listening to music. Richard was hilarious. He would jump up to the window every 15 minutes to exclaim, "Look at that view!" Black mountains supported a sky filled with stars and melted into the lake. "These are the good ol' days," he would mumble as he flopped back down.

On Christmas morning, the sun peeked into the cabin and, when I could hold it no longer, I jumped out of bed, careful not to trip on Richard.

"Santa came! Wake up boys!" I exclaimed.

Richard found his hiking boot full of candy and a wilderness magazine. Tyago opened a present from us containing organic chocolate and one of my favourite books, *The Power of One*. Mike was thrilled with a new speedometer and bungee cords for his bike. Santa gave me deodorant (a hint, I think), lotion, a razor (another hint?) and a new bike chain. Tyago gave us a travel book and a gift card to the coffee shop.

For dinner, we placed the table in the middle of the room and I covered it with a Brazilian flag. Tyago lit a candle. We all put on our best clothes (except for Richard, who only had old worn clothes) and toasted to great friends, adventure and travel.

It was hard to tear ourselves away from the Cosmic Cabin. Tyago and Richard were newly treasured friends. But Mike and I were meant to be travelling, so we knew it was time to get rolling. Two days after Christmas, we found ourselves on the Otago Central Rail Trail. The trail was once a railway line bringing the central land food, relatives and sheep. It was abandoned in the 1960s and had since been turned into a cycling path. The trail was wide enough for Mike and me to cycle side by side.

We weren't on the trail long when three athletes passed us and boasted they were doing the entire trail in one day. It wasn't long ago when I believed going fast and proving endurance was the most fun I could have on a bike. Perhaps I was slightly envious, but by the time we hit the Otago Trail, I had already realized there was pleasure in slower travel too. I was now keen to stop at tourist information signs explaining the history and the land. I was happy to lay out in the sun, rest my head on Mike's chest and stare up at the clouds.

While we rode, we chatted with cyclists all along the trail. One family told us they were taking six days to complete the trail. Another mother explained her family travelled light and stayed at bed and breakfasts along the way. One set of parents were riding with their 4-year-old son. The boy cycled on his own for small bursts and when he got tired was towed behind his mom in a small trailer so he could cozy up inside and take a nap. The parents' bikes had panniers and they camped the whole way. It was really inspiring to see families outdoors.

In the late afternoon we met Mark and Wilma from Auckland. Mark came across as confident and forthcoming. "Are you going to join us for a brew?" he asked in a way that felt more like a demand than an invite. We followed the couple to the "next pub" (which seemed conveniently located every 30 kilometres).

"Where are you guys staying tonight?" Mark asked us as he dug into his chips.

"In our tent."

"You're camping? You're not going to find a place," Mark told us. When we left them, he wished us "Good luck!" in a tone sounding more like, "You're going to end up back here!"

Mike and I filled our water containers and continued along in search of somewhere to rest. We were now experts at finding spots to hide the tent and found one easily. We required water, safety and protection from the elements, and then we combed the ground to find a flat spot with the least amount of cow patties. We placed garbage bags beneath the tent to keep it cleaner and help waterproof us from rain. Tent erected. Mats blown up. Sleeping bags out.

"Welcome home!" we said to each other, smiling.

The space was higher than the trail with an uninterrupted view of a gorge. A modest breeze blew and the northern sky threatened with jet-black clouds. I boiled a pot of water to wash with. The sky held off and I pulled out our food. We had four potatoes, along with the oil we used for making popcorn, left-over pasta and a few bruised bananas.

"Looking grim," I said to Mike.

"Let's cut up the potatoes and use the oil to make french fries," Mike suggested.

"French fries!" *How had I never thought of this before?* "Now this is bush camping redefined!" Mike heated up oil and we dropped in cut-up potatoes. For dessert, we fried bananas and put cocoa and icing sugar on top. A delicious meal.

In the morning, goats bleated outside the tent. I opened the door and watched them graze, shuffling their hooves in the dry ground. We stretched and shared our morning cuppa while cyclists pedalled below us on the trail.

"Hello down there!" Mike yelled to Mark. The Auckland couple straddled their bikes and turned from the goats to our direction. Because of the awkward angle, cyclists passing only saw us if they looked up and backwards.

I stood beside Mike and watched Wilma push her hand into her husband's shoulder. "Well, they found a great campsite after all, didn't they? Look at their view!" Mark swallowed his words. "I guess they did."

I smiled and thought of Stacy, who had encouraged us to free camp. She'd be proud of us. I was proud of us.

The Auckland couple taught us something in return. Mike decided he liked resting in pubs, ordering burgers and beers. He wondered out loud why we didn't start visiting pubs months ago.

The baaing of sheep woke us on our final day of the trail. It seemed our tent stood in the way of their morning routine. It was still early when we cycled into the town of Middlemarch, which marked the end of the trail. Mike took a nap in the shade. I noticed a spigot attached to the outside cement wall of what looked like a storage facility. I grabbed our dirty clothes and washed them under the cold water. After I was done, I took a quick look to see no one was in sight and then stuck my head under the spigot.

I turned off the tap when a family of six came into the park for a picnic. "Wow, look at all your stuff!" The father stared at our panniers spread across the grass. "Don't you think you've overpacked a bit?"

I shook my head no. "I think our packing is pretty good. Even though we often find something else to get rid of. Just this morning, I gave away a T-shirt I don't need," I explained. Now I only had two. "Plus, I like books."

"Where are you going?"

"We're biking to Dunedin tonight, and then we're going to bus and train to Nelson to be with friends for New Year's Eve. From there we'd like to ride the Rainbow Track." I was excited. We had a plan!

"Doubtful," said the father. "The Rainbow Track is more demanding than the Otago Trail. I don't think you're going to make it, and you most definitely won't get to Dunedin today," he told me. "It's already late in the morning, very hot and another 80 kilometres."

It was not the pep talk I'd hoped to hear. But I remained upbeat. "We'll be okay. You just finished the trail with four kids!" I pointed out. "I would've thought that was impossible, but you did it. That's pretty amazing."

We waved goodbye and set out. We cycled for hours. The heat seared and the hills were indeed relentless. Our water ran out. My saliva turned to paste. We were parched and neared exhaustion in a remote part of the country. I lost confidence we were going to make it to Dunedin after all.

"Look, there's a farm," Mike said, pointing to a home a kilometre away.

"Finally." We had passed very few homes. We cycled up the driveway and I immediately spotted a hose beside the house. I walked up to the door to ask for water.

"It doesn't seem like anyone is home," Mike said, and turned on the hose. "Here, pass me your water bottles and then you can leave them a thank you note," he suggested.

The sky remained bright and cloudless and the thermometer pushed toward 40 degrees. We were hot and came upon needed salvation – another pub – an oasis in the middle of nowhere. We walked through the open doors, flies drifting lifelessly around our sweaty bodies. A solo local sat on the corner stool chatting up the barmaid. Faded posters hung on the wall. One showed a big man in overalls with his chest bursting out of the straps, restraining a large sheep with one hand while the other ran a pair of shears across it. The poster read, "Now he deserves a DB." (Meaning draught beer.) Another showed a tattooed Maori resting a chainsaw across his thighs, exhausted from shaping a lounge chair from a massive tree. "Now he deserves a DB."

I looked over at my husband. Sweat dripped down Mike's brow. His tank top hung soaked and his arms perspired. We had cycled 80 kilometres in the heat with another 30 to go. "You deserve a DB," I told him. I ordered him the beer with two scoops of chips and we relished the break while the man in the corner attempted to explain to us the merits of cricket.

"Hurry! Lots of presents have come for you!" Two girls tugged at our hands, dragging us into their house. We had arrived seconds before in Nelson, on the very north end of the South Island to visit our friends Shawna and Cam and their three kids, who had moved to New Zealand for one year. The girls, Taylor and Dylan, were 7 and 5, and their son, Tylin, was 2 years old.

"Come on!" the girls squealed.

"Ta-da!" they exclaimed together as they opened up the door to their guest room. A pile of packages and letters sent from home were spread across the bed. Tylin came running through the door with Shawna directly behind.

"Girls, maybe give Mike and Katrina some time to get settled. They can open up their presents later." The energy in the little bedroom dropped. We couldn't take this excitement away from them.

"This is like Christmas all over again!" I said. "Would you like to help us open the gifts?" Shawna smiled at us from the doorway.

Taylor ripped into a package and held out the gift. My friend Dawn had sent me a gorgeous leather bracelet with two balls of silver on it. Dylan grabbed for a box from my sister and we struggled together, getting the tape to rip away. She finished jubilantly and then held up three tiny thongs.

"What's this for?" her small fingers intertwined in the thin straps of the underwear.

"They're panties!" Taylor laughed so much the bed shook.

"With no bum!" She rolled onto the floor in a fit of laughter and Tylin, not knowing what was going on, jumped on her with a big grin spread across his face, his light blond curls jostled up and down from the excitement.

"Ew, gross!" Dylan shook the thongs away and reached for another parcel. A new sleeping pad for me, slightly thicker and longer than the one I had been using. We also received sheets that spread over our mats and clipped together so Mike and I wouldn't slide away from each other anymore.

We spent the next couple of days reading and rereading the letters and Christmas cards from home. The kids and I decorated their guest room with the notes. My nephew Anthony had drawn a picture of a bicycle in green crayon and my sister wrote that it was his first drawing of a bike. Mike and I taught them how to make sushi and took them for ice cream cones. I watched Mike swing them around and play tirelessly. *He's really good with kids*, I noticed.

On New Year's Day, Shawna and I were on her deck enjoying coffee.

"Katrina, what's your New Year's resolution?" she asked, her coffee cup cradled in her hand.

"It's that time of the year I guess," I said, looking up into the sun and stalling on an answer. New Year's resolutions always make me think about the past year. And, although I was sure I'd made resolutions the year before, I couldn't remember what they were. Perhaps I'd been too depressed and upset then to follow through on any of them.

I thought about the last four months on the bike trip with Mike.

"I'd like to continue to work on my relationship with Mike. Figure out what our dreams are – not only for this year but for our future." I pursed my lips and looked directly at Shawna. "Mostly…my New Year's resolution is to be happy."

CHAPTER 11

CATTLE COUNTRY
In the Groove

It seemed like the biggest obstacle to happiness had always been my inner conflict. What did I need and crave to feel complete contentment? There were so many reasons to be happy and it felt incredible to feel pleasure again, and yet I couldn't help but wonder: *Could there be a balance between my wild self and the part of me that wanted a life with Mike?*

It was relaxing to be with Shawna's family, but I soon craved our tent, which, after all, had become my home. Our home. With Mike.

The ride out of Nelson headed west on a cycling trail along the ocean before we meandered inland to the start of the Rainbow Track. The gravel road wound south through the Wairau Gorge, over Island Saddle Pass and onwards to Hanmer Springs. We set up our tent 70 kilometres into the Rainbow Track, sheltered from the wind by a pair of large hills and a briar rose thorn bush with flushed pink flowers.

I started the stove and boiled a pot of water. I made hot chocolate for me and tea for Mike, then poured the rest of the hot water into my bowl to wash up. Mike always let me use the bath water first. I stripped down as much as the bugs would allow and cleaned off the accumulated dust from the day. On this night, there was water nearby, cascading down from Island Saddle Pass, but it was way too frigid for bathing. After my bird bath (as I called it), I pulled on big wool socks, thick pants, a fleece and an insulated jacket and topped it all off with a toque on my head. Clouds swirled and charged through the valley as we sat peacefully outside. The sky turned dark. The Southern Cross was hidden.

"I'm really happy we chose the three-man tent," Mike said while I passed him the food bags to hide away from the possums. "Could you imagine if we had to fit all of these panniers inside with us in a smaller tent? We wouldn't be able to play cards or anything." Mike piled the bags up at my foot of the tent before stretching out.

"No kidding. And I wouldn't be able to create such a comfortable back rest to lean against so I can write and read while you sleep."

"I'm working hard, you know, I'm tired." He smiled. I grinned. It was a friendly tease.

I placed my clothes bag against his hip and sat down, resting my mug of hot chocolate between my feet. The screen in the tent was zipped closed to keep the bugs out, but I left the flap open to have a view of the clouds.

"You did really well today," I said, completely serious until I burst out laughing, remembering one part. I reached for the camera and found the video of Mike ascending Island Saddle Pass.

We had stopped to take a break and then Mike went ahead while I filmed. In the video, Mike is lifting his leg over the frame of his bike and pushing down with one foot on a pedal. He tries to catch the rotation of the opposite pedal with his other foot but cannot create enough momentum on the steep gravel hill to keep the bike going and, with each rotation, his foot slipped off to push along the ground. It was like he was trying to kick-start a motorbike, and it was hilarious to watch as he basically hopped his bike up the hill.

"Am I that bad?" he asked. "The road doesn't look steep in the video." He began to laugh too. We watched it over and over.

The next day, Mike rode in front, providing me more such entertainment. For the second time on the Rainbow Track, his bike crashed to the ground. But, instead of him falling, he leapt up, hurdled his bike and landed on two feet. I had lost count of how many times he did this. He possessed a spidey sense of when to jump off and let the bike fall. It reminded me of when we travelled through Morocco years earlier and rode camels through the Sahara desert for a few days. Surrounded by sand and only sand, once a day Mike's camel would act up and bounce him off. Putrid spit escaped from between the large lips of the beast while Mike leapt into the air, performing a flying maneuver. On his way back down, I always imagined the destruction, yet, every time, Mike landed on his feet.

Mike gathered up his bike from the loose gravel to get back on.

"I think you missed your calling!" I shouted. "Maybe you should have been a high jumper." I rolled up to him laughing.

"I was a goalie," he reminded me.

"But that has nothing to do with it." I shook my head in amusement.

"I can react. I can anticipate what's going to happen, and I have super amazing reflexes," he boasted.

"You're hilarious," I said.

The gorge opened and we rode into a wider valley of scrubby bushes and brown hills. We passed Lake Tennyson, a large, crisp-blue lake left behind from past glaciers, still fed from surrounding snow-topped mountains.

We headed up the final hill, Jacks Pass.

At the top, we stood in the middle of a panorama. Snowy mountains set the backdrop and clutched the town of Hanmer Springs. We set up the camera and took a picture of us and our bikes, proud finishers of the Rainbow Track and well deserving of the hot springs to come.

"How do you like riding back roads now?" I asked Mike before we descended into town.

"It was enjoyable," he confirmed.

"So do you want to do the Molesworth Track?" I asked hopefully. My voice sounded as if I was 4, asking for a new toy. I loved travelling on gravel in the backcountry and didn't want it to end.

"We can talk about it after the hot springs," Mike answered.

"Deal." Back on the bikes, we flew downwards.

Hanmer Springs is in the bottom of the valley, but the Molesworth Track starts from the top of Jacks Pass. We would have to travel back up that same last five kilometres we had gone down. I promised Mike we could hitchhike up it if he said yes.

He said yes, and a few days later we were back at the bottom of the hill.

"We might as well cycle until we can find a ride," I said, no longer optimistic about hitchhiking. Low fog hung in the valley. Grass, flowers and trees were covered in a layer of fresh dew. Mike and I had slept poorly in a noisy campground and gave up in the early morning to begin riding. The rest of the town dozed.

No vehicles passed. I waited for Mike to bring up my promise that we wouldn't have to bike up it, but he never did.

At the top, we savoured the view once again and then took a right into Molesworth Station. The property is 181,000 hectares, which makes it the largest farm in New Zealand. We passed fields of tussock and blue borage wildflowers blowing in the wind. There were also 10,000 cows. The track rode through their pasture land, so we became close and personal with many of them. The cows often hung out at gates, or they blocked the road and we'd have to squeeze past.

The rules against free camping within the station brought a rare opportunity to camp with other cyclists just on the outskirts of it. We had already been conversing with a few people when another cyclist rode in.

"Come camp here," I said.

"Hey, thanks, I'm Tony." He spoke in a thick sharp Dutch accent. I shook Tony's sweaty hand and got a better look at him as he stepped off his bike. A large man but not tall, with a head of curls sticking to his scalp in layers like gummy toffee.

"Would you like a drink?" I offered.

"That would be great." He plopped down in the grass right beside our tent.

"We have tea, coffee, hot chocolate, juice or milk." Once the words were spoken, I realized how funny they were. For backcountry cycling, we sure had quite the selection of drinks and even condiments. The milk and juice were new to our diet. Mike got tired of drinking only water and, since half the water we drank came from an outside source like a stream, river or lake, it didn't always taste great, so juice crystals gave the water a nice flavour. The milk we carried was dehydrated, which was great for cereal or oatmeal in the mornings.

Tony chose juice and then pulled out his dinner from his pannier: a very small portion of tuna and seven crackers.

"Is that your dinner?" Mike asked.

"Ya, I eat the same thing everyday: tuna and crackers for dinner, hydrated peas for lunch and a granola bar for breakfast. It keeps the weight down." He patted his stomach. "These hills are killers aren't they? You don't want to carry any more then you have to. I'm not very fast, but I sure am organized," he flattered himself. "When I get to a large town, I splurge on a hotel and a steak dinner. I pack the calories in so I can travel light when I ride." Tony sat in a cross-legged position; his belly relaxed and spread itself like an overflowing muffin top over his cycling shorts. He reached into his bag again and pulled out a carton of cigarettes, which I hoped suppressed his appetite since they alone added to the weight.

"You have quite the bike," Mike said.

"Ya, they custom made it for me." He lit a cigarette and drew in a long drag, the tip glowing red. "My baby there has a Rohloff hub, made out of chromoly steel. It's really strong and if it cracks then it can be welded. I've been riding for weeks now and haven't had anything break."

Mike attempted to pick it up.

"Ya, she weighs quite a bit, good steel though," said Tony.

Tony talked nonstop, but he eventually paused for a quick breath. "You two already eat dinner?" I shook my head slowly, and Mike looked over and smiled at me.

"Would you like to join us?" Mike offered. Tony had a quizzical look in his eye beneath his curls. I imagined he wondered if he'd be as lucky with dinner as he was with drinks. He would not be disappointed.

"Well, Tony, I hope you're still hungry because we have a feast compared to your tuna and crackers. We left Hanmer Springs this morning with 12 frozen burgers, potatoes we'll do up in gravy and a pasta topped with broccoli and cheese. Before dessert that is," I said.

Tony couldn't restrain himself and fell onto his back with his legs still crossed (showing amazing agility for one so stout). His yellow bike jersey crept up and the black curls on his stomach bounced as he laughed. His legs sprang open and he rolled around on the ground.

"Ya, I'll eat with you. You are two crazy motherfuckers!"

Mike and I grinned as if he'd just complimented us. We've always loved having people over, feeding them and sharing our time with friends. Welcoming Tony to our camp stove felt like we had a friend to our home for dinner.

Mike and I were back in our groove.

The rain clouds followed us the next day and gently pushed us on. White gentians pulled in the last remaining sun and shimmered on the side of the road. Every hill, saddle and turn brought views of the valley. Clouds twirled, rhythmically dancing around jagged rock of the steepest peaks. We hid behind a large tree out of the wind for lunch. I pulled out the maps and finished highlighting the places we'd been to in New Zealand.

"It's been a good time, hasn't it?" I rested my head on Mike's shoulder and we leaned against the tree. The rough bark tickled my back.

"I could use some hydrated peas for lunch," he joked. I smiled. I enjoyed living in the outdoors and camping and watching Mike grow to love it as well. We sighed.

"Where to next?" I asked. I felt like I could live like this forever.

CHAPTER 12

MALAYSIA
Dodging Monkeys

Mike and I took a break from the road, staying at my friend Kobie's apartment in Singapore for a week. It should have been comforting to let someone introduce us to Southeast Asia and to sleep on a large bed, but each night I stared at the ceiling, willing myself to sleep. My head filled with worries of pedalling into countries neither of us knew. I worried we wouldn't find places to stay or enough food. On our last night in Singapore, I turned over to look at my watch – 2:00 a.m.

I put my arm around my husband. His breath was calm and even and I tried to match mine to his. We were six months into our trip and I felt closer to him. We agreed we were closer. But how could we not be after spending 24 hours a day together?

I flipped over and fluffed up the pillow. Yes, we agreed, we were closer. We also acknowledged, without so many words, that while we cuddled close in the darkness, and although we felt connected, we weren't exactly passionate. The night wore on and I continued to contemplate. I covered my head with the pillow, smothering relationship matters out of my mind. When I managed to let go, other worries surfaced: the heat, the bugs and the possibility of thugs. *Oh great, now I'm rhyming*, I thought. There were so many unknowns. My nerves kept me restless until morning. Like a tiger, anxious thoughts stalked in the dark and rested when the sun was high.

After a week in Singapore, we said goodbye to Kobie, who stood at the door of his highrise, wishing us the best for our ride. I held him in a big squeeze before he and Mike gave each other a hug with firm slaps on one another's back. Mike then hoisted himself over the frame of his bike and let out a big sigh.

He had caught a cold a few days earlier. I was antsy to go, but now I worried he was putting his needs aside and leaving for me again, just like six months earlier.

"Are you sure you're ready?" I asked Mike, concerned.

"Ready as I'll ever be," he laughed and winked at me.

Oh, that blue-eyed wink. I steadied myself on my bike and we pulled onto the clean city streets of Singapore to ride 30 kilometres to the Changi Ferry Terminal. There, a short ferry ride brought us to a small customs building nestled in the jungle on the southern tip of Malaysia. The officer drew us a map with an arrow toward the city of Kota Tinggi. Our tires rolled onto the rough road and we began our journey in Southeast Asia. Towering palm trees replaced skyscrapers and the succulent smell of greenery replaced the pungent smell of durian.

My legs circulated with ease and familiarity. I sat taller and settled into the rhythm, with renewed confidence on my bike. The bike, my other companion, knew my body as well as anyone, and I knew it. I knew when I had been ignoring my bike and not giving it enough love, either with cleanliness, oiling or more air. I never fought with my bike, or was mad when it wouldn't go faster or if the chain skipped and it wouldn't run smooth. I just accepted my bike, loving all its faults and everything it had to offer. I shook my head, remembering how early on in our trip I'd realized I'd better treat my husband as well as I treat my bike.

Over the last half a year, the bikes had become more than a ride. They were our marriage counsellor and our dream board for discovering what we wanted in life. Being back on them, riding alongside Mike, my worries dissipated. For a moment my smile was as pure as the sky – limitless. It felt like us. We were together and our untravelled future was waiting patiently somewhere, across many more border crossings.

My nerves settled. I cranked down on the pedals with determination, beginning to believe, after all my mulling, that I was now ready for whatever came our way.

Then a monkey ran onto the road.

My body stiffened, and I clenched the handlebars as more monkeys leapt from the jungle.

"Mike! Watch out!" I yelled. We swerved left, then right, to avoid running over them.

Mike and I had encountered monkeys before. Years ago, while hiking in Costa Rica, Mike had put down his backpack and, within seconds, a monkey had slid open the zipper and stolen our lunch. Another time, in Brazil, a male howler monkey masturbated while staring at me and screeching. Needless to say, I don't trust monkeys. Not five minutes into Malaysia, Mike and I were weaving our bikes as fast as we could down the road, dodging monkeys.

I was staring to my left, into the dense greenery of moss, ferns and palms, and noticed a lizard the size of my leg sunning itself in the afternoon sun. Mike rode beside me and yelled, "Kat, stop!" We hit the brakes and stopped right in front of a three-metre-long snake slithering across the road.

When the snake passed, we started again. Perspiration trickled down my chest from the relentless heat. I had decided in Singapore that out of respect for Islamic beliefs, I would dress more modestly in clothes that were long and loose-fitting. It meant leaving my usual tight bike shorts and fitted tank top in my pannier and donning Mike's garb. His blue surfer shorts were baggy and hid my legs past my knees, and his navy blue, long-sleeved top draped over my shoulders. I was not used to the extra covering, which in the humid heat felt suffocating. I pushed up the sleeves to my elbows and looked over at Mike.

His clothes were drenched. Drops of sweat dripped down his tanned hairy legs and soaked his socks. Then I noticed his broad chest rose with laboured breathing – the day before, he could barely walk from the bed to Kobie's kitchen. He was in no shape to ride the 100 kilometres we had planned.

But Mike kept riding. He even smiled while he rode. I travelled beside him, amazed not only by his fitness but by his mental strength to stay happy. And, good thing, because stopping to camp was out of the question. After we exited the monkey- and snake-infested jungle, signs on vast palm plantations clearly warned that trespassers were not welcome. Not that we could read the script writing on the signs, but the picture of a man being shot clearly translated what we needed to know.

I looked into the rows of palm trees. Malaysia is the world's largest exporter of palm oil and these plantations cover thousands of square kilometres. We had read that the palm industry increases the standard of living for many Malaysians, but the plantations, along with rubber plantations, have wiped out immense swaths of rainforest. This was easily visible from the seat of a bike. It made me feel sorry for the cheeky monkeys.

Despite the heat and Mike's cold, we pedalled the full 100 kilometres and reached Kota Tinggi: pavement seemingly plopped in the middle of the jungle, with colourful buildings and wide streets. Our white skin attracted attention and a profusion of hand signals soon directed us to the hotel area. At Grand Waterlilies Hotel, Mike went inside to inspect a room while I stayed on the curb, taking in the neon signs blinking over the doors of shops and restaurants. The buildings were old, but they had been put together with thought:

soft corners, immense awnings and intricate pillars. Balconies were lush with potted plants. The concrete I stood on was rutted and worn and bore tales of flooding. Cars, bikes and people crossed in every direction. Sweet and spicy smells from food stalls nearby made my mouth water. It was our first stop, and we had already smiled at and communicated with people who were ethnic Indian, Chinese and Malay. The wafts from the food stalls told me the food would be just as diverse as the population.

Mike came back and started to take the panniers off his bike.

"The word 'hotel' is an overstatement, but it looks clean, and it's only $12!" Mike said excitedly. "I can get used to these prices."

The Islamic call to prayer rang before first light. The sound penetrated the thin walls of the hotel and I smiled, having forgotten it would be a part of our days in Malaysia. The voice was deep and low, reverberating in my chest. It is not a song per se, but to my ears it sounded musical. The chords are long, powerful; they rise and fall as if they move with the wind. Similar to the varied flutters of a bird's wings, the muezzin's voice is strong, soft, fast, slow and melodic. I visualized thousands of faithful, performing their ablutions, washing their faces, hands, forearms, feet. I imagined them rolling out prayer mats in candle-lit corners of their homes, greeting the day and their God in perfected silent movements.

Shadows of light crept through the window as a call from another mosque rang moments later. I smiled again and reached for Mike's strong hand beneath our sarong sheet.

"We might as well get up, lazy bones," I murmured. "How are you feeling?"

"A lot better," he replied. I watched him pull on his black socks. He did look better. His eyes were clear and his face, though covered in thick brown stubble, had colour again.

By 11:00 a.m., we had cycled 65 kilometres northeast toward the South China Sea. We had only been eating leftover bread and were famished by the time we came across a food stall.

Mismatched pieces of tin lay fallen like a deck of cards on the roof of the restaurant, and bare light bulbs hung low from string tied to the rafters. The walls and tables were made of raw wood and opened onto the street. We laid our bikes in the dirt and sat at the table, big black ants scattering away from us as we relaxed, beside each other, into sturdy chairs.

My guess is Westerners rarely stopped at the food stall as there was no town nearby, but it was busy with local villagers, which I took as a good review of the food. A few men arrived on faded pink mopeds, wearing tattered clothes caked in dust from working in the fields. Others drove up in a rusted truck with thick tires and weed whackers in the back. We had seen such men hacking back the rainforest that dared encroach the road. They wore long-sleeved tops and cotton scarves to protect themselves from the sun and no doubt deserved the iced coffees they ordered.

Three kids on old steel bicycles stopped and made a commotion over our bikes, touching our panniers and making faces in my mirror with an eruption of giggles. They each bought a bright green drink. A woman with a pale pink headscarf ladled the drink from a bucket on the floor and poured it into clear plastic bags. She wrapped a miniature elastic around the top, closing the bag, before punching a straw into it.

The Daffy Duck mug holding my sweet coffee seemed out of place. Like us, it was brought in from another world. Even so, I felt comfortable. The coffee was delicious, a dark roasted blend poured over a half cup full of sweetened condensed milk. As soon as I finished it, I ordered another one. *I, too, could get used to this.* The other customers peeked at us from behind their drinks. Mike and I grinned a lot, trying not to spill our drinks or the food we had ordered.

Everyone ate with their right hand, scooping rice, fish, chicken and long greens easily into their mouths. Before Mike and I had a chance to try, a woman rushed over to place spoons down for us. Left hands comfortably hid beneath the table. Except mine; my left hand kept sneaking up onto the table like it had a mind of its own. Finally, I held it under the table, squeezed between my thighs. I tried to debone my chicken and fish head with a spoon. That didn't work so well. We ate clumsily.

When I was done, I put my spoon on my empty plate and told Mike I'd be right back.

"*Tandas?*" (toilet?) I asked a woman wearing a full black veil.

She motioned for me to follow her and we slipped to the back of the restaurant, brushing aside a thick curtain, into her home. We walked through and out the other side to the backfield. I followed her over two creaky boards laid over a muddy ditch, prancing precariously in my bike shoes across the planks. She pointed to a rough concrete structure. I opened the door and went inside.

The door swung closed behind me, faint light filtering through tiny triangles cut into the cement just below my head. Murmurs of goats and chickens were muffled beyond the walls. The stench wasn't bad. Other than a bucket of water, there was nothing else. No toilet or seat, no bucket for waste and no tissue paper. There wasn't even a hole in the ground. I did a few mystified circles and went back outside to find the woman.

"*Tandas?*" I asked again.

"Yes, yes," she said, encouraging me to go back into the concrete box.

If only I just had to pee, I thought. I stood inside again, jostling from one foot to the other. I finally noticed a slit between the back wall and the floor. The floor itself was angled. Previously, I thought it was just badly engineered, but then I understood: you do your business then slosh it all through the back crack in the wall toward the outside. I had toilet paper on me, but I realized I didn't know what I'd do with it after I'd used it.

"That was enlightening," I told Mike when I sat back down. "It dawned on me why we shouldn't eat with our left hands." He laughed but didn't ask details. I told him anyway. "I thought this right-hand business was a tradition from the past. But, nope, it's alive and well. And there was no hole."

Mike, a lot more private than I am, changed the subject.

"I paid 12 Malaysian ringgit ($3.50) for our meals while you were gone. It seems typical to eat and pay the bill later," Mike rattled on. "I don't think we were overcharged at all. Everyone so far has been kind and honest."

"I'm loving it," I told him.

I did love it. The road we were on extended from the very south of Malaysia to the Thailand border, about 700 kilometres away. The Malaysian peninsula is shaped like a tongue hanging from the head of Asia, drinking water from the surrounding seas. We travelled with the South China Sea on our right, its blue shimmering water lapping onto sandy beaches. The land was lush, fed with afternoon showers.

We passed our first water buffalo, wading in a muddy pool. Silver in colour, its long horns and ears stuck straight out as it caught the sound of our approach. In between the palm and rubber plantations were swaths of rainforest that seemed to burst at the seams with monkeys and snakes.

The traffic was steady but gentle. Mike and I switched back and forth, taking turns riding in front. We stayed close together, often with only inches between our wheels. People leaned their entire bodies out of car windows – even if they were the ones driving – to say hi. They waved so enthusiastically, full bodies escaping from the inside of the car, I thought surely their legs were going to slide out of the window to run after us. Young couples on mopeds slowed to wave as well. The men wore their leather jackets backwards, with the zipper in the back never done up. I didn't know if it was for fashion or wind protection. Women sat sidesaddle on the seat behind them, wearing headscarves in pink, turquoise and beige, each turning around to smile long after they passed. In small villages, children yelled "hello," and moms and dads held up babies, pumping their little chubby arms at us. Our arms got sore from all the waving.

The friendly welcome we received made our worries of cycling into the unknown fade away. We didn't have a guidebook (we had looked but hadn't found one) and I navigated from a tourist map that was dodgy at best. It was written in English, but all the signs along the road were in Malaysian so we couldn't match the two. I often didn't know our exact location.

We simply travelled, with our dodgy map, not knowing where we were going to stay, or eat or if a storm was coming in. And we got along just fine.

Then we met Becky and Scott.

In the town of Kuala Rompin, Mike and I were unloading our bikes to take to our room when they came to help. They introduced themselves and offered to carry our bikes upstairs.

"Hi! We're Becky and Scott from Canada, also travelling by bike," said Becky, all in one chipper sentence.

"Great to meet you," I said. "Thanks for the help! It gets tiring loading these bikes up and down the stairs all the time, but I sleep better when they're in our room."

"We do that too," said Becky. "Do you want to join us for dinner? There's a restaurant nearby that's recommended in our guidebook."

"We'd love to," I said, eagerly accepting company.

Our bikes stowed in our room, we walked to the open-air restaurant. Mike and I sat across from Becky and Scott, a quick friendship forming around our shared experience of cycling and travel. We shared what motivated us, our goals, reasons for leaving and what kept us going. We wanted to know about their lives, the past and the future. And they wanted to know about ours.

"How do you plan to go into Thailand?" Becky asked after we ordered.

"Up the coast until we hit the border," I answered.

"Do you have visas yet?"

"No, we'll just pick them up at the border."

"Well, I hate to be the bearer of bad news," Scott interjected as he moved his spoon around the bean curd he was having for dinner, "but the border on the east coast of southern Thailand is in upheaval right now. There are riots and travel is not recommended there." He pushed up his glasses. "You don't receive emails from the Canadian government's Travel Advice and Advisories?"

We answered him with blank stares.

"Well, never mind," he said. "Anyway, even if you still do decide to bike there, Thailand is no longer giving long tourist visas at the border. You have to apply in Kuala Lumpur or Kota Bharu. That's the only way you have the possibility of getting 60 days."

Becky and Scott, we soon realized, had a plan. They were methodical in their research, and they always knew where they were headed. They had a phone, maps and a GPS attached to their bikes. They carried guidebooks and a vast amount of cycle tourist stories downloaded onto their computers. They were the opposite of us.

Maybe we should have made a plan, I thought to myself. When you up and leave home like we did, planning seemed impossible. All along, it seemed difficult to make more than the most basic plans. Often, the most I figured out was how many kilometres we had to travel to reach the next town and where we might find water along the way.

"Why are you two on this trip?" Becky asked. My mouth clammed shut. *Because our marriage was failing and I wanted out.* I said nothing.

Mike answered instead. "We'd grown apart and we wanted to spend more time together." He looked over to me. "And now we do, hey hon? Six months for 24 hours a day of pure bliss." He reached out his arm to grab me closer. My chair skidded a couple of inches toward him. It took me by surprise and I started laughing. Mike grinned from ear to ear and I knew he meant it.

"Sick of me yet?" he asked, beaming.

"Not yet," I answered with another giggle. I realized I never tired of his company or his witty one-liners. I loved his relaxed attitude toward life. I smiled and realized even though we still had work to do in certain aspects of our relationship, I couldn't imagine life without him. I stopped laughing to study him as he conversed with our new friends. I was happy he had said no to a divorce.

Back at the hotel, Scott, a computer genius, took our laptop and downloaded dozens of other cycle tourist stories. Mike went to lube our chains, while I spread our maps over the bed and began to make a plan.

"After Pekan, we're going to Kuala Lumpur to get our visas there. You're welcome to join us," Becky said.

"Unfortunately, we're short on time in Malaysia because we're due to meet our friend, Eleasha, in Thailand," I explained. "I think we'll just head up the east coast as fast as we can and apply for visas in Kota Bharu, then ride this road through the jungle to the west coast." My finger traced a small yellow line on the map. "Let's ride to Pekan together though."

"We're waking up at 4:00 a.m. to beat the heat," Becky said.

Wow, I thought. "I'm not sure I can convince Mike of that, but we'll try to catch you."

Becky and Scott, true to their word, left extremely early. Mike and I rode 95 kilometres, hoping we would see them around each bend. We didn't. Pekan is a royal town, and when we arrived the town was in the middle of a celebration.

The smell of spicy food filled the streets as throngs of people hung out along the Pahang River.

We went to a dozen guest houses, hotels and hostels, looking for Becky and Scott and an available room. We finally found space in a small guest house for $2. We carried our bikes up rickety wooden stairs, following a trail of ants to our room. We were on the second floor facing the busy street. Mike pushed two small, lumpy beds together and brushed off hairs left by previous guests. I leaned my bike against a bedroom wall that looked like it hadn't been painted or washed in 20 years. The floor was covered in dust that stuck to the legs of the spiders crawling casually across it.

The shower and toilets were at the end of the hall. Male hotel patrons lined the hallway, smoking, and snickered at me as I passed. Secretly, I loved the attention. (When else could I pretend I was a full-fledged celebrity?) I stepped into the bathroom, which was about the size of a laundry chute. The toilet, a hole that fell down to the first floor, was caked in feces. It was the dirtiest toilet this celebrity had ever seen. The shower door shut with a rotating piece of wood on a handle. *I'm sure we'll see worse*, I thought as I hung my clothes on a rusty nail and stood beneath a green garden hose jutting out from the wall. I was not much cleaner on my reappearance in the hallway.

The owner, who may have realized we were a little out of our comfort zone, brought us a fan, blankets and soap. The men in the hallway, friendlier now, used hand gestures to ask us if we were hungry. We were. They led us downstairs to a restaurant where we ate delicious noodle soup with fish balls, beef and shrimp.

Late into the night, music from the restaurant wafted through our open window. We lay on top of the used sheet beneath our sarong while the fan blew warm air over us. I marvelled at Mike's ability to hit the pillow and immediately fall asleep. I stared up at the ceiling, curious about what had happened to Becky and Scott.

We found out later their guidebook flagged our hotel with this simple review: "Do not stay here." The two of them had continued down the road to a resort they found on their GPS for $100 a night, while Mike and I "cozied" up in our dirty, cheap and ultimately welcoming hotel.

Most days, finding a place to sleep proved to be time-consuming. Mike loved this part of the day. His patience for finding the perfect home for us was beyond me. He would go and meet owners, have a look at the room, ask some questions and then thank them and go look at the next place. We often went to about five different places, which, after a few weeks, I realized was pure entertainment for Mike. I would stay outside and watch the bikes, often snacking from street vendors.

Further north, in the city of Kuantan, I announced I was going to look for a place. Right away, I spotted a tall, narrow hotel and stepped inside from the afternoon monsoon. I wrung out my shirt and stamped my feet to try and dry my shoes. Here, as was often the case, there was no reception on the first floor, so I kept climbing until after the fourth flight of stairs, where I found the owner, a Chinese man, eating a bowl of noodles. Before I could greet him, he held his chopsticks in mid-air and barked in English, "No air conditioning!"

"That's okay," I replied. I couldn't remember the last time we'd had air conditioning.

He swallowed his mouthful and peered at me. "It's 35 ringgit" ($10).

"That's okay," I said. He sat up straighter and seemed to become interested in me as a customer. He put down his bowl then motioned for me to follow him up more stairs.

The small man opened a door to a spacious room whose walls had faded and peeling paint, but it was furnished with a queen-size bed and equipped with its very own squat toilet bathroom. *Luxurious*, I thought.

"Perfect," I said. The owner stared at me. My guess is he didn't get many foreigners. Being on a bike allowed us to access parts of towns and cities that don't see tourists. My language barrier didn't allow me to tell him this room was quieter and much cleaner than the one from the night before. He tucked in his shirt, as if putting himself together, and started the process of taking payment.

"You had to pick the one on the fifth floor, didn't you?" Mike said in jest, amused by the fact I picked the first room I'd visited. We made a number of trips up and down the stairs to bring up our gear and bikes. But by this point, we had this down to a science. One of us stayed at the bottom while the other carried up a first load of panniers and then made a second trip up with a bike. On the third trip, we could go together, managing to get everything up to the room.

The owner, now in full hospitality mode, drew a map of where to eat and, at the door, handed us a massive umbrella to protect us from the continuous rain.

We found the suggested large, open eatery beneath a tin roof. As I breathed in the scent of all the dishes, my stomach suddenly felt really empty.

Dozens of food vendors with uncovered vats of hot dishes lined the eatery. Each stall, vying for attention, called out to us, advertising their offerings. Fires and boiling oil heated the air and perspiration materialized on the cooks' foreheads. Mike piled his plate with fresh rotis, soft naan bread and spicy seafood. I walked to our table carrying a fusion of Chinese, Indian and Malay cuisine. On one side of my plate, I had *ikan bakar*, a grilled fish served with sweet *nasi lemak* (coconut rice) wrapped in a banana leaf. On the other side of my plate, I had *nasi dagang*, a coconut rice with a piquant fish curry. I garnished it all with peanuts, boiled eggs, vegetables and what I thought were fried little minnows. Lastly, on top of the heap, *murtabak*, an Indian-influenced stuffed pancake filled with ground goat, egg, onion and garlic. Time to eat.

Water jugs were placed on the table, but there were no cups. Mike observed that the jugs were used for washing and held the jug over my hands as I scrubbed at the dust and dirt, before losing my right hand in the mound of food.

The next morning, I woke with the call to prayer, kissed Mike, grabbed my journal and borrowed the umbrella again. Even though I never tired of Mike, I relished time alone to write and reflect. He, in turn, appreciated the sleep-in. I stepped outside. The rain had stopped and the wide streets were beautiful in the solemn quiet of morning. Men and women in mini markets, electronics stores and gadget emporiums selling everything from toothbrushes to vacuum cleaners swept the entrances of their shops in the soft light. Mud and trash swirled in a stream of water down the street. Near the Kuantan River, I stood for a few minutes outside the state mosque. It sits on the edge of a large greenery space, flanked with palm trees and bright pink flowers. The sun gave an orange glow to the massive dome roof. Flanking the dome, four minarets stood like rockets, arrowing toward the peaceful sky. I took a deep breath in and felt lucky to be there.

I explored until I found an Indian Mamak stall, which I had decided was my new favourite type of breakfast. I watched tall, strong men roll up balls of dough, tossing them high into the air until they were as thin as a crepe yet larger than a pizza, folding them in four and punching at the dough on a wooden table again. I could have watched them cook all day. I chose *roti pisang*, which is similar to a banana pancake served with a side of dhal. It was set before me, light and fluffy with promises of delight for my mouth.

Mike was still conked out by the time I returned.

"Come on, hon. I brought you coffee." I sat down beside him on the bed and stroked his arm, waking him from his slumber. "I've been doing the math and I don't think we'll make it to Thailand in time to meet Eleasha if we don't take a bus."

"That's still a month away," Mike said, sitting up to hold the coffee.

"I know, but we're averaging 100 kilometres a day and we'll have to spend time in Kota Bharu applying for the visas. Who knows how long they will take to process?" I explained.

Mike looked at me, green flecks sparkling in his blue eyes. He studied my tanned face.

"What did you do with my wife?" he deadpanned.

"Very funny," I said. "I guess we could double up the distance we bike each day..."

"No, no. Let's take the bus," he chuckled. We packed our panniers to go down and up, down and up, and then down the five flights of stairs and ped-alled toward the bus station.

The bus station was loud with chatter and blaring loudspeakers. It took the morning to figure out how to buy tickets. Then we waited until mid-after-noon for the bus, squeezing ourselves onto the overcrowded vehicle. It was weird to see the land move so fast. We were used to the slow pace of our bikes. On the bus, kilometres rushed by.

The bus stopped at 7:00 p.m. at a tiny mosque for dusk prayers. All the men and boys, except Mike, clambered off the bus and bathed beneath four taps protruding from the wall. They took off their shoes and washed their feet, then their heads and hands, each taking on the same movements, the mo-tions of a daily ritual.

Mike went to look for food for us. I had to go to the washroom. There were three squat toilets, but two of them were out of commission because they had no bucket of water to clean with. So, like in many parts of the world, we women were lined up, waiting our turn. I was the only woman not cov-ered, but once the lineup was inside, women slipped off their headscarves and brushed their beautiful hair in front of a cracked mirror on the wall. Each woman's hair looked like silk, polished and immaculate. When they all smiled at me, it was like being let in – part of the cool crowd. I wondered what they thought of me, since my hair, which was always on show, was ratty and quickly tied in a tight knot at the back of my head.

I was awake the entire 350 kilometres on the bus, yet, afterwards, I could barely recall the scenery. Travelling by bus felt like we were going the speed of light compared to pedalling. Kota Bharu was concealed in darkness when we arrived. I hate arriving in a new city in the dark. The bus stopped on an underlit street and Mike and I were told to get off. I was tense and nervous as we gathered our things. We had two bike frames, two handlebar bags, four wheels and eight panniers, which made a total of 16 items to keep track of. We amassed them into a stockpile I hovered over while Mike put a bike together. Men materialized out of the shadows and we found ourselves surrounded.

"I should've had a headlamp ready," Mike said. His hands, generally steady, fumbled with the skewers that were needed to attach the wheels onto the bikes. The men edged closer. With cigarettes dangling from loose lips, they talked over us, studying Mike and peering into the night. One shined a feeble flashlight from a keychain. I realized then they just wanted to help. I shook my hands in front of his light, making fun of its dimness. Everyone laughed and my tension subsided.

I grabbed a tourist map from a nearby kiosk and we cycled into the veiled metropolis. But, with us lacking a guidebook and not knowing where the bus had dropped us off, the map proved useless.

"Where you go?" asked a man from the street corner, riding up beside us on his scooter.

"Do you know of a hostel?" Mike asked.

"Yes, yes, come." He peeled off in front of us. We followed, taking too many turns to count. I lost all sense of direction and, considering Mike never had one, I thought *this isn't good*. The man on the scooter turned left down a pitch-dark alley. My jaw clenched and my pulse drummed in the moonless night.

I pulled my bike to a stop and Mike stopped behind me. "I'm not comfortable," I admitted.

"We can turn around if you'd like," he offered, though I could tell he wasn't concerned.

"Let's just follow him a little further," I said. We turned into the eerie lane. I could hear our tires bite into the muddy gravel and focused my eyes on the only light that came from the man's scooter. Dogs barked and swarmed the bikes, their smell mixed with a sharp whiff of garbage. We just missed hitting the dogs as we pedalled through their shadows. We stopped at a small house with a candle burning inside a window. Our self-appointed escort went inside and conversed with the bare-bellied man who had flung the door open. Their exchange escalated to such a volume that, as I gave a look to Mike, he tilted his head in the direction we had come from. We jumped back on our bikes and raced away from our chaperone, the dogs and the black night.

Then I spotted a name I recognized from Becky and Scott's guidebook: Leck's Traveller's Inn. I knew where we were now. Unbeknownst to our escort (or known to him, we weren't sure), he'd brought us to the area I hoped to be in.

"There's the place! Leck's Traveller's Inn."

We pulled into the lane, my anxiety gone.

"Welcome, welcome!" Mama Maeena brought us inside and showed us a private room that we could wheel our bikes directly into. Minutes later, a taxi arrived from the airport, expelling two guys from Spain and two sisters from Brazil. Suddenly, the hostel was full. We took turns showering and making friends on the couches lining the common room. At 11:00 p.m., we spilled into the dark alley, this time confident in numbers, and walked to an open Chinese restaurant on the corner of the street.

All eyes were on the Brazilian sisters. Both had long, sun-tinted brown hair and long legs in tight-fitting shorts. One wore an open-back tank top and the other wore hers falling off a tanned shoulder. I couldn't stop staring either: they were gorgeous. I, of course, was wearing the same stimulating outfit I'd been in for weeks: Mike's surfer shorts and baggy long-sleeved shirt. Seeing the sisters, I wanted to be dressed in more alluring, clean summer clothes. Although, for Malaysia, the Brazilian beauties would prove too revealing – something they'd realize as the night wore on, being gawked at by locals and tourists alike.

The menu was unreadable, even though we were given a poorly translated "English" version. We played the guessing game and I lucked out with an enjoyable meal of sweet and sour fried chicken with lots of veggies. Mike liked his as well, a noodle soup. The Brazilian girls, on the other hand, didn't have the best fortune. One of them, a vegetarian, ordered a salad from the menu. The waiter came back with a steamy plate of deep-fried pork smothered in congealed fat.

"Salad?" she asked.

"Yes, salad," said the waiter.

The Brazilian did try some of the dish and attempted to keep her repulsion to a minimum while the rest of us convulsed with laughter.

"It's 1:00 a.m.," I said to Mike when we left the restaurant.

"Whoa, we're party animals." He laughed and wrapped his arms around me. My stomach did a flip in his embrace. The night was warm. "Careful," he said, pulling me to his side to avoid a gaping hole in the sidewalk.

"It's past midnight, which means the date is March 17th," I whispered in his ear. Mike's arm slid from my shoulders, across my back, and he took my hand. He rubbed his thumb back and forth on mine. It was a light touch, familiar, and it sparked the memory of our first date, exactly 12 years earlier. As timid and excited as I was then, I began to glow.

"Happy anniversary," I said.

"Happy anniversary." He smiled and we walked back to the guest house, giggling at each other like we were 18 again.

CHAPTER 13

NORTHERN MALAYSIA
Enter the Jungle

"Katrina, *kopi* is ready for you!"

I rolled over in bed and smiled at Mama Maeena through the door. I'd been only four days in her house, yet she knew me very well. I came out of the room, took hold of my coffee and slumped down in bliss on one of the couches to watch Mama Maeena as she took care of everyone. Her skin was coconut brown and her body was larger than that of most Malays. She ran her hostel like a conductor: signing guests in, signing them out, making food, organizing day trips to the jungle or snorkelling – all, seemingly, at once.

I put my coffee down, stood up and gave Mama Maeena a huge morning hug. She laughed in my ear, perhaps used to Canadians squishing her. I had only watched her for a few days, but I was going to miss her. When we released our embrace, Mama Maeena confirmed, "Today is the day." It was time to pick up our passports from the embassy and move on. Since we had met Becky and Scott, Thailand had again changed its requirements on Thai visas, and they were now free. Recent upheavals in Bangkok had closed the airport. Free visas and faster processing times were offered to attract travellers back into the country.

"Banana pancake now?" Mama asked sweetly.

I woke Mike up. We ate and picked up our passports with our Thailand visas stamped inside, and then maneuvered our way through the chaos of the city, somehow, miraculously, riding on the correct road headed west. I estimated it would take four days to cycle from the east coast to Jeti Kuala Kedah on the west coast of Malaysia. Our first day we cycled 105 kilometres into a mild breeze and found a place to stay in a village called Jeli.

The next morning, mist hovered near the road. We lifted the panniers onto the bikes, but I hesitated. I checked the map again and called Mike to have a look. He stood over my handlebars with a quizzical look on his face. All the map showed was a yellow line with kilometres of nothing. We knew we were heading into the jungle, where villages would be scarce, but the map told us nothing about the road conditions. My anxiety poked its nose in again. My palms became sweaty and I wiped them on my bike shorts. I then suddenly dropped my bike down and ran to the bathroom for what was the third time.

When I came back, I said to Mike, "I'm nervous. It's so weird. I feel like it's a race day."

"It's a big day. We don't know much about this road, but we have everything we need. We'll support each other and I'm sure it'll be good." Mike said. I couldn't help holding back a few more minutes. It was as if I was waiting for the start gun to go off. I yearned for a kiss from my mom and her encouragement. Something like, "Good luck you two. Have fun."

But no one was around. There was no reason to delay any longer.

"We'll be great," Mike encouraged, and leaned in for a kiss. "Let's go."

We turned to look at the hotel we had stayed in and said, "thank you" into the morning air. It was our tradition to thank the place where we had slept safely before setting out. No one cheered or clapped. No one noticed we left. It was just the two of us and the road was peaceful.

We chased fog around bends as we headed up and up into the sun. Towers of rock formations stood above the jungle. There was no respite from the heat. The wind was pathetic, as if it, too, struggled to pass through the humidity. I ached to take off the long-sleeved shirt and the hot shorts that stuck to my legs and, I was convinced, sucked all the energy out of me.

After 30 kilometres of hard uphill riding, we came to an open stall with rickety tables and faded plastic chairs. The roof awning was extraordinarily large and, when I ducked under, my eyes were overwhelmed by the darkness. I stood still for a few moments, my eyes adjusting to the small amount of light. I then noticed a small boy with jet-black hair, shiny from a recent wash, sitting alone eating rice with an egg on top.

"Good morning," he said to me, sounding out each syllable.

"Good morning. How are you?" I said slowly.

"Fine," he paused in concentration. "And you?"

"Great, thank you. Can I buy water please?" The boy's mom came through a door in the back, which I assumed was the main room of their house. Then, one by one, three more heads popped into the dim light. The girls, young teenagers, each held a wooden brush, which they slowly pulled through their hair as they stared.

"Hello. How are you?" One of the girls said, breaking from brushing her hair and taking a step forward from her sisters.

"Good. And you?" Giggles were muffled behind tiny hands and then much chattering ensued. I caught the word "America."

"We're from Canada," I said.

"Ooh, Canada." Six girls from the house had now come beneath the awning's darkness, hair brushing abandoned. The little boy explained I wanted to buy water. The mom pulled two dusty bottles from a shelf: one Fanta and one orange drink called 100 Plus. I was made to understand there was no water. The family was then engrossed in a tremendous discussion, which I realized involved trying to figure out how to say the price for the drinks in English. Mike and I had studied Malay numbers, so I started counting in Malay, but after a few numbers I felt like they really wanted to converse in English. After what seemed like much debate, they could not come up with how to say the numbers in English, and because I couldn't understand when they said the numbers in Malay, even after all our practising, they ended up writing the price down on a piece of paper.

"Perfect. *Terami hasi*," I said, wishing them a great day in my best Malay accent. They peeked out into the sun to watch me walk back to the bikes, and more giggles erupted when they had a good look at Mike.

"Sounds like a party in there," Mike said as I attached the drinks onto the back of his bike. I strapped my helmet on with a grand smile on my face.

"That was fun," I told him. This was one of those small daily experiences of trying to communicate over a language barrier. I enjoyed every second of it. As we pulled away, the girls shouted in unison, "I loooove you!"

Mike and I grinned at each other and yelled back, "We love you toooo!"

Sounds from the jungle pulsed with each push of the pedals. We were in the Belum-Temenggor rainforest, one of the world's oldest rainforests. I tried counting the chorus of sounds. I gave up when I heard 15 different animals at the same time. It was a symphony of sweet birdsong, deep-throated calls from hornbills and screeches and yells from monkeys and possibly apes. Whistles and squeals I knew might have been from a huge Malayan tapir. The diversity of animals in the jungle was incredible – at least it seemed so from the "orchestra" whose music escaped beyond the impenetrable wall of coconut trees, ferns and orchids. The smell was overpowering: wet, fresh and natural. I stared into the greenery, searching for movement. I pictured the Asiatic elephant, white-handed gibbon, Malaysian sun bear and the Malaysian tiger somewhere beyond the trees.

"Kat, look out!" Mike pointed to a large mound of elephant dung. Elephant caution signs lined the side of the road.

As we climbed higher, our view expanded. Green hills appeared, undulating like notes on sheet music all the way to the horizon.

We came across a waterfall with a small pool at its base. I was hot. I ignored the pile of litter nearby and lay down to dunk my head in the water. I undid my ponytail and let the strands of my hair float around my face, holding my breath until I could feel my brain stop sizzling.

I was wringing out my hair when Mike pointed out a massive pile of used diapers nearby. *Gross*. Garbage was everywhere in Malaysia, even in the most beautiful places. Forty-five minutes later it began to rain. I stopped and Mike pulled in beside me. I took off my helmet to wash my hair – this time in nature's shower. I felt much cleaner and refreshed. The greenery brightened as the rain continued, our bodies welcoming the cool-down.

For five and a half hours we climbed uphill. Around 4:00 p.m. the rain stopped and we came to an outdoor restaurant. A bus pulled up at the same time and I walked over to talk to the driver.

"Are we close to the top of the hill?" I asked him. I really wanted to be near the top. According to my not-so-reliable map, I thought it would be another 30 kilometres to Banding Island, where we planned to camp.

The driver and I carried out an animated conversation made up of hand signals until he blurted out, "Uphill. You. Three hours." Disheartened, we cranked down on the pedals to climb again. My bum screamed in protest. My hamstring was tight and I thought I had strained it. I willed my body to go on, to get as far as we could before darkness came.

"You know, Mike, Malaysians tell it like it is. If it's uphill, then they say it's uphill." As soon as those words were out of my mouth, I felt my wheels begin to spin beneath me and my hamstring relaxed. Downhill at last. There was no need to rotate the pedals. I lined my feet up behind my front panniers, lifted my tailbone and leaned forward to get the most out of the aerodynamics. Thirty kilometres later (and, frankly, one of the most satisfying downhills ever), I made it to a bridge spanning Temenggor Lake. Mike sailed in a few minutes later and we leaned on the railing together, marvelling over the bright blue water and colourful boats bobbing below.

"Kat, I think the bus driver was pulling your leg," Mike said. "Either that, or the two of you were having completely different conversations."

I smiled. We had crossed over the peninsular divide; the watershed would now be draining into the Indian Ocean.

At the campground, we set up our tent on a bamboo platform beside the lake. No one else was there. I thought the platforms strange until thousands of ants discovered our panniers. They lined up like army troops and marched in procession from the ground, up one of the platform posts until they reached our bags, where they scattered like children let out for recess. We set up our tent as fast as we could and zipped up everything inside.

Clouds from the afternoon storm settled like whipping cream on top of the trees. Two rainbows sprouted from the jungle across the lake and breathed colour into the sky. Temenggor Lake dazzled in the afternoon. I felt content.

Dust and mud caked our bodies and trickles of sweat left streaks down our legs and arms. I was searching in my bag for my bikini when a family of eight arrived at our lakeside camp. I kept Mike's clothes on and wallowed in the water up to my neck. The clothes needed a wash anyway. Dengue fever was prevalent in this area, so when we retreated from the safety of the water we put on more loose clothes to protect us from the mosquitos.

Mike set up our stove on a picnic table near the lake. I sat across from him and watched him start the stove with ease. The hum of our noisy cooking apparatus brought five kids over. Their eyes exuded shyness and intrigue. They dangled on the edge of curiosity, inching closer every few seconds.

"Come and see," Mike patted the bench beside him, inviting three tiny boys and two girls to come over. Their father joined us and explained they were on vacation from the city of Kuala Lumpur, staying at the resort up the hill.

Two women looked on from the edge of the sand with pale pink and blue headscarves that matched the fading light. I assumed they were the father's first and second wives. Islamic tradition recognizes that as long as the man can treat his wives justly and love them the same, then polygamy is allowed. The family set up a picnic dinner, which quickly transformed the wooden table into a buffet of food.

"Please, you two bike hard. You should eat our fish," the father invited us in near perfect English.

There was no need to ask us twice. The children delivered plastic plates with fish, fruit and rice balls, as well as a bowl of soup. The father warned us about the soup, thinking it might be too hot for our foreign tongues. We each dipped an edge of our rice ball in the soup and, in one bite, our mouths burned. We huffed and puffed and hopped around like bush turkeys. Mike grabbed for his water bottle to wash away the heat. The kids giggled like it was the funniest thing they had ever seen. They brought out their camera and took dozens of pictures of us.

The sun dropped behind the hills and the clouds turned gold, the colour of tinfoil on a chocolate coin. The moon rose and a light breeze rippled warm air over the lake. We brought out our headlamps. The kids put them on their heads and ran all over the beach and around the table, playing games with them and then with our camera. I looked at Mike. He had a beautiful relaxed smile on his face.

At the end of the evening, the smallest girl stood in front of Mike with a large purple plastic bag and, though timid, courageously said, "We have a gift for you." Inside were lychee juice boxes, guavas, oranges, apples, a dozen donuts and pastries stuffed with spicy vegetable filling. We were so thankful. It took all I had in manners to resist reaching out and squeezing each of the kids in a big hug.

As they left, the father shook Mike's hand and then touched his heart. It was a slow purposeful movement. His hand rested a few seconds on his heart while he nodded to me as if he wanted to capture a part of this moment to take with him. His wives came over to stand in front of us and each enveloped our hands in theirs. They had stood off to the side for hours and never participated. The corners of their lips curved up just enough so we could visualize their happiness, to show they had enjoyed the evening as spectators, just as much as we did as participants. The children then put their little palms in ours before bowing their heads. Their hair brushed against our hands.

We stood near the beach and waved goodbye until they were out of sight. The night was suddenly silent. Only a gentle wind ruffled the lake. Stars were beginning to shine in the darkness; just soft pin ends of lights.

"What a wonderful family," I said, and gazed wistfully at Mike. "It's interesting, isn't it? How different cultures and religions are from one another. How what is accepted in one society is not accepted somewhere else."

Mike laughed and said, "Kat, you're not allowed two husbands." My stomach dropped. My body lurched and trapped my breath for a few seconds. I looked at him and his body was at ease. He held in nothing. No destructive feelings. *Was he joking?*

I collected myself with the realization that Mike had forgiven me for loving someone else. What's more, I realized, he had probably forgiven me a long time ago.

"Okay. But if *you* were allowed multiple wives, I'd really appreciate one to cook dinner and do all the cleaning," I joked. I thought I would never be ready to make jokes about our past.

Mike took my hand in his. "Sorry. You're stuck being my *only* wife, and you're so good at those things." He smiled. "Although, the cooking part could use some help." He turned to wink at me. I smiled back at him, happy to be his one and only.

It was still warm outside. The mosquitos, thankfully, had gone to sleep. We undressed and waded hand in hand, naked, into the lake. That night, I lay in the tent with my head on Mike's chest, staying wide-awake for hours. I was pleased and thankful he had forgiven me.

Even so, it made the work I had yet to do on *myself* that much more obvious. I realized I had to forgive myself for hurting my husband. And I needed to learn how to love *me* again.

CHAPTER 14

LANGKAWI ISLAND
Rock the Boat

"You're really starting to smell, you know," Mike said from behind me. We'd been riding for three hours since our campsite.

"You can smell me from there?"

"Yup."

Oh, that's lovely, I thought. Our stuff did reek. We had been getting rained on most days, splattered with mud, then baked in the sun. And then there was the sweat. We hand washed our clothes, but the high humidity in the evening didn't allow them to completely dry.

"We can do laundry tonight," I suggested. We stopped in the town of Pengkalan Hulu and found a room with a shower. At the laundromat, the woman weighed our big bag of clothes and then counted out every single item. I plugged my nose to indicate how bad our laundry smelled.

"Come back nine," she said, laughing.

At 9:00 p.m., I left Mike stripped down to his underwear while working on his bike and walked the little town on my own. We were definitely the only foreigners around, but I felt safe.

I opened the door to the laundry and the woman and her daughter were sitting on the floor, folding our clothes into a small pile. The woman looked up. She wore a traditional purple flowered dress and a light violet head covering, which lit up her face. I smiled, remembering a story my mom told me about one of her favourite memories with her own mom, sitting on the floor with socks draped over their legs as they sorted the laundry together for her nine brothers and sisters.

I perched on a small plastic stool watching them. I had trouble being a spectator, but I forced myself to just watch and listen. The room smelled delicious. The mom held up Mike's padded cycling shorts to her young son as he bounced around. I heard admiration in her voice and caught the words "America" and "racing."

"We're from Canada," I peeped up.

"Ah, Canada, ooh," she said, smiling.

"We biked from Singapore."

"Ah, Singapore," she responded. The son looked up with big eyes. I wanted to share with them so I said, "Kota Tinggi, Mersing, Kuantan, Kota Bharu and now Pengkalan Hulu." I mapped out the locations with my index finger on my palm.

I blushed as the young daughter folded my tiny thongs in perfect folds.

They handed over the laundry in a package taped like a present. I walked back to the hotel with my arms out in front of me with care not to squash anything. Our clothes and laundry had never smelled so good. We hadn't used a dryer in months and the warmth from the material practically made my body tingle. Back in the room, I spread the clean clothes around me like my mom would have done and watched Mike work on his bike.

In the morning, accustomed to the call to prayer ringing though the walls, Mike and I snuggled closer. I knew he didn't want to wake up. It was always me who woke up first.

"How much would you cycle most days if I left it up to you?" I whispered.

"None."

"Really?"

"I'm kidding." He wrapped me tighter in his arms. I wanted to believe he was joking, but I doubted it. I realized I didn't mind, though. The fact that he did it and enjoyed doing it was enough. At eight, I finally made myself get up and opened the blinds to another bright day. Rolling hills and jutting rock penetrated the sky.

Once we were on a back road, I gave up on the terrible map I owned. I trusted my instincts and sense of direction instead. We passed our first Buddhist temple, covered with intricate carvings and bold colours. People smiled and those on mopeds and bikes waved or stopped to take pictures of us.

A sign appeared for Alor Setar: 95 kilometres away.

"Only 95 kilometres to go – awesome," I said. Trees with seeds, massive seeds bigger than bananas, hung down from vines. The insides, which looked like cotton, spilled from the seeds like feathers from a pillow fight. I spotted another tree with a fruit similar to a lime, but I knew it was not a lime tree. Everyday there were new mysteries to solve.

My legs dripped with sweat. I looked over at Mike, who didn't have a dry patch on him either. In fact, to look at him, you'd think it was raining. The next few hours were slow and painful. I seemed to have pulled a muscle in my hamstring, which also made my butt ache. We were closer to the west coast now and rice fields spread toward the skyline like a large lake. I stretched my arms above my head, one at a time, and took deep breaths. I then leaned forward and twisted one way and then the other. I rested my left foot on the top tube of my bike to stretch my glute while my right foot did all the pedalling.

"Did I miss something? Did yoga practice start?" Mike asked me.

"It's the perfect place for it. I'm really sore," I responded. Mike chuckled. Not because I was hurt, but because I moved like a clown on a unicycle. I thought about healing blood flow and sent positive energy down to my butt.

At a hut on the side of the road, we pulled over for popsicles. Thanks to roadside stands, our popsicle intake had increased to one popsicle every 25 kilometres. I forgot my sunglasses on the counter and the woman found us in the shade around the corner to give them to me. I was so thankful but realized I must be tired. Her young son came to sit near us in the shade. Not much conversation was to be had since Mike and I were exhausted and he seemed shy. Then he walked over to my bike and, despite his small size, picked it up like it weighed nothing. He reached his little leg over the frame and began riding in circles.

Mike smiled and then turned to me, "It looks like we might make it to Alor Setar and the ferry today after all. This morning, when we saw that sign for Alor Setar and you said 'awesome,' I thought, 'no way are we riding that far! It's so hot.' But look at us. I think we'll make it."

"I never had a doubt," I said. "We better get going." I gave the boy a nod, asking if he was coming with us. A smile plastered onto his face and he ran to grab his own beaten-down bike. He joined behind Mike as we finished our last kilometres on mainland Malaysia.

We made it to the ferry terminal one minute before the last ferry to Langkawi Island left for the day. We threw our bikes onto the top deck, then walked downstairs to collapse on a row of seats.

When we stepped onto the dock of Langkawi Island, it swayed beneath us like a waking snake. I went to lift my bike from the dock.

"Mike, the camera is gone!"

Mike dropped his bike and ran to the edge of the dock as the boat pulled away. "Stop!" he yelled. Our hearts sank. "Please stop!" We pierced the air with our cries, willing the ferry we had just stepped off to come back. A boy in his late teens coiled a large rope while he laughed down at us.

Another deckhand heard our pleas and waved his arms, directing us to turn around. "Maybe it's going to moor," Mike said. "We can go find our camera then."

The watercraft grunted and rocked while easing itself among the tight marina before coming to rest a pier over. We grabbed our bikes and jostled with them as we made our way toward the boat. Once close enough, I put mine down and leapt onto another vessel, ran across its slippery deck, then jumped a metre gap over the black water, coming to land on our ferry.

"No!" The boy coiling the ropes yelled at me.

"My camera is gone," I tried to explain. He ventured to lead me away, but I forced aside his hands. I went down the stairs into the belly of the boat. I walked in on a group of teenagers cleaning the passenger benches. They turned to look at me.

"My camera is gone," I announced.

"No. No camera." An older man took charge to get rid of me. I stood my ground. I knew someone had my camera. It was attached to my handlebar by a string and a carabiner and zippered into a case permanently fastened to my bar. Though obviously not a theft-proof system, it was not capable of falling off. I had made a mistake in not removing the camera after rushing onto the ferry. We had expected to be able to sit beside our bikes before we were told it wasn't allowed. The camera itself wouldn't be hard to replace, but it held photos from Malaysia we hadn't yet uploaded: pictures of the child riding my bike, pictures of our camp under rainbows, photos of sticky rice and fish goo with the family, proof of the mounds of fresh elephant turds.

I kept saying, "My camera, my camera." Any Malay I had learnt escaped me, so I continued in English. "Malaysia has been incredible, such beautiful sights and the people have been so kind" – I paused for effect – "I'd really like my photos back." As I became more hysterical, so did the crew. They laughed and continued to do their own work, aside from the same helpful boy who kept checking our seats because he was convinced we'd just dropped the camera.

There was a shuffle of footsteps behind me and I spun around. It was an older teen with a bulge in his jeans that I immediately convinced myself was our camera. "What's in your pocket? Empty it!" I challenged him. Everyone hushed. I took authority in what was clearly their domain.

He obliged and slid his hand into the pocket of his jeans and leisurely pulled out a pack of cigarettes. I stared at it then slowly lifted my eyes from the pack to his face before I looked around the room.

The men glared at me. Men I was accusing of theft. The stupidity of the situation I had put myself in suddenly rose like bile in my throat. Even though I knew our camera was stolen, I couldn't accuse all of them when I didn't know who it was. It was night. We were in a place we didn't know, and these men were looking increasingly unhappy that I was slowing them down from going home. I turned and ran up the stairs. I threw myself through the door and breathed in fresh air. The stars of the southern hemisphere were coming out, illuminating the sea. *Life without the camera won't be so bad*, I thought.

"Did you find it?" Mike asked. I shook my head no.

"This is ridiculous! I'm going to get it!" Before I could stop him, Mike took off across the first boat and I could see the shimmer of his bike helmet as he made the leap onto the next one.

A burst of wind squalled up and splattered me with water. The dock rode the choppy waves and with each swell slammed into the adjacent boat. The darkness of night engulfed the island. Lights from the town were far, far away. A deckhand's laughter cackled in the gloom. A sign nearby grated against its rusty chain.

"Mike!" I screamed in panic. I wanted him to come back. I wanted to chase after him, but I couldn't leave the bikes. It wasn't the camera I worried about any longer. The seconds slid by like hours. Overwhelming love was awakened for my husband. I longed for him to be back at my side. We had recently celebrated six months on our bikes. The last few years of our relationship were mirrored in the tempestuous seas, but the material want of our camera was a trifle compared to the need of having my husband safe.

Then I saw him, striding toward me. My body relaxed. His jubilation radiated as he held up the camera. "They 'found' it!" We must have wasted too much of their time, so the boy gave it back. Mike wrapped me up in a triumphant hug. "Now let's go look for a place to sleep," he said. We slept heavy. My arm wrapped around my husband all night.

The next day, swimming in the ocean, Mike's hand brushed up against my thigh in the water, and a passionate memory was sparked from years earlier. We had been travelling through Ecuador and were exploring the Amazon. In the evenings, by the gleam of our headlamps, we spotted fresh water crocodiles, and during the days we paddled a dugout canoe. On one of the swims from our boat, I wrapped my legs around Mike's waist as he held the edge of the canoe. Pink dolphins sailed past, piranhas nibbled on our legs. Water slapped against the hull of the boat. We hadn't cared.

Now we smiled at each other and Mike leaned in for a kiss. It was time to rock the boat.

CHAPTER 15

THAILAND
Getting "Manipulated"

I turned back toward the island with a mournful look. We were leaving places before we got to know them. The worst part of it was I now found myself researching the next place we were headed to rather than learning more about where we were. I studied maps, figured out visa requirements, health and food. That was the problem with planning. I felt rushed ever since the middle of Malaysia because we wanted to meet our friend in Phuket, Thailand. *How, with all this time, could there not be enough time?* I asked myself. The boat landed in Thailand and we began riding north. I pedalled harder.

At the first large gas station, I bought a map book that labelled roads, towns and cities in both Thai script and English. We pulled to a stop at a crossroad and managed to match the road sign to our map, like a game of matching cards. We turned left.

Banana plants towered above with red, umbrella-like flowers, which skimmed the tops of our helmets as we rode by. The sun blazed down, making us sweat in our saddles. Our hands slipped on the handlebars. I wiped my brow onto my wet arm and then looked at Mike. Perspiration puddled beneath the rims of his sunglasses and fogged the lenses. We both hung our tongues out like dogs, licking moisture from the air.

I heard the toot-toot of a horn behind me.

In my rear-view mirror, I saw a vehicle the size of a golf cart homing in on us. Mike moved closer to the side of the road to let it pass and I followed him. We had been honked and waved at by families of six, who all shared the one seat of a scooter; drivers who carried loads of five-metre-long bamboo poles sticking out at awkward angles; and dozens on mopeds with birdcages clutched in their hands. (In my evening research, I'd found out bird-singing competitions were held twice a week and taken very seriously. The red-whis-kered bulbul was the most sought after for its musical whistle.)

The vehicle honked again and pulled up beside me. I nearly fell into the jungle.

"It's an ice cream truck!" I called ahead to Mike.

The driver's smile was as large as mine. He knew he had happened upon the easiest sale ever.

I loved Thailand right then and there.

Mike laid his bike down in the thick brush and paid for our treats while a cow with saggy skin hovered close by. Mike handed me my coconut-flavoured ice cream cone. It was creamy and cold and disappeared in seconds. My body cooled down as if an air conditioner had been turned on. We bought two more from the driver, who couldn't stop smiling. We savoured our second one, pausing to giggle at each other between licks. Mike seemed so happy.

Back on the bikes, we watched from our saddles as the land changed from dense jungle to towers of limestone swathed in broccoli-green mangrove forests. Late afternoon rain came and washed the rest of our sweat onto the streets.

We took advantage of a long breakfast the next morning. I assured Mike we had a shorter ride, only 80 kilometres, so we waited until 9:30 a.m. to leave. When we did, construction went on for hours. Dust billowed like a sand-storm. We kept to the left-hand side of the street and moved as slow as camels. Cars flew by.

"I'm feeling squashed from the traffic and construction!" I yelled to Mike, who had taken to riding in front of me since I'd caused an accident a few days earlier. I had stopped suddenly to talk to someone but didn't give Mike our hand sign and he ran into my back wheel. The force jolted me forward and kicked Mike sideways into the road. We were lucky he wasn't hit by a vehicle.

"It's scary!" I called again.

"Scary? Do you not remember the highway in New Zealand?" he asked over his shoulder.

I remembered. And he was right. At least the drivers in Thailand were used to obstacles in the streets: cows, chickens or kids. A couple of bikes were nothing for them to move around. Either way, we stopped for a break at the next roadside stall. Bunches of bananas hung from wooden rafters. I pointed for some to buy, but the stall owner shook her head no.

"No?" I didn't understand. I really wanted a banana. I watched as she filled a bag with peeled bananas that looked well past their expiry date.

"*Gloo-ay ya,*" she said with a smile, the curves of her lips seemed to reach for the sky. It was as if she pulled positive energy right from her toes. Her eyes smiled too, their corners crinkled from her cheeks constantly pushing upwards. She handed me the bag but wouldn't take any money from me before she had me try a bite. *Gloo-ay ya* – deep-fried banana – instantly became one of my favourite Thai treats. For ten baht (30 cents) I cycled away with a large plastic bag of deep-fried bananas swinging from my handlebars.

The southwestern edge of mainland Thailand is connected to the island of Phuket by a bridge. Mike and I hung over the edge of it, watching men sort fishing nets in long wooden boats with prows decorated with scarves and flowers. I was excited for the beach.

Phuket was originally an ocean stop for the major trading route between India and China. The area had been rich in tin and rubber, but now its wealth comes from tourism. Phuket is either derived from the Malay word for "hill" or from two Thai words meaning "mountain jewel." Either way, I didn't register this at the time, and had mistakenly assumed since we would be cycling along the shore that our ride would be flat.

As we cycled toward the town of Patong, the hills grew in size. The roads were crowded with trucks, scooters and people. Signs went from Thai script to English and tourists were everywhere. My legs slowed and my energy waned. I was cut off by a scooter and had to dig into my reserves to follow Mike, who was a couple hundred metres in front of me, pointing, probably at different holes in the road to be avoided. He still thought I was right behind him.

"I have to get him a mirror." I chuckled and pushed as hard as I could to catch up. I caught sight of his blue helmet as he made a turn.

It was the busiest road we'd cycled on yet. Exhaust pipes from scooters scorched our legs and nearly burnt holes into our panniers. Many of the vehicles were driven by tourists, who I assumed were not used to driving in an Asian country with its countless obstacles on the road (ourselves included).

I caught up with Mike and we pushed up another hill. The sun, alone in a clear sky, beat down on us and sweat poured down my forehead, stinging my eyes. Hot air blew into our faces and dried our mouths. Every vehicle honked its horn. It was oddly motivating. I wiped my brow and my legs pumped with renewed energy.

At the crest of the hill was a gorgeous temple. Its entranceway was lined with dragons and a sweeping roof, covered in red, green and gold tiles.

The honking increased.

"*That's* why all the honking! I didn't know what was going on," Mike said.

"I thought the honking was to cheer us on!" I laughed.

The honking, we learned, was for respect and to keep bad spirits away. Mopeds, cars, buses and tuk-tuks honked for good luck, honked for happiness, honked for wealth, honked for safe passage – not for us. We coasted down the other side and it felt great to ride free without having to spin the pedals. At the bottom, we pulled over to look at the map.

"Oh no," I said, staring down at the map.

"What's 'oh no'?" Mike asked in a voice that signalled he already knew the answer but didn't want to accept it.

"Did you not see a sign for Karon Beach?"

"No," he said.

"We missed our turn," I announced. "I'm tired today and *hot*! I don't think I've ever sweat so much. Seriously, I had to work so hard to keep up with you," I rambled. "I'm sorry, I wasn't paying attention."

"We have to ride back up that hill?" Mike asked.

I nodded.

Mike sighed. It was barely audible. But I knew him well and my ears were attuned to it. He reached for his warm water bottle and drank until it was dry and stared at the hill for a minute. His face, though flushed, still looked calm.

"Thank you for not being mad," I said.

"Why would I be?" He asked.

Because I messed up. Because it's hot out and I'd predicted we would cycle 80 kilometres, but at 110 we've well surpassed that, I thought to myself.

"Let's get it done. I'll buy you a Slurpee on the other side," he said, and reached his leg over his bike frame to start.

This time, I really did believe the cars were honking for us. And some of them were. People on scooters saw us working hard and shot their fists up into the air congratulating our efforts. Scooters, tuk-tuks and cars all laid on their horns, creating a symphony of mass honking.

"Woo-hoo!" I let out a huge cheer at the top once again because it felt appropriate to cheer to the world.

I hadn't minded cycling the hill twice. There was so much to look at. Along with the temple, there were many offerings along the side of the road of flowers, incense, drinks and food. We saw these shrines everyday while we cycled. One couple stopped in an old black truck to place an offering. They had brought a gold shrine shaped like a doll's house and sat it at the base of a tree. It had mini decks, windows and an intricate detailed roof. It stood over a foot tall. We had learned these offerings give the spirits a place to live and show respect for them. Buddhists like to care for the spirits because they are believed to protect people and bring good luck, fortune and health. The man took out a bottle of red Fanta, opened it and placed a straw inside before offering it up to the shrine. We watched quietly as they prayed. I grabbed Mike into a sweaty hug, thankful we were doing this together and that he was so accepting of my faults.

The next day, at Karon Beach, I woke up hungry and sore. We walked outside into the pandemonium; too many people in a small town. Locals vying for tourists' attention outside guest houses, kiosks and stores; tourists in sarongs, flip-flops and bikinis buying pancakes, coffee and ice cream; street dogs following along, begging with moist eyes. The streets were colourful and smelled like dust and chocolate. I loved it.

"Hello, massage for you?" rang a street hawker in a long, drawn-out, high-pitched voice. Massage parlours were plentiful. We had already passed dozens that morning; each one with its own lady or transgender person coaxing people inside.

"Yes, please," I answered and told Mike I'd meet him afterward.

Seemingly surprised by the sale, she motioned to follow her through the open door. *After months of cycling, I'd think I wouldn't be sore anymore,* but this wasn't the case. I was handed a menu of massage options, but I could only understand the length of treatment. We settled on a price of 200 baht ($6) for an hour. I didn't drive for a hard bargain, as I assumed doing so would only hurt the quality of my massage.

The woman motioned for me to follow her down a hallway. At the end of the hall, she pulled aside a pale purple curtain and instructed me to get changed. I undressed and climbed onto the massage table. Once on my belly with my head supported in the headrest, I took a deep breath, letting the air out slowly.

Breathe in and out. *This is just what I need. Some prime relaxation and time to unwind.* My eyes softly closed. The days of riding through the scorching heat had taken their toll. *I deserve this break.*

Swoosh, the curtain opened and the sheet covering me was whipped off and floated to the floor. My eyes popped open and a tiny massage therapist pounced onto the table, miraculously found enough room to kneel down and proceeded to pound on my back.

"*Well, this is different,*" I said under my breath, somewhat in shock. My eyes searched across the floor through the gap of the headrest. The therapist picked up one of her dainty legs and straddled my bottom. I became quite conscious that my bum, saddle sores and all, was bared to this woman. She reached back for my ankles and pulled my legs up – and up and up – back and behind until they touched the top of her head. I felt like a windup toy. Back and forth she worked my legs, eventually letting them fall back to the table, as if defeated.

She scooted down to straddle me behind my knees. I felt her lean forward as she reached to grasp the front of my shoulders and pull me backwards. Her hands slid down to my wrists and she heaved on them until my upper body followed. My bare breasts received a breeze from the curtain that was still open. I noticed this, since my head was now out of the headrest, searching around like a centipede, with my arms stretched and clasped behind me.

It was in that moment of centipede glory when I had the eureka moment. *Aha, a Thai massage*, I thought. I was in Thailand after all. (When I was a kid, I loved the movie *Back to School*, starring Rodney Dangerfield. The main character had a Thai therapist who walked all over his back to get him ready for competition.) *Well, at least she's not walking all over my back*, I thought, as she graciously let me crash back down to the comfort of my headrest.

I heard her begin to converse with another woman. They both laughed. I assumed they were laughing at me and the fact I was the only one dumb enough not to wear clothes. And then I felt it: small feet walking up my calves, one at a time, and then pressing into my hamstrings. Then the other woman stepped on my back, her foot pushing the tightened muscles across my shoulders and back.

How tough am I now? I thought. *I can support the weight of two women walking all over me!* I was no longer embarrassed. *I'm strong like a warrior! I am Jane of the jungle, no, make that Xena: Warrior Princess!*

They jumped off, landing with a soft thud on the linoleum floor. One of the ladies began to pull at my neck and ears, while the other one walked to the back of the table, took hold of my ankles and, with all her might, pulled on them, stretching me like I was on a rack. They then grabbed my digits and cracked each of my fingers and toes. The lady at the back gripped onto my ankles once again and proceeded to spread my legs wide apart. Very wide apart.

What the—, I thought in a panic.

At the end of the hour-long muscle manipulation, I was spent. Certainly no more relaxed than when I went in.

"How was the massage?" Mike asked when I dragged my beaten body into our room.

"Really interesting, you should go for one," I said, and collapsed on the bed in exhaustion.

CHAPTER 16

PHUKET

Cleansing the Spirit

Time for a break. It was good timing because our friend Eleasha from Canada had come for a holiday and was due to be picked up at the airport. Mike hailed a taxi outside our guest house.

"Only 1,200 baht," ($36) said the taxi driver.

"1,200! That's crazy! We'll take the bus," Mike said.

"Oh no, you no take the bus, there's many people on bus, oh no," the driver said, drawing out each "oh no."

Mike gave him a look and a crooked smile lit up his face, "That's okay, we like people."

The driver waved us into the vehicle. Mike sat in the front. He loves to bargain. I sat in the back, entertained by the constant chatter up front. They initially haggled over a price for the taxi to go to the airport. When our driver realized he could have a customer to the airport, wait for us while we found Eleasha and then drive us back, he kept bargaining.

"Mr. Alee is a good man. No smoking, no drinking alcohol, pray five times a day," Mr. Alee stated proudly. "Only 1,200 baht." He turned around from his driver's seat and gave a smile, providing me a full view of his black, stringy goatee. It shone as if it were silk.

"700 baht," Mike countered.

"Oh, you are funny!" He slapped Mike's thigh in jest, again sounding out his "oh" to the point where it became a sentence on its own. "That is only one way. I will take you one way."

"Just to the airport is good then. The bus is cheap."

"Okay, okay, you crazy man. 1,000 baht."

"700 baht," Mike countered again, in the high-pitched voice he uses when bargaining. "It's good for you and good for me. And it's a nice drive."

Mr. Alee slapped Mike's thigh again. The sting of it caused Mike to shift his position in the front seat.

"Aho, okay. Mr. Alee a good man. Take care of you. You happy, Mr. Alee happy."

"Great! Pull in here," Mike pointed to a 7-11 convenience store.

"What's this?" Mr. Alee asked after we had come back to the taxi. He held the cup we'd given him, condensation dripping from the container onto his lap.

"It's a Slurpee. The finest drink in the world," Mike told him, and we watched while Mr. Alee took a sip from the straw.

"Mmm," he said, and started to drive with one hand while taking long draws of the Slurpee.

"Aah!" Slamming the Slurpee in the cupholder, Mr. Alee's hands shot up to hold his head.

"And *that* is a brain freeze. I should have warned you," Mike laughed. Mr. Alee steered with his knees while he recovered. I thought we were going to smack into the colourful bus passing us.

Winnipeg, we explained to Mr. Alee, is the Slurpee capital of the world. Considering our city is frozen half of the year with temperatures often minus 20 degrees Celsius and colder, frozen pop makes little sense to be known for.

Mr. Alee recovered from his brain freeze and said he enjoyed it, but finished off his Slurpee with more caution.

"Look. Muslim mosque," Mr. Alee pointed out.

"Are you Muslim?" I asked from the back.

"Mr. Alee is a good man. No smoking, no drinking alcohol, pray five times a day," he repeated.

"Where are you from?" Mike asked.

"Muslim," he stated. Mr. Alee pointed out mosques, churches and Chinese temples with pillars wrapped by dragons and lions supporting gentle sloped roofs. We passed hundreds of monks in procession, walking along the road near a Buddhist temple with a high, golden-leaf roof and brilliant, gold, Buddha statues. Mr. Alee acknowledged the pictures of the king that were strung out on massive billboards.

Mr. Alee took a sharp right down an alleyway. "Shortcut," he said matter-of-factly.

Everything moved fast: people, vehicles, signs and streets. We kept the windows open and the sounds bombarded our senses. Horns, exhaust, screeching. It had been a long time since we had been in a car. I realized how easy it could be to get sucked back into a fast-paced life, one where answers needed to come right away. Where people must know their careers for life, choose their partner, respond immediately to texts, emails, never being without their cellphones and working long hours.

The only thing that had become clear was I chose Mike. But as for a career or something I would like to do for the rest of my life, where we wanted to live or whether we would have children...those were questions that must wait. I was not at all ready to go home, I realized.

Jenga blocks towered eye-high atop the plastic tablecloth. I carefully reached for a middle block four rows down. The tower shook but steadied and I let out a breath.

We were with Eleasha on the island of Koh Phi Phi, playing Jenga at our new favourite restaurant. The first time we found it, we had weaved our way from the beach, along sand tracks tucked in behind makeshift stores selling wares to the throngs of tourists. The stalls, made with wood, bamboo and tarpaulin, sold everything from jewelry and sarongs to sunglasses and oil paintings of the islands.

The restaurant was hidden in a narrow gap snuggled between two shops. Poles held up woven tarps and planks of wood for the low roof. One had to crouch to come and go. The bright sun was virtually shut out once you entered, and it took a moment to adjust to the dim light. The owner, who had introduced himself as Sakda, motioned for us to sit down. I don't remember being hungry, but his twinkling eyes and gesture led us to settle at one of his tables. Sakda wore a large blue chef's hat that comically sat perched on his head like *The Cat in the Hat*, and a smile that told a story I immediately wanted to hear.

When Mike and I stay in one place for a while, we tend to pick a favourite venue and eat there over and over. So here we sat, same restaurant, same table. The two of us eating at the same stall gave us the impression we belonged, that we had friends and the familiarity of home. It was nice because travelling sometimes feels fast-paced. I was figuring out how to slow down and relax into the calm of our surroundings. I had learned a lot from watching Mike.

It took three days to work up the nerve and then figure how to communicate well enough with Sakda that I wanted him to teach me how to cook. When he understood, he took me by the arm into the kitchen. We made pad Thai and then a yellow curry. We cut up cloves of garlic and he taught me to leave the skins on as they added more flavour and texture to the dish. Vibrant yellow and red peppers, purple and green onions and bright chilies danced in the much-used wok. Then Sakda poured in sauce, sending up steam into the small space (and making my eyes water). He stuck his baby finger in to taste. Then he added more chilies and tasted again. The tips of his mouth curved into a smile.

I tried to be serious and write down what Sakda told me, but I had missed half of it in the translation. Mike was thoroughly entertained as he watched me cook, and we laughed when the dishes I made went off to other guests in the restaurant.

Our table soon displayed vegetarian coconut-milk curry, rice and yellow curry with prawns, chicken garlic with noodles and pad Thai. To me, Thai food portrays all the desirable elements of an ideal life. It's the perfect combination of sweet yet spicy. It's satisfying but leaves one wanting more. Mike pushed aside the Jenga after winning the last game, and we dug in.

As we got to know Sakda, we learnt about his story of the tsunami that hit five years earlier. Until the devastating tsunami, Koh Phi Phi was an island known for its serenity, simplicity and beauty. The populated part of the island lies only two metres above sea level on a sandy isthmus. Each side of this narrow strip of land was hit with its own wave. One wave was three metres in height and the other over five. Within minutes, the island was decimated.

Sakda described how he was caught and thrown around like a bath toy. Many others were pulled into the current and struggled to hold onto trees as their homes crumbled around them. Sakda became trapped under rubble from the makeshift shops and bamboo huts. He took what he thought was his last breath, convinced his life was over, until foreign hands dug through the chaos on top of him and he saw the sun again.

Over 2,000 people died on the small island that day. Every time I sat down on the blue plastic chairs I thought about the power the world has over us. The power of destruction and sorrow but also the power of people to build it back up again. Many countries and individuals reached out when food and water were needed on the island in the middle of the Andaman Sea. Now, years on, we still found remnants of the disaster tucked away, burning in piles on more remote parts of the island.

Sakda lost everything. He lost friends, his home and his possessions. Listening to Sakda's story made me think about the part of the world I come from and how attached we were – I was – to our "stuff." North Americans have so much stuff that it's trendy to downsize, to pare all belongings down to only 100 things. If only this part of the world were so privileged, I thought.

Over the week, Eleasha, Mike and I had spent hours playing Jenga. The joy that abounded within the reconstructed walls of that restaurant was fresh, alive with an understanding of what it means to live. While we played, we watched apprehensive Westerners stumble into the restaurant to be swayed to sit down as we had been.

I found myself thinking of Sakda's world. It had tumbled down around him like Jenga blocks, but he was resilient and stacked the pieces back up again. I thought Sakda must be exhausted from trying to win over new people every day. But it never showed. He smiled as bright as I'm sure the sun had felt when his head broke through the rubble.

Carefully sliding out a block, the tower shaking before collapsing on the table, I took a quick breath. I reached beneath the table and grasped the top of Mike's leg. In the next moment, his hand was on mine. Sparks shot from his hand to my heart, nearly leaving me breathless. I couldn't imagine losing him now. His one hand interlocked with mine while the other built us another tower.

Morning came slowly, but when all you have to do is get yourself to the beach and eat food, life is pretty easy. On the sandy path from our guest house, Eleasha walked back toward us, laughing.

"I realized the fastest I've moved all week was to run after the donut lady," Eleasha said with a huge bite-sized piece in her mouth. Most of the food in Thailand is worth running for. After many days, the crepe lady was already making our orders as soon as she saw us walking toward her. We could hear the thud of dough slamming on the table until it was thin as paper. It was already sizzling on her pan by the time we stopped in front of her trolley. She sliced a fresh banana and laid the pieces on the crepe, which was ready to accept the trail of chocolate that flowed from her bottle. With a swift, practised hand, she rolled the crepe up like a tube and cut it into bite-size pieces placed on a plate. She stuck a toothpick in, handed it to me and began to work on Mike's order. Pure heaven.

After a day of snorkelling in the cove of Koh Phi Phi Leh (where Leonardo DiCaprio's movie *The Beach* was filmed), Eleasha, Mike and I drank coconut water from coconut shells and devoured chocolate, banana and strawberry shakes on the beach. Grains of sand massaged our toes while the sky went from bright orange to red to blue. Paper lanterns were taken away by the wind. Mike laid back and took a nap.

"I hope our friendship lasts forever," I told Eleasha while we watched a lantern fly high into the universe. Eleasha, Mike and I had been friends for ten years. Over the past decade, she had often spent Sunday evenings at our house regaling us with tales from her dating life, which I invariably found hilarious and entertaining.

"It will," she paused, smiling. "Mike and you seem to be doing great."

"We are." I smiled. "It's been an amazing opportunity to be able to spend so much time together and to really get to know each other."

Another pause.

"Do you ever hear from Alex?"

I hadn't heard his name said aloud in months. I let it settle but noted that hearing his name didn't make me anxious or fall apart.

"No. I stopped phoning him," I said. "I hear about him sometimes from Dawn and it seems like he's doing well – which is good. I miss him. Sometimes, I think a part of me will always miss him, but going on this bike trip was the right decision for all of us."

I dug my feet deeper into the sand and continued. "You know, it hasn't always been easy. Some days were extremely hard, and I really wanted to reach out to Alex, but, as the months went on, I became better at communicating with Mike and he began to learn how to communicate with me."

I paused to look at my beautiful friend with her dark curls frizzled by the sun. "I think Mike forgave me a long time ago," I said.

She laughed and said, "I'm sure he did. What about you though? Have you forgiven yourself?"

I shook my head back and forth. "I'm still working on it."

"Kat, so many relationships go through problems. The main thing is what you are doing now. You're reconnecting. You're saving your marriage." Eleasha took hold of my hand. "And I'm glad you did. You're so much happier now. I can really see it."

I looked over at Mike, still asleep on the sand. He laid on his back with his head tilted in our direction. He looked peaceful and content. My heart skipped a beat as I reaffirmed what she said. "I am."

When the stars came out, we made our way to a dance bar. Music blasting from speakers seemed to reverberate off of the sand and pulse with the waves of the ocean. Loops of fire streaked through the black sky as fire dancers moved with grace and precision. The flames from their sticks lit up the beach. I arched my back and reached my head to the stars. Eleasha moved her hips and body in time to the music; she had better dance moves than me. Mike sat and watched from a barstool, drinking rum from a large blue sand bucket.

"The Norwegian couple are fighting!" Eleasha yelled to me over the music.

"What?" I asked. "They seemed perfect." We had gone snorkelling with the

Norwegians a few days earlier and they'd been fun to hang out with. They had even come with us to Sakda's restaurant.

"I don't get it!" I yelled. Eleasha shrugged her shoulders and kept dancing. It turned out the Norwegians' relationship, which looked so light and transparent, was difficult and rocky. *Relationships are one of the great mysteries of the world*, I mused. I didn't have a hope of figuring them out.

I spotted an elderly couple sitting near Mike at the bar holding hands. The woman leaned her head onto her husband's shoulder. I loved seeing couples that had been together for 50 years and still showed affection. But an eternal connection is tough and, for some, unrealistic. I couldn't see the point in getting to a golden anniversary if life would have been better without one another.

"But they seemed so amazing together!" I cried.

"We have no idea what goes on in another relationship," Eleasha said. "We can only guess." She was right. I had a habit of mistaking outward appearances for private realities. It was a habit I found hard to shake.

Take Mike and me. We went to a very low place in our relationship and I bet most of our family had no idea we were having problems. I had promised forever on our wedding day, yet, less than a year ago, I had wanted to take that back. Mike fought for me to stay. We don't know what triggers the slipping of a relationship, when a relationship will fall or if it will get put back together. Ours, thankfully, was standing stronger everyday.

A few days later we said goodbye to Eleasha. Back on Phuket, Mike and I biked to the Shanti guest house, a tropical rainforest nestled between the dust and heat. Rock steps led from a saltwater pool to our room, which was made of gleaming hardwood and bamboo and, for an extra $3, included air conditioning. Mike stretched out on the bed, looking blissfully content.

The next morning we were led by the hand into a group of men as they laughed, danced and poured water down our backs, chests, then over our heads. The men swung our arms and shouted, "Welcome! Welcome!" I wiped the cool water from my eyes and watched a truck pull up, filled to the brim with people pointing Super Soakers in our direction.

Today was Songkran, the celebration of the New Year in Thailand, marked by the passage of the moon and sun into the zodiac sign of Aries. Songkran is a Sanskrit word that implies to ascend or to move on. Water is used to wash off the past year in order to start again fresh. People spring clean their homes and scrub Buddha statues. Traditionally, the water used to bathe the Buddhas was considered blessed. Families paid homage to their elders by sprinkling their hands and feet with this water, which was often scented with jasmine flower petals. It symbolized the cleansing of negativity from the past and provided a natural path to renewal.

These days, Songkran in Thailand is the world's largest water fight. Hundreds of people lined the streets, congregating around huge barrels of water, armed with hoses, buckets and the biggest water guns I'd ever seen, while the rest of Chalong Bay seemed to be driving around.

The parade seemed to never stop. Scooters slowed and drivers cringed as water was tossed on them. A pickup truck drove up, armed with 15 people and a massive barrel of water in the back. It was all out war! Dust and heat washed away and the entire country seemed to cool down a few degrees. With the coming of spring, hearts were unfurling. We dripped like Bodhi trees from an afternoon monsoon. The festivities left us feeling lighter, even though we were soaked.

Mike was given his own bucket, and I was handed a container of white baby powder to smear on people. Baby powder mixed with water is used to bless others and for good luck. My finger traced white lines beneath brown eyes as passengers from the trucks put their cheeks out for me to whiten. It was hot, but as the day wore on the water became surprisingly cold. Scooters with sidecars attached and loaded with massive blocks of ice stopped at each group to add ice to their barrels of water.

Mike and I continued down the road, our clothes dripping and our sandals sloshing in puddles as we walked. Music pounded from vehicles and boom boxes covered in plastic. I'd been practising how to say "Happy New Year" in Thai, which sounded to me like *Sawadee Mai*. In the streets, people yelled, "Happy New Yeaaaa!"

We were invited into family groups and given shots of SangSom, a cheap rum. Cans of beer were passed down from trucks and thrust into our hands. Men and women would take hold of us and dance and spin on the side of the street. Others smeared paint on us, only for it to wash off when the next buckets of water cascaded over our heads.

Mike and I felt grateful and fortunate. When baby powder leaked into my eyes and I had trouble seeing, a stranger came up to me, attempted to clean his own palms on the back of his wet jeans and tried to clean out my eyes by wiping them with his hands. When that didn't work, he poured a bucket of water on my head.

All the children were out. Some were so tiny, they sat in their own small buckets of water, splashing and giggling. The bigger kids were loaded with water guns half their size, with water packs strapped to their backs.

One young boy came over confidently. He wore a yellow shirt that gaped at the neck and held a red bowl of white powder. Mike bent down to his level so the boy could reach his cheeks. I then knelt down to do the same. The boy's hands were bright white with powder and his smile radiated. His hair, soaked, clung to his forehead. His brown eyes shined with purity and he moved them to look at me, then Mike and back at me. Those eyes stared into mine and I felt that through him I was being understood and forgiven. I crouched there, frozen, until Mike stood up and held out his hand for me to grab onto.

I was baptized a Roman Catholic, but my family cherished the breeze blowing through the aspen trees and ripples across the lake more than the insides of a church. Mike's mom converted to Judaism to marry his dad, but Mike didn't have strong beliefs. I never made it to confession. I hadn't welcomed that part of Catholicism into my life, but, here, in the middle of another country's religious festival, I found myself internally confessing with every splash of water. Letting my sins wash off me, soak the ground and flow into the gutters.

Thailand had turned into a place of personal sanctuary – a place of security, happiness and love. It was the place where I found myself back to loving Mike – fully and completely. It was the place where I began to learn how to love myself again. With every bucket of water, I took in a sharp breath of air and, as I let it go, I let go of my sins. I shed self-loathing. I accepted that I might never live up to the standards of what I had imagined "the best partner ever" to be, but, with every smear of powder on my cheeks, I made a vow I would try.

Mike took the key out from his shorts pocket and opened the wooden door to our room. The air conditioning welcomed us, cooling our skin and evaporating the evening sweat. I went into the washroom and shut the door behind me and smiled. Everything was so clean. White fluffy towels hung from stainless steel racks. I slid open the immaculate shower curtain and turned the hot water on. The room steamed up as I lathered myself with a new bar of soap. A steam cloud escaped like mist rising from the ocean as, wrapped up in a towel, I walked back into the main room toward our queen-size bed.

Mike opened the duvet cover to welcome me. I slid in, tossing the moist towel onto the floor. I gathered my book to begin my ritual of reading myself to sleep. Mike reached for my other hand. His fingers entwined mine. His thumb slid softly up my thumb, around my wrist and back down to my pinky finger. He rolled onto his side and his other hand glided from my shoulder to the crook of my waist, slightly passed my hip. It was so gentle. His caress was so soft.

His hand came back up again, feeling the curve from my hip to stomach, then lingered on my hip before pulling me in tight to his own body. I put my book down. His lips brushed against mine as if they were gliding along a rose petal.

The room was quiet except for the singing hum of the air conditioner. It was as if the whole town had gone to sleep. Even our breath was quiet like a whisper. Yet I felt loudly awake to his touch. My heart pounded in my chest, beating like a hammer in the quiet room. Mike rolled away slightly, enough to create a gap and make me want more.

"I love you," I whispered in his ear.

"I love you too," he said, while he pulled me in tight. We took a moment, feeling the raw emotion of connection. My body, now eager, grasped at Mike in desperation. We let go.

Later, I marvelled at our rediscovered passion for one another. *Finally*, I thought, no one else mattered. No one. It was Mike and me. I smiled, certain it would *always* be Mike and me.

CHAPTER 17

KOH TAO
Taking a Dive

"Mangos!" I yelled. I collected five and brought them to our tent where Mike was sleeping. We were camped in Sri Phang Nga National Park on a grass patch surrounded by lush jungle. During the night, I woke up several times from a thumping sound. The noise turned out to be falling mangos. I pulled out my knife to cut up our sweet breakfast and began dismantling the tent around Mike.

"Are you sure it's morning?" He moaned.

"Yes, I'm sure." I smiled at him through the mesh screen. "We should get going. It looks like it'll be hot again."

I pulled the last stake out of the ground. Mike didn't shift. His body lay beneath the orange sarong and his chest rose with each breath. I couldn't dismantle any more of the tent until he was out, so I laid my mat on the grass. I took a deep breath and looked around. The sky was bright blue, the grass wet from the rain. Some days I was more successful in waking Mike up.

The two of us were different in so many ways. *That's okay,* I reminded myself. *I'll make him coffee in the mornings, and he'll remember to buy batteries for our headlamps and maintain my bike.*

I was coming to love our ebb and flow. It was subtle, delicate. Spending so much time together, we learned each other's rhythms in a new way. But more: we were learning to love what the other brought to share. I, for one, was learning how to enjoy the moment; how to stop moving so fast and to listen. Everything was amplified when I listened.

The birds were singing.

We were in no rush. Mornings came and he woke slowly.

I was always out first to start the water boiling.

"Coffee is ready," I told him, in another effort to wake him.

"Coffee's always ready when you're around," Mike replied, and pushed himself up onto one elbow.

Mike stayed in the tent to pack up sleeping bags and roll up his mat. He tossed them outside and I put everything in its correct pannier. When Mike finally emerged, he flipped the tent upside down to dry the bottom and joined me on my mat. Breakfast was our usual peanut butter and banana sandwich on squished bread. I tilted my head and he leaned in for a kiss.

We were interrupted by a young Thai couple, the only others who had spent the night in the national park. They smiled as they slowed their scooter in front of us. Last night they had taken Mike on the back of their scooter to the main road to buy dinner. The three of them had bumped along the gravel road without helmets. I had stayed with the cicadas that hummed like electrical lines. It wasn't long before I missed Mike. I ached to hear the drone of the returning scooter. I had felt so alone without him.

"Sà-wàd-dee" (may goodness be with you), they said.

I cupped my hands together, touching my thumbs to my chest and bowing my chin to my fingers.

"Sà-wàd-dee," Mike and I both called out, and then waved as they drove away.

The wasps arrived – drawn to the sweet smell of the mangos. All but one had worms inside anyway. I grabbed them and threw them back into the jungle. Mike is allergic to wasps.

We cycled 15 kilometres before our first break and stopped again at 30. It was not going to be a record-breaking day. From Phuket, we had been travelling up the west coast of Thailand. The sun burned as if we had personally offended it. Our tires melted into the road, and I ached for the afternoon rain to come. Large, lazy water buffalo wallowed in a muddy pool, making me jealous of their cool mud bath.

A storm finally hit in the afternoon. The clouds shot us with needles of rain. The cold water felt rejuvenating, even though the drops stung. The jungle changed to farmland, with patches of rubber plantations, coconut palms, pineapple fields and fish farms. The sharp smell of fish fought with the sweet smell of bright wildflowers.

We found a small roadside stall, seemingly in the middle of nowhere and busy with locals. There was so much chatter going on, it was like a Starbucks, except open to the dust and surrounded by bamboo and tarpaulin. A teenage girl pointed to the menu nailed onto a bamboo post, while some men made room for us at their table. The menu was entirely in Thai script. I looked at it, giggled, then shrugged my shoulders and put my hands up in the air to demonstrate I had no clue what it said. Everyone laughed.

"*Ow an nan na*" (I'll have that), I pointed to a neighbour's bowl of curried chicken with rice. One out of ten times my lousy Thai was understood, but my hand gestures were deciphered more easily.

"*Non pet*" (not spicy), Mike insisted, which meant we only received three hot chilies instead of 18. It was still too spicy.

I wiped tears from my eyes and used an entire roll of toilet paper blowing my nose. The men at our table laughed. I told the man across from me that he was big and strong, as he added more chilies to his bowl. I grabbed at my tongue and waved it around in the air, panting to show him how numb it was.

The men enjoyed teasing us. One man stood from the table and walked over to a large container of water and scooped me out a cup. I drank it greedily. No one was in a hurry to leave. The rain fell thick and fat, bouncing off the sand beside the tarp and creating a symphony of sound between the plastic, wood, ground and pavement. I smiled. I love the beat of nature's music.

We bid goodbye to the ocean and pedalled up and down hills. The hills were full like the belly and bosom of a woman blessed with a child. Myanmar now cradled our side, spooned in an entanglement of greenery and delicate ferns swelling with morning dew.

I had come down with a cold during Songkran five days earlier. My throat was sore, but I was happy. I convinced myself that my body was performing the finishing touches of its cleanse and that I was nearly pure. I sat in silence on my bike behind Mike. I smiled and waved to everyone while Mike yelled, "Hello!" In every village, children and parents ran to wave and welcome us as we rode past.

We dropped our bikes on the side of the road and walked into a market, so full of colours, it seemed to vibrate. Large circular baskets bore fruits and vegetables. Blue plastic twine mixed with red and orange rope was wound throughout the baskets, which overflowed with bright red, orange and green peppers. Ginger root lay stoically next to brilliant yellow bananas. The smell of garlic and spice filled the air beneath the tarps, and my stomach began to dance, making space for our next Thai feast.

"*Chemchy king chen few pheaw*" (my compliments to the chef), I said, beaming at the man and woman who cooked our meal. He looked at me and then at his partner with bewilderment.

"*Chmchy khng chạn kuu pluaa*," I tried again. A woman called over another woman from the other side of the market.

"What are you trying to say?" she asked.

"You speak English!" I enthused. "I said my compliments to the chef," and showed her the sentence in our Thai dictionary.

"*Chmchey ǩhxng čhạn pheǔx phìxkhrạw*," she called out to our chef for us. That was what I'd said! I was sure I sounded just the same. Everyone laughed. Thai is a tonal language and every syllable is said with a certain tone – low, mid, high. I rarely got the tones right.

The woman who spoke English sat with us for the rest of our break and we practised how to count.

"*Nèung, sŏng, săam, sèe, hâh …,*" Mike and I had already memorized all of the numbers. Each day, we memorized ten new words by writing them on pieces of paper that we slid into the map cases attached to our front handlebar bags. Our mouths would form loops around the musical sounds of the Thai language as we pedalled.

Our impromptu language teacher sat down and helped us be understood. We choked out attempts, struggling to copy the rising and falling of her tones as she sang out the numbers. Soon, there were a dozen people in the market helping us count to 20 over and over again. Our interpreter slid closer to me and rubbed my arm back and forth.

We left the market with 15 donuts and a bag of apples that were given to us. We were really excited for the apples because it had been a long time since we'd seen any.

A few hours later, we took another break, avoiding that afternoon's monsoon. I noticed my shorts were feeling tight. By no means was I large. I mean, I have good Dutch genes, so I've never been petite, but the beach holidays and treats everyday had caught up to me. I slipped my fingers into the waist of my spandex shorts, ripping apart tiny fragments of elastic so I could breathe better.

"Perhaps I shouldn't eat so many ice creams," I said to Mike.

"Why?" Mike asked. I could have guessed he'd say something like that. Mike couldn't care less what I looked like. I could lose a ton of weight and I'm not sure he would notice. "As long as you're healthy," he said. Easy for him to say. For all the weight I gained, he lost. He was now looking lean and muscled. I ripped the band on my shorts a little more and reached for a donut. Mike laughed as he bit into his apple. He held out the sticker for me to read: Product of the USA.

"That's funny." I laughed too. The apple had travelled a long way and so had we. We left the Myanmar border and biked toward the east coast. For days time floated by like the tiny seed strands drifting from spring trees. It hung in the air with no rush to get anywhere, almost as if we could catch time in the palm of our hands, blow softly and watch it go on its way. Despite my tight clothes, it was one of the most peaceful, serene times I could remember us sharing.

On the east coast, in a town called Chumphon, we followed a young girl on a scooter. She worked at the guest house we spent the night in and offered to lead us to the pier where Mike and I wanted to catch a boat to the island of Koh Tao. It was certainly nice not having to negotiate with the map. The Thai people we met had been unquestionably authentic in their desire to help, either telling us how to get somewhere, or calling friends to aid us. They let us know how to find a place to sleep, where to set up our tent and where to put our bikes in order to keep them out of the afternoon rain. This was often help we didn't ask for, but the people we met took great care in making sure we were well.

The sun was cresting the horizon. The alleys were quiet except for crowing roosters and yelping dogs. When we reached the pier, backpacker reality set in. A busload of tourists had just arrived with big backpacks, guitars, snorkels and smiles. It had been a week since Mike and I chatted with another Westerner.

I watched Mike scrutinize the backpacks. "I was here ten years ago," he realized. Mike had been to Thailand with one of his best friends to island hop and celebrate at the full moon party. "Those were some great parties!" he laughed. "I loved staying in the tourist scene then. Plus, it would've been all I was ready for. There's no way I could've handled some of the situations we find ourselves in now."

His blue eyes looked over his bike and then to me. "Travelling by bike had never even crossed my mind, but now I love it and I see the benefits everyday. Did you read what our travel book said about where we've been this past week?"

I laughed, "Yes, 'Not really worth going unless you need a visa renewal.'"

"That's what's crazy about this travelling business. If I'd been on a bus, I would have slept! Maybe I'd be dreaming about the next destination, but when I'm on the bike I feel so awake the entire time! It's hard to miss anything – a waterfall, for example, because I'll see it for ten minutes. Plus, we've met so many wonderful people."

Listening to Mike talk about how much he loved travelling made me go weak. I gazed at him for so long that he began to blush.

I knew I was living *my* dream, but it was even better sharing it with him. Mike reached out and cupped his palm around the back of my neck. Then, as if it were getting too steamy, he grabbed his water bottle.

"I'm so happy we biked," he continued.

"One person's paradise is another's version of hell," I laughed. "Can you imagine me at a full moon party?"

Mike choked on his water, trying to stifle his laughter, "Not your best attribute." My partying skills are dismal. Nothing frightens me more than the thought of an all-night party or not knowing when or how I'll get home or when I'll get to sleep – funny since I have no problem staying up in the bush all night. Admittedly, though, I looked forward to a break from our usual adventure and the easy living that a bona fide tourist outfit brought – especially the availability of pizza and fries on the island.

We bought tickets and boarded the boat, this time sitting beside our bikes. We chatted with other travellers for the entire three hours while we watched the hills of the mainland melt away.

Koh Tao came into view. It was affectionately called "Turtle Island" for its shape: a large body emerging from the sea, a head and one flipper all covered in thick green palm trees and golden sand. Our high school friend Lorna had invited us to Koh Tao. She found us as soon as we came off the boat and grabbed me by the hand, introducing us to her boyfriend Elliot.

"He's a dive instructor," she told us. Her eyes gleamed.

"Aren't you the perfect match," I said. Lorna was an underwater photographer. They looked lovely together.

That evening, another friend, Billy, whom we had known since early school days, joined us on the island. Billy had toured abroad for eight years with Cirque du Soleil as a stage carpenter. He was due for a holiday and when he found out we were in Asia he decided to meet us on Koh Tao.

Billy looked the same as he did in high school. He had a slight build, short brown hair and intense eyes that conveyed his intelligence. Billy, similar to the Thais, laughs with his entire body. His laugh was easy-going and contagious, and Mike and I thrived in his company. Billy had planned to spend only a few days with us, but, as it would turn out, we would spend the next two weeks together.

We caught up on years past while hiking in the jungle and over coffee in the early mornings at an open-air, beachside cafe. One morning, the confident male waiter asked Billy if he would like milk in his coffee. Billy signalled he didn't understand, so the waiter grabbed his chest and pretended to milk it. This put us in hysterics. It was the best sign language we had seen yet.

"Want to go diving now?" Elliot asked. Elliot had taken it upon himself to refresh our dive knowledge in the pool. Mike and I both had our PADI dive certificates. He loved it, but I had done my course purely to try something Mike was passionate about and to push myself to accomplish something I didn't really want to do. The fact was I was afraid of diving.

While in Koh Phi Phi, I saw a T-shirt that read:

> What – You Don't Dive?
> And you call yourself a TRAVELLER!
> 70% of the World is covered in water,
> Have fun with your 30%!

Maybe that helped to sway my opinion. Either way, an hour later, I found myself leaning over the side of a boat. I spat in my facemask, smeared it around and then washed it in the ocean. The boat bobbed over a wave and a light spray wet my torso. The smell of salt stung my nose.

My hands shook as I tightened the mask around my head and wet the mouthpiece. I went over the instructions Mike had taught me. Then I pulled the mouthpiece out.

"You'll stay beside me, right?" I clarified.

"Always," he smiled. "Trust me. You'll love it."

I wasn't so sure. The equipment scared me. Give me climbing, mountain crevasses, or double black diamond skiing any day. Having to put my entire trust into a breathing apparatus that could explode, implode or leak was not my idea of fun.

"Ready?" Mike asked. I nodded yes and rolled backwards off the boat, careful to not catch my flippers on the railing. It was easy to float. I put my face upwards to the sun. *Now, this is nice. Why would I want to leave the sun?*

Mike came up beside me and pointed down.

Down we went. We slowly dropped through the ocean that sparkled like diamonds with the sun's rays. My eyes darted back and forth, making sure Mike was right there. He was. He pointed to a manta ray.

My heart beat faster. Never mind that water covered 70 per cent of the world, it was another world unto its own, one that breathed delicately and pulsed with its own heartbeat. I waited for anxiety to rear its head, but instead my breathing slowed. I followed Mike as he pointed out sea urchins as thick as my leg, then blowfish and blue-spotted stingrays. The colours were more brilliant than midsummer's alpine flowers, all found in water so clear it seemed invisible except for the bubbles created by our exhales.

Mike's flippers calmed, and he turned back toward me and grasped my hand. I gripped onto him as he guided me through a tunnel of rock. The sun seared through the water, again turning it into the perfect aqua blue.

We communicated easily. Mike directed me where to look, but my eyes were stuck on him. Effortlessly, my body glided beside his.

CHAPTER 18

BANGKOK
Tuk-Tuks and Tricksters

Weeks later, in Bangkok, the mist at dawn steamed like my morning dumplings. I sat with my journal and breakfast at a tiny coffee shop while Billy and
Mike still slept. A woman swept the floor around me – the light reflected
along her cheekbones, bronzed from the hard sun.

"You. Today, happy?" she asked me.

"Yes, I'm happy," I told her. She and I had developed a friendship. I'd been
visiting her for a week since discovering she made the best coffee. Hours had
gone by seated on her hard chairs with my journal on her worn metal table.
The first time I came in, I found a Southeast Asia Lonely Planet book on the
shelf in the corner. I tried to buy it, but the woman and her husband gave it
to me for free. The next time, she undercharged me and wouldn't take more
when I let her know. Since then, she'd brought me a free tea with the coffee
I always ordered and given me free cookies, homemade muffins and a green
gooey rice concoction I would rather not have eaten. The entirety of their
home was on display through the back of the stall: a small television with
large antennas sticking out like palm trees in a desert, blankets spread out on
the floor for their bed and a Buddhist shrine sitting in the corner.

Mike, Billy and I stayed down the street at the Tavee Guesthouse, which
was walking distance to the tourist district of Khao San Road. Khao San did
not sleep, therefore neither did Mike and Billy. Mike snuck into the room in
the early hours of the morning just before I snuck out. I reached for my journal and tried to catch up on all we'd experienced and seen.

Bangkok has over six million people jostling in harmony for their place.
We had explored the intricate city by taxi, bike, tuk-tuk and boat. The Chao
Phraya River is an integral part of life in Bangkok. Monks in varying colours

of orange and red lined the rails of the riverboats, sometimes standing so still I couldn't imagine anything more peaceful, other times talking on cellphones. We had joined Buddhists and monks by purchasing bags of bread pieces to toss into the water, creating turmoil among the catfish. It was one way for a Buddhist to have good karma in this life and the next. For us, it was fun.

For days we moved around, visiting markets and temples. The elaborate temples were beautiful, gold-plated and rimmed with characters and Buddhas of every size. We had walked slowly through open markets. Slowly, because it was hard to move fast and see the daily life of the city. Young girls in tank tops washed hundreds of quail eggs and thousands of chicken eggs. Then cracked yokes into well-worn tin bowls. Men fried cockroaches, beetles, worms and maggots to a crispy crunch. Massive washing bins held live snakes, catfish and frogs, waiting to be bought then placed back into the river for good luck.

From the fish market, we had gone to Pak Khlong Talat – the flower market. At first, the colours overwhelmed my eyes like sunshine after days of rain. Then the sweet smell took over. It was a refreshing smell one wouldn't think possible in the otherwise smoggy metropolis. Thousands of roses, daffodils, lilies, jasmine, orchids, forget-me-nots and birds of paradise were displayed in open buckets or loosely wrapped in newspaper. Pickup trucks overflowing with fresh-cut daisies navigated through the tight lanes. Our bodies were thrust into vendors as they passed.

I bought two large bags of the national flower, *ratchaphruek*, known as the golden flower. One bunch was for the woman who ran our guest house. She was often grumpy (which seemed rare in Thailand). When I gave them to her, she said, "*Kob khun ka*" (thank you), smiled and sprayed herself with water. I took it as a sign she was pleased with the gift. The other bag was for Megan, a Warmshowers host.

Megan was hosting Scott and Becky, the super-organized couple we'd met in Malaysia. I plied them with questions about visa requirements for Laos and China. Zach and Elise, the cyclists we had met at the airport in New Zealand, were also in Bangkok, and we all met at Megan's house for dinner and to tell stories of our adventures. Since first meeting, we had followed each other's websites, shared emails and developed a bond that felt like we'd been friends for years. In the days that followed, we ate our way through the city with Zach and Elise.

I glanced up from my journal to take a sip of my coffee and noticed two young men in their late teens standing over a ceramic bowl of water, taking turns with a bar of soap. They scrubbed their muscular bodies and long black hair, sending streams of water to pool in the broken pavement at their feet. An elderly woman walked by, dipped her hands in the same water and washed her face and then the back of her neck, before moving on. The boys wrapped towels around themselves and slipped off their wet shorts from beneath. A man then walked out from an adjacent market and pretended to snatch one of the towels away. I giggled.

The ceramic bowl sat precariously on top of a pile of baskets, a bag of cans and a massive mound of garbage. The rubbish was bagged, but dogs had torn into it – its contents fell to the ground. The boys lived beneath a green tarp right beside it. Laughter erupted once jeans were pulled on, and they ducked beneath the tarp to grab something else before leaving. I watched them walk away, laughing and jabbing each other in the ribs. It was hard to have a miserable day when there were constant reminders of people who have very few possessions yet seemed to have an abundance of joy in their lives.

My favourite example of making the best out of life could be seen down the street, where faded red, yellow and blue scarves were knotted around a massive tree trunk. It was a very large specimen. One branch reached all the way across the road as if protecting everything beneath.

Scarves often encircle this type of tree, named *Ficus religiosa* in Latin but known as the Bodhi tree or sacred fig. Buddhist legend claims that, while meditating beneath a Bodhi tree, Lord Gautama Buddha attained enlightenment. The colourful scarves display love and peace and mark trees with a spirit. Buddhists wrap the trees to please the spirits living within them, and this keeps the former souls happy so they will not wreak havoc in the land of the living. I learned that Buddhism and relationships are like the tree. They need to be constantly nourished in order to grow.

This particular tree also housed a thriving mechanic shop. The tree trunk spanned two metres wide and metal bins of tools were scattered at its base. Sizeable engines lined the shop's perimeter. Hoses, pipes, gas canisters, wires and tires were stashed high into the crux of the tree. Every day, the mechanic opened the shop and proceeded to pull apart scooters, tuk-tuks and taxis. At night, when he closed up shop, his tools and engines either hung from the tree's limbs or were gathered close to the base of the tree trunk. He then covered it all with a dirty sheet of clear plastic, the worn Buddhist scarves underneath still visible. In the morning, no matter how early I arrived, he was awake and at work. *How many places in the world could someone run a successful business out of a tree?* I wondered.

My thoughts were interrupted by a new customer in the coffee shop.

"Where's your husband?" the man asked me.

"He's with his friend."

"Why is he not with you? He should be with you."

"Trust me, we spend a lot of time together."

"How long you together?"

"12 years."

"How many children do you have?"

"No children," I said. He pondered this for a moment before changing the topic.

"Thailand is relaxing, peaceful and fun. We don't have real jobs. If you don't make your own fun, who is going to make it for you?"

"I totally agree," I said, but then noticed my new friend was playing with his crotch an awful lot, which was not the sort of fun I was interested in.

"You go to Pat Pong?" he asked.

"Yes, we did, actually." My answer really had this man squirming in his seat. A few nights earlier, we had found ourselves in Pat Pong market, which is the "red light district" of Bangkok. The streets were packed with tattoo shops and piercers. Vendors and stores overflowed with pirated goods, knock-offs of glasses, watches, DVDs, Levi jeans and Gucci and Prada bags.

"Pop." Men stalked the streets whispering "Ping-Pong show" and making popping noises with their mouths. "Pop." Another man followed right behind us, whispering for a long time before we conceded to curiosity. The man brought us to a stairway leading down to a bar for a "cultural show." He told us we would each have to buy a drink and we agreed on a price of 300 baht ($9). Darkness devoured our boldness and I held Mike's hand as we were led inside. A stage with purple lights encircled the edge and amplified the gloom. As my eyes became accustomed to the dark, I noticed the place was nearly empty. For the next 30 minutes, the women on stage seemed bored. Talent, on the other hand, was spot on. One woman blew out candles with her vagina. Another wrote with a pen on paper. Still another used it to smoke cigars.

It was clear the women were not happy, and I shied away from watching. Many were refugees from Myanmar or had come from labour jobs in factories. *For what*? Their better life was spent performing all night, every night. They didn't seem proud to be doing what they were doing.

I sank lower in my seat and Mike, Billy and I looked at each other more often than we looked at the stage. What had started as a joke for us was obviously someone else's reality. We were uncomfortable and made to leave.

Five intimidating people instantly surrounded us.

"You owe another 3,000 baht" ($90), the largest of them demanded. Pressure at the table mounted. The three of us were in a booth and they blocked the edges so we couldn't get out. Mike lifted his chest and shifted his body to block me. They pounded on the table, while vajayjay cigar smoke circled over their heads.

"I'm sorry for the misunderstanding," I said. "We'll leave now and you can have my drink back."

They didn't want my drink back. I'd probably just insulted them all further, but I was desperate to get out of there. An argument ensued, as we didn't have that much money. Mike left 200 baht on the table and Billy left a few hundred as well. Mike and Billy pushed their way from the table to get out. They wouldn't let us leave the way we came in, so we spilled out into an unlit alley. Mike put his arm around me and held it there for a long time. I remained stressed and on edge long after we made it back to the neon-lit main street.

"Did you see Ping-Pong balls?" The man leaned over my table to ask the question.

"No."

"Ya, they lie about that now. The ladies used to do it all of the time, but now it's all ribbons and bows." He looked sad.

I didn't tell him about the shooting darts.

My friend, the shop owner, cut in, bringing me another tea and pretending the table needed to be cleaned at once. "Say letters for me!" she asked, saving me. The man slinked away into the chaos of the streets. She and I had been practising each other's language. She loved it when I sang in English.

"A-B-C-D-E-F-G," I sang. She smiled wistfully.

Bangkok, I concluded, is the beauty and the slime together. Without one or the other, it wouldn't be the raw, honest place it is.

Eventually, Bangkok spat us out.

CHAPTER 19

CENTRAL THAILAND
Missing Home

"I don't want to bike tomorrow," Mike said.

"What do you mean?" I was ready to bike. Although I had found a love for Bangkok, I was eager to cycle away from the smog, the smells, the appealing and amiable parts of the city. It was time to move on.

"This city is crazy and it'll take us forever to get out of it," he said.

"What do you want to do?" I asked.

"Take the train to Ayutthaya."

I looked up at Mike stuffing his clothes into his pannier. "Oh come on, it'll be fine," I insisted. I wanted to bike. I wanted a workout. I wanted a challenge. But, also, I was concerned others would question our decision to bus or train instead of bike. *We're on a bike trip after all.* Our friends and family, other backpackers and cyclists following our adventure: *Won't they be disappointed*? It would be a long time before I realized no one else cared. I don't mean that in a negative way, but, really, no one stressed if we biked, trained, skipped or rode a camel to the next town. No one except me, that is.

I stomped into the bathroom attached to our room.

"Be careful packing the razor. It's a new one," Mike warned me at the same time as I, in my cantankerous mood, nicked myself by accident while I packed our washroom kit. I ran the cold water over the cut and bandaged my finger.

"Choose your battles" – my mom's voice entered my head and, after some stewing on my part, I relented, likely more grudgingly than she would have had in mind. On the way to the station, I raced off in front of Mike, pushing down on the pedals in annoyance that he didn't want to bike out of the city. *It wouldn't have been that bad*, I thought. We could have done it in a couple of hours. It irritated me that he didn't require the same amount of body movement I seemed to need. I ignored my mirror so I couldn't see Mike and released some frustration by riding fast. But Mike was now as fast as I was on the bike and I couldn't get away. I slowed down and led us through the chaos of Bangkok. We found space on the road among the concrete, shacks, people, buses, taxis and tuk-tuks. Miraculously, they flowed seamlessly around us like milk in a bowl of Cheerios.

At the train station, we came across a hairdressing school. Mike had trimmed my hair a few months earlier with the mini-scissors in our Swiss Army knife, but I was ready for another one.

I took a seat, thinking a trim would only take a couple of minutes. A young woman began to brush my hair. After over 100 strokes, she spritzed water on it, found my natural part at the top and continued to comb. I turned my head to look for Mike, found him and smiled. He was standing on the edge of all of the chairs. I realized this was going to be longer than I expected. My hairdresser laughed and waited until I sat up straight again. I was reminded of my mom. She was my hairdresser growing up, cutting it quickly in the family living room. My mom would calmly tell me to stop fidgeting and to sit up straight while I struggled to be immobile.

An audience began to gather. They gave me the thumbs-up. I gave them the thumbs-up back and after ten minutes I stopped squirming. I breathed deep like I would at the end of a yoga class, when the body is finally relaxed.

The out-of-place beauty school on the train platform managed to stretch out my haircut for half an hour. She took two inches off my long hair, but when I tried to pay the hairdresser waved my money away. I got up from the chair in a room of spectators, feeling like some kind of supermodel.

Mike stood near the edge of the crowd conversing with a monk. The monk's orange robe contrasted with the grey surroundings. When I arrived in front of them, he beckoned me to reach out my arm and carefully tied a bracelet around my wrist. As a novice monk, he hadn't yet gained enlightenment and wasn't allowed to touch women.

The cotton-thread bracelet symbolized a sustained circle. We were now blessed for luck in our travels, our adventure and in our old age. We thanked him and he stayed with us until we boarded the train.

We stored our bikes in the freight car, located at the very end of the train. The panniers were still attached. "Trust the system," Mike said, as we walked virtually empty-handed several cars ahead to our third-class seats in the train. He sat by the window and I sat beside him and the train began to sputter and chug along the track, rocking me back and forth like a baby. It took time, but we left the city and the cerulean blue sky reached out in front of us, seemingly endless. I rested my head on Mike's shoulder, while feeling a wrinkle of ache for my mom.

Hours later we arrived in Ayutthaya, 85 kilometres north of Bangkok. Three rivers surround Ayutthaya: the Pa Sak, the Lopburi and the Chao Phraya. Chao Phraya, the largest, empties into the Gulf of Thailand. Thanks to this river, Ayutthaya had once been a thriving international port, and one of the largest cities in the world. Now it's a UNESCO World Heritage Site, with many historical wats, temples and ruins dating back to the 14th century. We spent hours exploring until Mike had flat tire number 23.

"Are you sabotaging me for not biking out of Bangkok?" he joked. "There's a thorn in here. I haven't even seen a thorn bush in Thailand." I smiled innocently and went to buy him a Singha beer while he fixed the tube. I was no longer upset. I'd realized that giving up on the adventure of cycling out of Bangkok had allowed others in: my hairdresser, the monk and the train ride.

From Ayutthaya, we headed north. Our ride split the country in two by following back roads up the middle, escorted by the Chao Phraya River. Cows and water buffalo roamed free along the slopes, wading into the water. Men speared fish and cast nets. Their catches lay spread out on the side of the road, slippery mud oozing off snails and piles of small fish. Women did laundry and kids played.

For a few days, the ride was rice-paddy flat. The rice fields were as varied as their colours. Some were the brightest green on Earth, dotted with men and women working. Others were flooded with water and rows of women wading in them, planting rice seedlings in the mud. The women wore tall rain boots and big hats held in place by fabric wrapping around the sides of their faces. With each bend at their waist, gloved hands and shovels disappeared into the muddy water. Deep soaking swamp swallowed the smaller women up to their hips. They worked as hard as the buffalo, and sang strong and beautiful like a red-whiskered bulbul, their melody floating above the fields. If one of the workers spotted us, they would all look up to greet us. If we slowed down enough, the bravest would run to the road and offer us water from their canteen. The water felt like everything we needed to sustain us on what were hot days.

In other areas, men pushed hand plows to turn the soil. Entire bodies were covered from the sun, including thick balaclavas worn on their heads. They looked like they could make it through a Canadian winter.

I could only imagine how back-breaking the work was, and in the hot midday sun no less, but when we talked with them, they thought we were the tough ones. And crazy for riding our bikes across the country. Perhaps we were. It was hot. For an entire week we travelled in 40-degree-Celsius heat. Mike would not consider camping again until the temperature dropped.

During one stretch of road, a woman drove her scooter alongside us for 20 minutes. She motioned to my bare arms, asking why I didn't wear long sleeves. I motioned to her head, since she wasn't wearing a helmet. She laughed. I was asked daily about my skin and questioned as to why I wasn't covered head to toe. I was even told, in the politest of ways, that my skin was ugly because it was too dark. Many of the women wanted white skin, because being white was considered beautiful.

Mike, willing to try anything to cool himself, began to wear a Thai-fashioned, long-sleeved cotton shirt. He still dripped sweat like a leaky faucet. The new shirt clung to his body as if he had just left the shower.

If the crops were not bright green, wet or being turned by hand or with water buffalos, they burned. As we continued north, more and more land was covered in flames. For days, the air filled with smoke and covered everything in a grey haze. Temples and distant hills were shrouded in clouds.

By now, it was an established fact that we had a lack of organization. I had known it would be hot, but I had forgotten to tell Mike. What I hadn't realized was that many of the fields would be in flames this time of year.

"Maybe we shouldn't ride here," I said to Mike one morning when the smoke was thick and ashes covered the road.

"What makes you think that?" he asked with a hint of sarcasm. "The fact that it has been nearly 50 degrees every day, the humidity or the smoke?"

Sure enough, a few days later, I pulled out our travel book and read a warning to not bike from Central to Northern Thailand during the months of April and May. The book read: "It's too hot and the crops are burning."

"Oh well, what's the alternative? Not to bike?" I asked, without expecting an answer. That seemed less fun. We rode on.

The fires nipped at the road. The burning grass crackled and hissed against water in the ditches. Flames pierced the sky and ashes fell on us like large flakes of snow. Our throats were sore for days.

One afternoon, we heard music from a distance. As we came closer, we found a party in a field in front of a Buddhist temple. Just off to the edge, a man barbecued chicken on skewers and we stopped to buy some and listen to the festivities. Before we could pay for our skewers, two men came from the party, took us by our elbows and guided us to one of the 20 plastic tables.

A stage had been set up for karaoke, but the singers were far from amateurs.

Some even performed dance moves. We sat down to a feast of Thai dishes, drinks and ice. After days of clammy heat, ice felt like a miracle.

Loud music screeched from large speakers, which made conversation hard. After an hour, I realized three of the men were discussing which one of them was going to take us home. One man clasped his palms together and rested his head on the back of his hand. He then pointed at us, then at his chest and said, "home" and "no money, no money," and then gave a general wave in the direction behind us.

I was up for an adventure. Mike, too, considering he was on the dance floor. One man, who had been drinking, invited me to dance, but the man who initially brought us over motioned I shouldn't go. Mike went up to satisfy the others. I turned around to watch Mike. There he was, clacking in his bike shoes and bobbing in his bike shorts. Mike, if convinced to dance, has the same dance moves for every song in any language: his arms, bent at the elbow, float in front of his body and bob up and down in time with his knees. The men nodded approvingly, a few even trying out Mike's signature move. I sat at the table, laughing to myself that he looked like he was shaking out a big bag of potatoes. It was cute.

Mike and I grabbed our bikes. "Do you think they're gangsters?" I joked. I loved the interaction we had just had – and the fact that our hosts fought over us to have us as their guests.

"No, I don't think so. Plus, we have our new Buddhist bracelets on, so nothing will happen to us," Mike said. We followed the men into the forest, along a path to their village.

"You home, eat, sleep, no money," Kiet, our host said. Kiet introduced his wife Lawana. Lawana was tiny, with a powdered face and red lips. She took hold of my hand and led us to a table in their yard with two other men from the party.

They didn't have a kitchen in their house, only a kettle and dishes, so Lawana, who never sat, constantly ran out and came back with more bags of food. Kiet knocked down mangos for us from their trees, and all the men drank rum and water for the rest of the day. Mike poured himself a drink and they yelled the Thai version of "Whoa!" making fun of him with drunk motions. One man took the bottle from Mike to show him how it was poured. With a steady hand, he splashed rum in the tiniest amount and then filled the glass with ice and water. It was no wonder they could drink all day.

After many hours, Lawana invited us for a bike ride through the village. Mike and I, needing a break from trying to speak Thai, wobbled behind her without our panniers on. We were so used to the weight hanging off of the frame now that we overadjusted every turn and nearly ran into her when she stopped.

Lawana had the most graceful mount and dismount. Her pointy high heels gently touched the sand. Her face was white as snow and reflected in the river when we peered over the edge. She took us to a temple and a monastery where her eldest son lived as a monk. We only figured this out once back at the house, when she showed us family photo albums.

Kiet phoned a friend and handed me the phone. I held the receiver to my ear. "I am a friend of Kiet's. He wants to welcome you into his home. It is his pleasure and they do not want any money from you."

"Thank you," I replied. "Please tell Kiet his family is incredible and we're happy to be in his home. Please thank them."

"I will. Goodbye." I passed the phone back to Kiet.

Lawana, pausing long enough to hear the phone call, then thought we needed to do laundry. We tried to explain that everything was clean, as it had only been a few days since Bangkok. She grabbed onto Mike's new Thai garb and, obviously disgusted, insisted it could use a wash. She piled everything together and did our washing.

We slept upstairs in their teak house. The large room was clean and cooled with a fan. It was bare except for a small dresser and twin-size bed. In the middle of the night, I crept downstairs to use the washroom. I was on my way back upstairs when I noticed Kiet, Lawana and their teenage son sleeping on the floor. We had not realized we were given the one and only bedroom.

Lawana was up earlier than us and already back from the market when we came downstairs. She sat us down to a breakfast of chicken, runny eggs and small bags of rice. Unwrapping banana leaves revealed a ball of congealed rice with a bean and some unidentified filling. I liked it, but Mike didn't. Kiet pulled out their camera to take pictures of us before we left, and Lawana gave us a huge bag of food, including caramelized bananas. She knew how much I loved them from the night before because I kept smiling and saying, "*Ah, roi!*" (delicious).

Lawana, in her high heels, stood near me as we packed the food on the bike. She was like a beautiful angel; present and watching over everything, yet at the same time she was quiet and never right in the middle of anything.

I didn't want to leave. There was so much I wanted to talk to her about. I wanted to know her dreams, her passions, her inner being. I wished I had the language to tell her what she meant to me; that I found her resilient like the river behind her house and bountiful like the bag of mangos she was now stuffing into Mike's front pannier. She was a mother, not unlike my mother – strong as a mountain and yet as soft as the petal of a tiger lily. I imagined she waved goodbye long after we turned the bend in the road.

We cycled for a bit on a high from being taken in, nurtured and loved by others. But after being in Lawana's home, which was comfortable and familiar, Mike and I struggled to settle back into a rhythm. We missed our own mothers – now more than ever. Meeting Lawana spurred our first strong bout of homesickness. We agreed we needed to find a phone to call home.

Two days after leaving Lawana's house, we found a place to stay just outside the town of Banphot Phisai. We went into town to search for a phone or the internet. We spotted a place with opened garage doors and a computer set up inside. Thinking it was an internet cafe, we walked in and said we would like to use the computer. Only, we had walked into someone's house. Despite our blunder, the homeowners were hospitable.

"You eat with me. Come," said Noy, who we soon learned was a young father.

Next door to the house, Noy rolled up another set of large garage doors and we entered his karaoke bar. "Tomorrow you bike lots. Eat! Eat!" Noy directed. So we ate. Chicken fried rice and coconut sticky rice served with mango for dessert. When we were finished eating, Noy's family came into the bar and he started the karaoke. He was fantastic. Then he insisted I take a turn.

Seven years earlier, while in England, my friends and I had actually won money for our karaoke rendition of "Sweet Home Alabama." I grabbed the mic (I wasn't worried) and strutted on stage like a professional karaoke star. I sang "Home" by Michael Bublé – terribly. The words of the song stuck in my throat like a lump of dry crackers as I tried to sing about home. I sucked so bad I was booed off the stage, which was particularly embarrassing considering there were very few spectators. Mike came up to finish the song for me. Noy's son took over from Mike, saving us. Neither of us was invited up to the stage again.

A couple of evenings later, in a town we never did figure out the name of, a man named Praci invited us into his place to sit and eat. We thought it might be a restaurant, but it wasn't. Praci just sent his daughter to go and pick up food. He explained that he wanted to feed us because he often has trouble finding good food when he is in another country. "Thai people have big hearts," he said. "Here everyone eats. No one goes hungry." We could attest to that. We certainly weren't going hungry. It seemed everyone wanted to feed us.

The next morning, Mike and I were sitting on the side of the road sipping cold drinks. My handlebar bag was flipped open and pictures of my 1-year-old niece Isabelle and my 3-year-old nephew Anthony were taped to the inside flap. The woman who had sold us the drinks saw the pictures.

"Babies," she said, and clutched her hands to her chest.

"Ḥlān šāw" (niece), I replied.

She touched my shoulder and looked into my eyes. I smiled.

We proceeded to have a 30-minute conversation – hers completely in Thai and mine mostly in English. Without a clue as what the other was really saying, we seemed, nonetheless, to understand each other.

I told her how much we loved Thailand. I told her the people were amazing and our hearts were touched every day by the kindness of strangers. I smiled when I told her how happy we were but that we missed home right now and we hoped to phone our families soon. She told me (I think) about her day and that she works with her sister and how important her family is to her. She told me I was brave and a kind person. She wrapped me in her arms and we giggled like schoolgirls. I felt so comfortable with her. When it was time for us to leave, she gave us a bag of mangos with sugar and chilies to put on top.

Hugs, families and generosity made my homesickness worse. Minutes, hours and days passed by and, with the rotation of pedal strokes, thoughts of my family circled in my head. Mental and physical exhaustion sapped our bodies and minds.

We arrived in the town of Sukhothai Thani. We planned to stay for a few nights and we went to many places before we found TR Guesthouse, which advertised Wi-Fi.

"May I have the password?" I asked the young girl at the front desk. I had our laptop out and wanted to test that the internet worked before we paid for a room because I was desperate to talk to my family.

"Only guests," she replied.

"Yes, I will be a guest if it works, but I want to make sure. May I have the password please?"

"Only guests."

We went back and forth this way for far too long, mainly because I was exhausted and, hence, unhinged. She must have thought I was a complete dunce and finally wrote the password down on paper. It turned out the Wi-Fi password was "onlyguests" (all one word). I laughed. It worked great. We paid 250 baht ($8) for a room with a fan.

My parents, at long last, had gotten a Skype account. When my mom's face appeared on the screen, my heart clenched like something had reached down my throat and grabbed my heart and lungs, barely letting me breathe. Tears flowed down her cheeks and then I began to cry too, smiling the entire time. It was the first time we had seen each other in nine months. She was beautiful: a pillar of spirit and love. We couldn't even talk. Mike rubbed my back and then took my hand and began a conversation.

My dad came on the screen and I grinned at him. My dad emits courage and strength. Whenever I had come up with a hair-brained idea growing up, his reaction was always support: "Yeah, why wouldn't you do that?" "I could do that," was his typical response. I never felt doubt from him.

My niece and nephew then came along and crawled up into my mom's lap. They were shy and tucked beneath her arms. They had grown so much, I exclaimed. I was smitten.

We then called Mike's parents to hear their voices and to tell them how much we missed them. The next day, Mike and I lay beside each other on mats to receive full-body massages (this time we kept our clothes on).

"This is great. Why didn't you tell me?" Mike joked as he was being walked on. I had been pushing him to get a Thai massage for six weeks.

Back on the road, even after the phone calls, I was still emotionally and physically exhausted. With my homesickness came a longing for all sorts of things. My dreams were disturbed, filled with family, good friends and my old job. I thought of Alex and wondered how he was doing and who he was hanging out with. I missed potatoes. What I would have done for mashed potatoes or french fries.

I shifted in my seat. For two months I hadn't been comfortable, but now I could no longer get the pain out of my mind. I had searched for a new saddle in Bangkok and other towns but hadn't found one worth spending money on. I'd bought a gel cover, which helped a little, but my backside screamed in agony everyday. Mike said he would order me a new seat.

We took a break and I sat defeated at a stall, convinced my coffee and food order was wrong. Most of the time, I could handle the charades and my inability to speak Thai, but, after hours of blistering heat, my patience was nonexistent and ordering a coffee felt agonizing.

"It's 36 degrees in the shade," Mike said after checking our thermometer. "48 degrees in the sun. It's okay to be tired. We've done 50 kilometres already." That made me feel a tad better because I hadn't realized we had gone that far. The woman from the stall came over with our orders. She served me rice. (I had tried to order noodles.) Fortunately, the meal was delicious. She set down two coffees and filled our water bottles with ice.

"I can't believe you can drink hot coffee in this heat," said Mike. "You're ridiculous." I smiled. I had only ordered one coffee but luckily found myself with two because of my poor language skills.

We told the woman running the stall that we'd biked most of the way from Singapore.

"You, no! I don't believe...You big!" she said. I laughed out loud. I heard that a lot. I actually felt pretty good about myself, despite the fact I'd been steadily gaining weight. But, of course, even if I were at my tiniest, I was still bigger than almost all of the women we met and most of the men too.

Back on our bikes, into the heat, our yearning for home returned. It was Mother's Day. Water buffalo and cows wandered along the side of the road, adrift in the heat like us.

"Where you go?" a monk yelled at us. We slowed to respond and he waved over a pickup truck, instructed us to get in and told us the driver would take us to the ruins up ahead.

"Free. No money," he declared. I didn't want to argue with a monk. Mike sat in the truck bed with the bikes while I was up front in the air conditioning. The soft leather seats and the cool air were luxurious. I reclined back like a prima donna and made small talk with the driver, using all my Thai words. In what felt like warp speed, we were dropped off 15 kilometres later. However, during that short truck ride, I realized how much I preferred the bike. Sore butt or not, high temperature or not, smoke or not, missing home or not, I wanted to ride.

That afternoon, we entered the town of Si Satchanalai when a Westerner drove up beside us on his scooter.

"Hey! Are you looking to stay in town?"

"Yes, we are," Mike answered.

"My name's Curtis. Follow me," and he proceeded to direct us to a guest house. The owners would not consider renting us a room without air conditioning. This was a little ironic because, 30 minutes later, all the power in town went out for six hours.

Halfway through the power outage, we were sitting outside our room on white plastic chairs when Curtis and his family arrived with his truck. "No use going out for supper here since the power is out," he motioned for us to get in. We eagerly jumped in the truck. Curtis drove half a day's bike ride away to another town. He couldn't have known my cravings better. He brought us to an outdoor buffet. There was fish, chicken, beef and shrimp in pots cooked over coals. Even better, there was a massive salad bar, chicken wings and the long-awaited french fries. I was sure they had never seen two people eat so much.

The next morning, we departed Si Satchanalai full and content. We left behind the flatness of rice paddies and pedalled into the hills. It would be our first ride in Thailand where we could go over 40 kilometres without seeing a roadside stall. We were caught without enough water.

A blue car stopped and a man with a mop of white hair and an infectious twinkle in his eye stepped out. "Want a cup of tea?" he asked as we slowed down. "I live just up the road."

"We'd love to," Mike answered.

"Welcome, come on in," Dwayne said when we arrived. We walked into a kitchen. "This is my lovely wife, Pim." Pim was Thai, young and beautiful with soft curves. The kitchen was westernized with appliances and a large fridge that held pictures of the happy couple. We enjoyed tea and then lunch while I asked them about their relationship.

"We met on the internet," Dwayne told us as he squeezed Pim's hand. "Buddha brought us together. I used to be Catholic, but I've come to forgive all my sins. I'm no longer concerned they'll affect my afterlife." He paused and looked at Pim. "It was fate."

Dwayne looked at me and asked, "Do you believe in fate?" I smiled but didn't answer. If fate is having no control over the outcome, then Mike and I had changed our fate. The idea of fate, however, clashed against the Buddhist idea that every consequence had a cause. Mike and I had not spent enough time together, leading me to grow too close to someone else and bring on our near divorce, for instance. Fate, destiny, soulmates: I loved all of it, but I wasn't sure what I believed in.

We biked away from their home and I asked Mike, "What do you believe in? Fate, destiny or soulmates?"

"I believe in you," he said.

I smiled just like a Thai, right from the tips of my toes.

My homesickness began to recede. I was heartened by the warmth mere strangers had brought into our lives. My heart was full from being with Mike. Along with my belly, I realized my emotions were well fed.

The temperature dropped into the high 30s and I persuaded Mike to camp. Curling up in the tent, Mike read by headlamp, his light casting shadows along his grizzled beard. I broke off from gazing at him and spread out the maps. I traced routes, added up kilometres and thought about the next part of the journey. I looked forward to it – bouts of cravings, homesickness, all of it. We didn't have an end to our journey in mind. We figured when it felt right, we would go back to Canada. And we weren't ready yet. Our home for the moment was with each other – on this road to somewhere.

CHAPTER 20

CHIANG RAI
Never Enough Bananas

My fingers, wet with lavender oil, traced over the bumps on Mike's arm, connecting them like the villages on our map. A long line of red welts paraded from the base of his head, down his neck, across his broad shoulder, tramping over his elbow and falling off at his wrist. We sat on the ground beside a monastery.

"Try not to scratch them this time. They'll go away faster," I encouraged softly.

"I'll try. Unfortunately, I'm getting used to them." It was Mike's third time feeding bed bugs in Thailand. I didn't react to them. That, or because I wore more clothes to sleep, I was less susceptible to being bitten. I dabbed more drops of oil on the pads of my fingers. Mike swallowed a bite of banana while I smeared oil on his skin and massaged his arm. The calming scent of lavender mixed with the sweet smell of Asian bananas.

"Let's leave the rest of our bananas here," he said, and gestured with a nod of his head to the monastery. His helmet rested on top of his bike. His hair, though we had only travelled five kilometres since our guest house on the Wang River, stood up like a rooster comb where the air vents from his helmet let it escape. Mike looked hot. The sun, not yet high, gnawed on us with an insatiable appetite. Dogs hung out nearby, waiting for us to drop food.

We had been in Thailand for two months and the longer we stayed, the more we craved. In return, we fed the country our leftovers. Fed it with our skin. Fed it with our energy. It drank our blood and licked up our crumbs.

The day before, large dogs had chased us, their tongues flapping in the air between menacing barks. Mike reached over to my bike, ripped off some bananas from my rack and, with his legs still spinning, threw them at the dogs.

It was not our first dog chase, as they seemed to make a sport out of terrorizing slow bicycles. Even so, we still had too many bananas. Villagers generously gifted us bunches of them, and though we ate as many as we could, the bananas were heavy, especially now that we were in the hills. Two dozen bananas strapped to the back of my bike felt like I was attached to a bungee cord, forever being pulled backwards.

"Good idea." I stood up and walked to the front steps of the monastery and left our bananas at the entrance.

We climbed more hills, rolling gradients of green toward Chiang Rai. We were far north, close to the borders of Myanmar and Laos and near the periphery of the golden triangle, one of the most expansive opium-producing farmlands in the world. Smoke from burning fields filled the air. We swallowed juicy bites of humidity – wet like a peeled mangosteen – yet the smoke ground against our throats like sand, raw and abrasive, and our lungs starved for oxygen.

Our fear of facing another extremely hot day was abated when dark clouds began to pour in from the mountain range. The rain hit us on an uphill – not necessarily a bad thing while climbing. Our clothes clung to our bodies like bathing suits. We reached the top and eagerly began the downhill, our reward for the tough climb. The rain, the wind and the liberation of moving our hefty loads 50 kilometres an hour felt incredible. I rode in front of Mike and tucked even lower as I took the lead.

Then, *bang!* I was about 15 metres ahead of Mike when I heard the explosion.

"Kaaaaat, I'm stopping!" I heard Mike fade off behind me. I gently squeezed my brakes. Water splashed as I slid to a stop. I turned around and headed back up the hill.

"Are you okay?" I puffed.

"I'm all good, but my tire exploded. It was hard slowing down. We were flying!" Mike stripped his panniers off his bike and turned it upside down. "I'm glad you had just taken the lead. It would've been nasty if I took you out when I put my brakes on," Mike said. He stopped looking at his bike and pulled me in for a hug.

When he let go, he dug to the bottom of what we liked to call the "Bike Fix It" pannier. He looked up at me with a funny smile. Then, from depths of the pannier, he extracted, like a magician, the extra tire.

"Yay! We get to use the tire!" I laughed and jumped in the air, dancing in the rain. We had hauled the tire around for eight months, 7407 kilometres, often asking ourselves whether carrying the spare was unnecessary weight. Mike was efficient at swapping out the tube and tire, and we left a few minutes later.

We were about 90 kilometres from the city of Chiang Rai when I heard another explosion. This time the noise was close. I stopped and looked at my back wheel, flashing Mike my big smile. (The smile that many Thais pointed out: "You big cheeks. Same same as Thai.") Mike's flat tire count was up to 24, but this was only my third flat. I took the panniers off and flipped the bike over.

"Mike, have a look!" I yelled. A jagged gash in my tire looked like Teen Wolf had torn it apart. "Can you believe it?"

Mike shook his head in disbelief. Within an hour we each had blown a tire. We concluded it was their time to go. After all, we had bought the tires at the same time and rode more or less the same distance on them. The problem was this time we didn't have a spare.

I held up the back end of my bike and walked to a restaurant we had just passed. Those in the restaurant stood up, eager to help us, and waved for us to come underneath the roof to get out of the rain. We tried to explain that we needed a new tire, not just a new tube. One woman from the restaurant called her friend who spoke English. The friend rushed down on her scooter and translated for us. They decided it was best for us to catch a *songthaew* (bus) to Chiang Rai.

The women waved down the *songthaew* when it came near. It stopped and the driver flung himself onto the roof and tied our bikes up there. Mike and I and all of our bags sat inside, at the back. I looked at Mike and we just started laughing.

We settled into the vinyl seats and I pulled out my journal and wrote, "You do what you can and prepare for what makes sense. Though, sometimes, you just have to sit back and ride the adventure unravelling itself in front of you."

A tall man with short copper hair welcomed us outside the BEST Guesthouse in Chiang Rai. "My name is Chup," he said, and took a moment to shake both of our hands. "Come in, come in." His easy smile displayed glorious white teeth. I could tell Chup was a proud man, but his shoulders drooped forward just enough that any arrogance he might have had fell away. Rather than walking us to a guest room, he surprised me by leading us into his home, which was attached to the guest house. It was small, with one bedroom and bathroom. The living room was clean and well cared for.

"Sit, sit," he encouraged us, motioning to a couch with a coffee table in front of it. My leg rubbed against Mike's as we sank into the cushions.

"I want to show you this," he said eagerly, as if he wanted our praise, as if maybe he wasn't the proud, confident man that I'd first thought. He brought over a photograph from his bookshelf. It showed him standing with the queen of England.

"Wow! That's amazing!" I exclaimed. In the past few months, we had met dozens of people who rarely left their villages. They never complained about it; the opportunity to travel wasn't an option so it wasn't thought about. Yet Chup had been able to travel, and to meet the queen no less!

"It was in a wax museum," he laughed heartily and chuckled until his back shook. "Looks so real," he said while putting it back in its honoured place on the shelf. We laughed.

"Do you travel?" I asked.

"I did before, but not anymore. There's too much money leaving Thailand. I'll only travel my beautiful country to keep my money here."

"Karaoke?" he then asked. He didn't wait for an answer and was already turning his system on in the corner of the room. *Not again*, I thought. I looked at Mike and he smirked. The corners of his eyes lit up, but he didn't offer to sing. I reluctantly took the microphone from Chup and chose a song. This time, I sang a Dixie Chicks song. Chup didn't boo me, so I considered it a success.

"Okay, you want a room?" Chup asked, and turned swiftly, motioning us to follow him. And with that we had found our new temporary home. Chup took care of us for two weeks, beginning by lending me a bicycle and leading us to different bike shops. We bought two new bike tires to replace our bad ones. They were the best ones we could find in Chiang Rai, but they were narrower and thinner, closer to a road tire than a mountain bike tire. We hoped they would be strong enough. We also bought taller stems for our handlebars. I thought we looked like prairie gophers, sitting tall, taking in the sites. My right hand had been going numb and we hoped the change of position would help my hand, as well as my bum.

The padding in my seat was gone, pressed down as thin as a mango peel. For months, it had begged to retire, but I hadn't been able to find one I liked. That is, until I met my first Brooks saddle. Mike had bought one in New Zealand, and I'd watched over the distance how happy it made him. After seeing me suffer too long on my current seat, he'd ordered me a Brooks saddle online and arranged to have it delivered to Chiang Rai.

I opened the box while Chup watched. He saw the price that was printed on the package for customs, which made his eyes pop, and he moved closer to me. He knew I'd been looking forward to the package, and I knew he was perplexed as to why someone would possibly pay so much for a bike seat.

I pulled it out and ran my hands along the smooth black leather. Then I turned it over and admired the silver rivets strung along the sides like pearls. I pinched the firm rails that would attach to my seat post and my eyes sparkled. A Brooks saddle for a cycle tourist is equivalent to toting the latest, most expensive Prada bag. I couldn't help but love it.

Yet, brand new, a Brooks seat is more Tonka than Prada. I knew, for the first month at least, it would feel like I was sitting on a block. But, like anything worth holding onto, it needs work. I looked over in wonder at Mike. He was thrilled for me.

I turned the seat topside again. Chup still stood by my side and shook his head with confusion. My smile broadened. I knew the secrets of my Brook saddle and stuck my fingers into the special hole of the seat. It was a hidden pocket, the place where I would tuck away my *delicates*. This strip of missing leather is a miracle of women's seats. It alone deserved a designer award.

The next day, Chup invited me to go to aerobics. "Anyone is welcome to join," he encouraged. The three of us rode up to the main square in town, where about 70 people were gathered, dressed in 1980s Jane Fonda aerobics clothes. Mike parked himself in the corner to hang out while Chup walked with me onto the paved field. High-energy music began, screeching from speakers. A man bounded up to the centre platform, belting out instructions. He shook his butt and the women squealed in response. I laughed and tried to keep up. Sports involving any sort of coordination were never my forte. I swung my arms into Vs and Xs and spread my legs into As and Ts.

I went to aerobics daily with Chup and it provided much amusement for Mike, who liked to laugh from the sidelines. Even Chup made fun of me as I bounced around like an elephant attempting to be graceful.

Chup wore the tiniest white shorts. His long brown legs stuck out like trees in a field. *And I stand out?* I thought to myself as we assembled for another morning aerobics class. But I did stand out – I was the only white person there and many took notice. As the days went on, and I thought I might be getting better, Chup seemed increasingly embarrassed by my antics and practised his aerobics further away from me. When the hour was over, though, Chup would come back to my side and introduce me to the women, happy to know me once again.

On one of our earlier mornings, Chup led Mike and me to the other side of the Mae Kok River to a school called the New Life Centre. We parked our bikes beside some old steel bicycles and walked into the open area of the school. Three classrooms lined each side of a cement square and at the end was a covered area with long brown tables. Chup's presence attracted a couple of girls right away, and he introduced them to us as Nin and Pinchamen. Nin wore a red T-shirt that matched her blushing cheeks.

"She'll play for you now," Chup said. Nin unzipped her violin case, taking a moment to brush back her smooth hair from her shoulder and adjust the violin beneath her chin. The song she played was soothing. We sat at one of the tables and Chup spoke: "Sixty women live at the school, most are 16 years old or older and are starting Grade 1 lessons." He explained that the women were from northern tribes in Thailand. Their families, along with thousands of others, had fled from Burma (now Myanmar) in the 1980s and 1990s to escape violence. They now lived in temporary refuge/tribal camps near the border.

"Thailand," Chup paused and inhaled deeply. "Thailand does not recognize the growing population, and the girls are not given opportunity to legally work. The New Life Centre, through education and training, create a positive change in their lives and help to develop a better place in society." He smiled and peered out into the distance before looking directly at Mike and me.

"I teach violin here," Chup said proudly. Nin smiled and swelled with pride as the song flowed faster and her small wrist flicked back and forth. "If you want, you can come here again?"

We did. Mike and I went to the school often. We sat in on English classes, helping to sound out letters and practise basic phrases. Melanie, who was a missionary from the United States, and volunteering as the English teacher, said to us, "It's really good you're here." She piled up papers onto her desk and studied one.

"As you can see, most of the girls haven't attended school before, but they're grateful for it." Her smile disappeared as she told us some of the girls' horror stories of being raped, beaten and working in Bangkok's prostitution rings. For most of them, this was their only chance at an education – one they were happy for.

Between classes, we played cards. We taught the girls how to play go fish and war with decks of cards we had brought. Since many of the girls were from tribal communities or Myanmar, they were new to the Thai language and so we would all shout out the numbers in English or Thai. As I listened to them yell "Go fish!" my heart melted enough to flood the Mae Kok, spilling water over its banks to drench the rice fields.

Mike melted my heart too. He took on the project of fixing all of the bikes on the grounds, adjusting the gears, tightening brakes, pumping up tires. One afternoon, I watched him from the outside of a large circle of girls. He towered over their heads and I could see the joy in his eyes as he showed them how to patch a flat tire and how they could do basic maintenance on their bikes. He had them smiling and laughing as well.

One afternoon, I told the girls I was going to organize an exercise class. I expected maybe ten girls to come but was shocked when I parked my bike at the front of the school the next day to find 50 girls ready to exercise. *What am I going to do with 50 girls?* I asked myself. I stared at them for a minute while my cheeks turned red.

"Nin, can you play music?" I asked. Nin ran for a CD player and came back.

"We're going to do aerobics," I told them. *Okay Kat, you can do this, you've been doing aerobics for a week now, clearly you're an expert*, I coached myself. I turned up the music to fade out my insecurities and we jumped, jived and shook all about. *If only Chup could see me now*, I thought. I taught them Mike's shaking potatoes dance moves too. Fifty smiling faces swam in the overflow of my heart.

Every day, when we arrived and departed, groups of girls gave us "*sawadees*" (thanks). Placing their palms together to rest against their chests, bowing their heads slightly. The tips of their fingers touched the tips of their chins. It was a sincere and touching gesture.

One afternoon, when we biked back over the bridge into town, we came upon Chup, who looked upset. "Is something wrong, Chup?" I asked.

"The girls need more vitamins. Yes, they have some now, more than they could have wished for before." He stopped his bike and looked out over the river. "I've tried to get someone to sponsor one banana a day for the girls, but they said no."

Tears welled in his eyes. "It's so sad. They could each use a banana a day," he said. My heart hit against my chest, making me choke down more air. I couldn't tell Chup that, in previous weeks, we had been flinging our excess bananas all over the place.

Chup brought us down a small back road to the stoop of his church. "This is my church, come in and see." He unlocked the door and showed us the alter he had built. "Jesus is my God. When I prayed to Buddha – no answer, but when I pray to Jesus, I have answers. I want to become a pastor," he told us. "I'm writing a thesis. I'll show you later."

That evening, we went to his office attached to the guest house. "See, my thesis," he showed it to us on his computer. "I'm having troubles. Do you know how I can save it?" Mike stepped back, understanding right away that Chup had worked for months on his thesis and had not saved it at all. "I'm not really good at computers," he admitted. Mike taught Chup how to save it, as well as how to email himself a copy. (We found out a year later that Chup did finish his thesis and became a pastor. He now has his own congregation.)

Our Thailand visa was about to expire, so we decided to bike to the Myanmar border in order to leave Thailand and re-enter. Chup waved and waved goodbye, even though we were leaving only for the day.

Hills rose near the border like billowed sails from a sea of water. Signs for tribal villages also marked the way. Over 40,000 people live in these camps, and it had become a tourist attraction to visit the tribal villages/refugee camps. The most common tribes for tourism are the Akha for their beautiful dress, and the Paduang for their "giraffe women." Heavy brass coils are worn around the Paduang women's necks, making it look like their heads float in fragile beauty. The coils don't lengthen the neck, but the weight of the brass pushes down the collarbones and compresses the ribcage. More coils are added every year from as early as 5 years old, and the body is distorted. Historically, it was thought the coils protected girls from spirits or a tiger's bite. Not every girl or woman wore them, as it was usually decided who would wear them based on the day they were born. But, since the giraffe-like women attracted tourists (and their dollars), more girls were now distorting their bodies.

Mike and I originally decided we didn't want to support the tourism of these villages because of the exploitation of the tribal people. Many people believe the tourist treks to the villages (also called "human zoos") don't actually benefit the tribes, only the tour operators. Some people thought the hill tribe people were oppressed and not allowed to leave the villages. Rumour was if they did try to leave, they would have to pay the tour operators to do so.

The signs continued on our way back, and I noticed I was braking in front of one of them. I wanted to understand the situation more. But I was conflicted. Some people we had met had nothing good to say about the villages. Others praised them.

"Why don't we just go and see what it's all about?" I said to Mike. "Then we can decide for ourselves?"

"Lead the way," Mike replied. The ride took us down a narrow road up into the hills, past bony cows and lazy dogs. We turned onto a dirt track and mud stuck to our wheels. The sparkling green of the trees enticed us to continue on. We picked up stones from the ground in case one of the dogs decided to give chase. None did.

After half an hour the end of the track brought us to a large restaurant with teak floors, thatched roofing and an entrance gate to a village. Two Akha women with dark chiselled faces gave us a shy smile. They crouched on the floor dressed in fisherman pants with wide silver belts and bright-coloured necklaces swooped around their chests. They each held a naked baby. The little wiggling bodies were placed in a pink tub of water. (There were no diapers, so washing babies happened many times a day.) The babies' heads held brimmed hats with a hole in the top – essentially a circular visor. It was brilliant. Soap and water slipped over the hat brim and made its way through the floorboards, shielding the babies' eyes from soap.

Mike and I bought a bottle of water to cool down, and the woman who took the entry fee for the village was surprised that we didn't want to go visit the five hill tribes. "It's only 300 baht. It's good to visit," she encouraged. Two small girls played with a fruit nut on the floorboards beside her. They rubbed it back and forth and then touched it to their skin to see how hot it was.

"No, I don't think so. We wanted to come for a bike ride down this road and just see."

"These girls would love to take you." To emphasize her point, she told two girls and they stood up, ready by my side to lead me in. "How about only 200 baht and you can go and see all five tribes?"

"Kat, why don't you go? I'll stay here and rest," Mike said.

What to do? I was curious. It wasn't the discount of a few dollars in price but the fact that this woman seemed genuine. She held the girls as if they were her own and I could tell she really loved them. I nodded yes.

The girls were tiny, barely as tall as my belly button, and wore a school uniform of white blouses with blue skirts. Their hair was tied in tidy pigtails that swayed as they skipped down the path. I followed them down steps and through a wooden gate, known as the spirit gate, into a village. The ground was as clean as if it had been recently swept. Women scurried to put on their traditional hats and the girls led me by vendors selling crafts – woven purses, water bottle holders, hats, silver bracelets and rings.

The little girls then sat me on a bench in front of a wooden stage beneath a thatched roof. Twenty villagers ran to take their place inside. This was the Akha tribe, a decorated tribe with conical headdresses made from beads, wool pompoms and silver coins. Multiple beaded necklaces hung down their chests and heavily beaded sporrans were tied around their waists. The women wore handwoven dark skirts and jackets dyed from the indigo plant and brightly coloured leggings above bare dusty feet.

The performance began with a dance and song. Bamboo flutes, cymbals and a harp created a melody that their strong and crisp voices clung to. It was powerful yet delicate like a light breeze. I sat up straighter and tried to take it all in. The Akha people looked happy to be playing for me. They smiled with toothy grins stained from the betel nut.

One of the girls placed a large bamboo basket in the middle of the floor. The donation basket, I realized. I was wearing only my tights, tank top and helmet on top of my head, and I hadn't thought to bring any money with me. It wasn't as if I could sneak behind the rest of the crowd – I was the only one there. The performance continued and, with each minute, I felt more and more embarrassed that I had nothing to give.

The girls grabbed my hands when it was over and we walked through another field and into a village with bamboo homes. Chickens and pigs scuttled nearby. We walked a similar route, first through an artist village and then into the showground. This new tribe was gathering for another presentation. I sat and watched and tried not to feel self-conscious in my bike garb while they entertained their lone spectator. It became obvious there would be five shows, one for each tribe represented. I squirmed on the hard bench and didn't want to watch alone any longer. Once the show finished, and I wasn't able to place coins in the basket, I asked the sweet girls to take me back to the front gate.

"No, no." They tried to pull me in further and it took a few minutes to explain I wanted to go back. Once at the restaurant, the main woman didn't understand why the girls hadn't taken me to the long-neck village. They leave the Paduang tribe until last.

"They wanted to. I felt bad because I had no money to purchase crafts or put in the donation bucket," I said. Mike looked up from where he was playing on the floor with a younger girl.

"That would've been okay," she said. She was a wonderful woman. Older children had come back from school and were sitting at a table in the restaurant, giggling and doing homework. She called one of the girls over. The girl stood proudly beside her, and she reached for her school blouse and pulled it down to expose her long neck. "See, she's Paduang. She just takes off her rings to go to school." (Contrary to much belief, the women are able to take the coils off – though, from what I understand, it's quite a process.)

"The money from these villages help pay for school," she explained.

We got back on the bikes. I was quiet, contemplating the mixture of thoughts in my head. Eventually, I spoke, telling Mike, "Even though I felt awkward, I'm glad I went."

"Did it seem fake?" he asked.

"Yes and no. The grounds were swept clean and there weren't a dozen dogs running about like most villages we see. Yet laundry was hung out and the people seemed happy." I slowed down when the track widened so we could cycle beside each other.

"I appreciate that tourist villages may help to keep a tribe's culture, traditions and language alive to pass on to their children. But, at the same time, I think they're being exploited. The tribes don't have enough outside support, and the disgusting truth is they don't have the freedom of a fair choice."

"You're something else, Kat," Mike said. "It's tough when you can't fix things, and I know you wish you could."

Back at the girl's school, we had another conversation with Melanie. "Many people in the tribal villages and even our school are not able to leave the grounds because they're not given citizenship cards," she confirmed. "Most believe living in a tourist village is better than the alternative, which is sex tourism or deportation."

Melanie raised herself from the table and her long hair swooped to the front of her shoulders. "This school is working hard with the government to get the girls cards so they'll have a fair chance to be in the workforce. It's tough, but everything done here is helping. We have to keep helping." I smiled at Melanie. I gave her hug and let her know how I admired her effort, determination and selflessness.

I left Melanie's classroom for the last time and Mike stood by my side. We watched the girls huddle around a metal table in the courtyard, now playing cards on their own. The air was fresh and clear, even though my mind was muddled. I had fallen for Thailand and this darkness broke my heart. I understood, though, why Chup didn't want to leave, why he wanted to help others in his country.

We said goodbye to Chiang Rai by tossing shots of whisky down our throats with the husband and wife who did our laundry. We said goodbye to the bike shop and coffee shop workers. The woman who made Mike smoothies said she would miss him, and I realized how much the french fry lady was going to miss me when I told her I wouldn't be coming anymore. Soeey, the maid at our guest house, gave us the biggest hug the morning we left. My eyes welled up with tears, spilling over when I embraced Chup.

Our last day in Thailand was a quiet and reflective ride. We stared into fertile fields in silence as we rolled along. When we did speak, it was to reflect on Chup's generosity. We cycled slowly, as if we didn't really want to move. I joked that I wished we had dozens of bananas to slow us down.

"*Soo-ay*," I said in the late afternoon. The sun was washed out. The sky was light pink and orange, fading beyond the hills, beyond the Mekong River. We realized we could now speak hundreds of Thai words.

"*Soo-ay*," Mike confirmed.

Soo-ay means beautiful.

CHAPTER 21

LAOS

A Security Breach

Mike and I stepped into the Mekong River, each carrying four panniers above our heads. Garbage and foam pooled around our legs, and with each step my sandals were enveloped into the depths like quicksand. We tossed our possessions into a long canoe and pulled ourselves in. A boy half my size stood stable in the back and began to steer the boat toward the other side of the river.

All we had travelled with for nine months was piled between us: bikes, clothes, kitchen gear, heartache and love. I reached over the pile and clenched Mike's hand as I felt my stomach rock with the boat and my lips turn upwards. His eyes crinkled at the sides and I thought about what we had overcome this past year. How we started with a wounded marriage, with loss, but now our relationship felt revived. We peeked back toward the shore then turned our focus ahead. Goodbye, Thailand. Hello, Laos.

Across the water, a wooden shack greeted us – the border crossing – where we were stamped into the country and back to riding on the right side of the road. After months riding on the left, it was an awkward transition.

A dirt road led to the canoe docks where we had decided to book a two-day slow boat to the ancient town of Luang Prabang. The long-tail boat looked like a jumble of wooden puzzle pieces with nails holding it all together. The operator threw our bikes onto the roof to lie with a mound of backpacks and enormous bags of seeds. We took a seat on a bench inside and waited as more tourists embarked in droves. I thought we might start popping out the windows.

Tracy from England sat down beside us. I had watched her, a tiny woman with burnt-red white skin, walk toward the boat. It looked like she suffered under the weight of her pack, which must have weighed twice as much as she did. Her smile came easy and her face beamed when she said hello. Patrick from Australia joined us too. He was a large man, tanned, and his voice was deep and heavy. We hadn't heard much English for the past month, and I leaned back against Mike while accents from around the world swirled around me like cream in coffee.

The engine at the back of our boat powered up. It took a few sputters, but then we skimmed slowly south. The Mekong begins on the Tibetan Plateau. The water is thick with deep-brown silt, splitting the border of Laos and Thailand in the north, eventually flowing through Cambodia and Vietnam before pouring into the South China Sea. I wondered how many months we might follow it.

We floated all day. It was a different way for us to travel. I enjoyed sitting back, observing life on the river. Saggy-skinned water buffalo lazed on sand-bars. Men with sun-kissed bodies stood in bamboo boats, fishing with home-made nets. In front of small huts, naked women and children washed clothes, bathed and swam in the water. I stared upwards to give them privacy and noticed puffy pillows of clouds move as if they were a river themselves, flowing among the green mountaintops. The mountains were high, covered in a gelatinous carpet of jungle.

As the sun dipped into the tangle of trees, the long-tail boat pulled up to the village of Pakbeng for the night. Mike, Tracy and I walked down the mucky road and chose a room at the Sivongsack Guesthouse. The village was lit by a petrol generator, which powered down shortly after we arrived. When the lights went out, Mike stayed up to watch a movie on our laptop while I peacefully slept beside him.

"Mike, where's our laptop?" I nudged him awake the next morning when I couldn't find it.

"Right beside the bed," he mumbled and rolled over again to go back to sleep. It was early. He was used to me getting up when the birds began to chirp and the sun made its way up from the horizon. It was my favourite time to write and reflect.

"I can't find it. Are you sure you didn't put it in your pannier?"

"I'm sure." He rolled back toward me to have a look at the floor, then steadied his gaze behind me.

"Did you leave the room already?"

"No."

Mike pushed aside the bedspread to check again where he had placed the computer the night before. "I think we were robbed. The door was locked before I went to sleep and now it's open."

Please no, I thought. I scrambled to find our passports and found them. Only the laptop was gone.

Only the laptop.

I went down the hallway and knocked on Tracy's door. She pulled it open, smiling to see me until she saw the look on my face. "What happened?" she asked.

"Our room was broken into," I explained. "Can you watch the rest of our stuff while we go to the police station?"

Tracy gave me a hug and said of course.

The police station was down the mucky road in a one-room building. I sat on a hard wooden chair beside Mike and two officers sat across from us. A rifle was propped on the right side of a desk. The report they were about to fill out lay lonely in front of me, the only item on the worn, wooden desktop. I focused on each scratch, notch and bump in the wood.

One officer reclined back in his wooden chair, tipping the front legs up as though he were relaxing in a recliner. The other officer sat close, leaning forward to let his elbows rest on his knees, while he stared intently at Mike, who wrote out our police report. My heart had sunk all the way to the bottom of my seat, weighing me down.

Only the laptop. Except, the laptop was everything. I had written daily on it for nine months. It contained countless late nights in the tent, pecking away on the keyboard; thousands of photos, pictures of smiling children, storms, sunshine, blue oceans, mystical mountains, dusty deserts and us. I had let myself be honest. Emptied my soul on pages and pages of writing. I taught myself over the months how to make a website and use the photography pages. We had downloaded travel journals, took turns at night to read each other stories from around the world. We watched movies, we Skyped with our friends and family. *The writing.*

I sank further down.

"It would help our case if you gave us something to work with," one officer said, as he smoothed his moustache.

Mike looked up from his report. "We've given you all we know. I wrote it down. All I can speculate is that the family who runs the guest house let themselves into our room in the middle of the night and stole the laptop," he told them. "There were two locked doors, so they must have had a key. No one else would have seen we even had a laptop. I bet the owners who live behind our room saw the light from the screen through the window."

The officer flattened his moustache again. Then he took off his cap and quickly slicked down his hair. "Yes, but if you gave us more to work with," he said again.

"We don't know any more!" Mike threw his hands up in the air.

"Only the report will cost 20 dollars," the officer said. "Do you want us to do more?"

"We want you to find our laptop," Mike answered.

"Yes, but it would help our case if you gave us more to work with," the first officer told us. He leaned way back in his chair.

"Mike, they want a bribe," I whispered. Then I yelled, "We'll pay you! If you find our laptop before we get on our boat. We'll pay you lots and lots of money!" It was the first time I had spoken.

"I think it's best if you pay us now."

"No!" I spat back.

They walked with us back to the guest house. Mike and I shrugged our shoulders at Tracy to let her know how useless our trip to the police station had been. The owners asked if we'd still like to buy lunch. *Are you kidding me?* The cops spoke with the owners and they all laughed. I assumed the worst.

Patrick, Tracy, Mike and I made our way to the boat and found a place to sit on the floor of the back deck. We were right beside the boat engine and the noise was constant, rattling my body, jarring my brain. A joint was passed around the circle, which Mike and I declined. The smell of marijuana mingled with diesel, and news of our theft spread like high school gossip throughout the boat.

"You're lucky you didn't wake up," Patrick informed us. "Yeah, man, my brother was in South Africa and they robbed him of everything! Tied him up, gagged him and took his whole lot but the whities coverin' his ass. It took him a long time to find someone to help him. He couldn't even make a phone call, nothin'."

Patrick took a long drag on the joint and passed it on. "You could have been shot, stabbed, drugged. Who knows? Good thing you stayed sleeping." A shudder ran through my whole body and I tensed up. Mike reached out for me and stroked my leg.

A girl in dreadlocks and bright-red socks piped up, "Yeah, my friend was in South America and had his one eye jabbed with a screwdriver while he was looted. He's blind in that eye."

Horror stories flowed. But soon everyone mellowed from the joint and started playing Monopoly. I was light-headed from the narratives, smoke and fuel, so Mike, Tracy and I made our way to the front of the boat. Other travellers moved over to make room for us on the straw mats. The long-tail boat continued to plow its way through the water, while the captain inhaled cigarettes as if they were air, with one hand lazing casually on the steering wheel.

"Take a look," Tracy motioned to our right, into the jungle. A large tree stood out, towering over the rest. Its vast root system had grown sideways, with the roots as giant as log beams. There were enough of them to create a ceiling over the eroded soil beneath it. A woman carrying a woven basket made her way beneath the roots. Tattered laundry hung over its limbs and blew in the soft breeze.

My shoulders slumped in shame. *I'm spoiled. Being upset over a laptop, when that woman lives in a tree and owns less than we carry in our panniers?* I chastised myself internally: *Why am I so sad about losing a material item?*

"Oh, bollocks!" Tracy shook out the contents of her lunch bag onto the matt. "Damn, those owners! I paid for a lunch and they gave me someone's unfinished breakfast! Oh, this is piss-poor! Look at this," she pointed at the water bottle that came with her lunch. It wasn't sealed, obviously a used bottle refilled. "Those owners are shite." Tracy sucked in her upper lip and stuffed the old food back into the bag.

"We can share our food with you, Tracy. We have tons in our panniers. As long as you don't mind eating peanut butter, we could probably survive if this boat runs aground for a few days," Mike told her.

The driver kept the boat afloat as he avoided the maze of shiny smooth boulders and rapids to arrive in the town of Luang Prabang.

Mike slept beside me while I lay rigid, scrutinizing every noise and movement within the guest house. We had looked at numerous places. We checked locks on doors, felt out different owners and searched for a room not on the first floor, all in an attempt to find one I'd feel safe in. But here I was, lying awake all night, reliving the robbery in my mind. *What if we had awoken? What would we have done? Would they have had a knife or a gun? Would they have used it? Was he or she only a child?*

I had relied on my systems. After what I could add up as years of travel, I had trusted my intuition when something was amiss. Depending on the situation, I would act confident and give off a "don't mess with me" vibe, or I would run. Literally. Either that, or I would bike somewhere else. I moved. Whatever it was, I felt I could take care of myself and take care of us. But now? *What had I missed?* I had let someone knock down my security door and breach the system.

I stood again to go look out the window. A delicate moon filtered through the clouds and lit the monastery across the street. I looked down to search the wall. *Could someone come in here?* The dresser and bed in our room were pushed against the door so no one could open it from the outside. I lay back down.

"All that matters is we're safe, Kat." Mike pulled me in to try and lull me to sleep. Morning couldn't come soon enough.

"Let's go get my journals copied," I told Mike as soon as we woke up. I took hold of his hand and led him down the street. When the laptop had needed charging, or if it hadn't seemed appropriate to pull it out, I wrote by hand. I was now intensely protective of my journals since it had become our only written memory. We made two photocopies and mailed one to my parents' place from Luang Prabang. I planned to wait until the next city to send the other copy to a friend, since I didn't want to put all my faith in one post office.

Luang Prabang seemed like a peaceful town, but I was agitated and restless. We stayed for a few days while I attempted to find peace again. Each morning, I woke early and observed the procession of barefooted monks as they collected alms for their sustenance. They were up before sunrise and left their temples holding large brass pots cradled in the palms of their hands, silently asking for food donations from Buddhist devotees. The power of religion in the town was inspiring. Women and children who looked like they had barely enough food for themselves knelt on the dirty sidewalk to hold out plain bread or balls of sticky rice.

As the sun rose, it illuminated the monks, surrounding them with an aura of light. In soft-orange robes they flowed down the streets, moving with energy and purpose, yet gliding easily as if they were water in a leisurely stream. Even though there were always many people in the streets, the place was calm and welcoming.

On the morning of our last full day in Luang Prabang, I awoke to dozens of ants crawling over the bristles of my toothbrush. Bright red, they moved swiftly, wriggling all over each other. I sprayed the ants off with water from my water bottle and then put the toothbrush back on the counter. I went back to reading my book for a few minutes before brushing my teeth, trying to ignore the fact that it had just been a rest stop for dozens of ants. When that didn't work, I convinced myself that surely ants must be good for me in some way.

At the market, black flies swarmed in masses around meat, dead and alive. Live bamboo rats and deer mice hung out lethargically in the bottoms of baskets. Large cut-up chunks of lizard hung from poles. Or one could buy them alive. Metre-long lizards were on display, with their feet tied in neat little red bows to keep them from scurrying away. I moved away from their staring eyes and found small frogs strung together on a length of shoelace.

"Mike, it's a frog necklace!" I exclaimed. The vendor took this as a possible sale and began to pack up the living piece of jewelry for me. I dissuaded him from finishing and we scurried to the sheltered end of the market where we bought fruit shakes and roasted nuts. Tracy and Patrick already had a taxi waiting and we jumped in to spend the day swimming beneath waterfalls and leaping off cliffs in the nearby jungle.

In the late afternoon, I sat with Tracy on the curb outside of our guest house to watch the town drift by. It was her favourite time of day. The weather had cooled slightly and her pale skin was less affected by the sun (she had been burnt since we met her). All the kids came out to play. They kicked a ball and ran up and down the street, giggling at us as they passed. Though maybe they were only laughing at Tracy. She continuously punched at flies swirling around us like she was queen of air boxing, having an English word with them as they buzzed around her.

"Oh, you want to row, do you?" she said to the flies. She then put her arm around me. "Thank you for fixing my rucksack. You're a proper hero!"

"You're welcome." I had adjusted her harness and molded the metal stays to her back. Maybe now she would be more comfortable and not look so ridiculous carrying it.

"Let's go have anotha *crap*!" She suddenly jumped up, pulling me with her toward the end of the street. Tracy's pronunciation of the word "crepe" always put me into stiches. I didn't stop laughing until we made it to the shake-and-crepe lady. It felt good to laugh.

In the morning, Mike and I passed by the early monks with our bikes loaded and ready to move south. We stopped at the market for a last shake and met Patrick. Despite his continuous traveller horror stories about people with hooks coming through windows and screwdrivers driven into eyeballs, he gave the best hugs. He wrapped me up in his large body and held me for a long time.

"I'm not saying goodbye darlin' as we'll see each other again." His bright eyes twinkled down on me.

I looked forward to being on the move again. My bike had become a comfort like no other. On it, I felt in control, less vulnerable, less fragile. Safer. As long as Mike was with me, there wasn't anywhere else I would rather be.

"Zion" is a word that describes a place of peace, refuge or sanctuary, a place where humanity connects with God. I didn't know this at the time, but we both felt it. Photo courtesy Jason Nelson.

It was on the back roads of New Zealand where we felt free.

Mike perfecting the art of the stove and popcorn.

Mike ordering from an ice cream cart in Thailand.

Creating positive karma in Bangkok.

Rising into the mountains in Northern Laos.

Busy highway in Laos.

Mike reading one of our heavy books in Laos.

Laotian family playing cards.

Mike always looked like he rolled through Cambodia.

With the kids in Cambodia.

Riding among rice paddies in Vietnam.

Flat number 50?

Steve, Zach, Elise, Mike and me.
Sapa, Vietnam.

My 30th birthday.
Celebrating our anniversary.

Potala Palace, Tibet.

Yamdrok Yumtso, the most beautiful lake. Photo courtesy Billy Riske.

The Tibetan Plateau. Photo courtesy Billy Riske.

Billy, laughing and smiling at the top of a high pass in Tibet.
Couldn't be happier. Photo courtesy Billy Riske.

The best downhill. Photo courtesy Billy Riske.

Zach, Bob and Kunchen with Nathan in front of the truck.

Welcome to Mount Everest.
Mike, Zion and Katrina.

Katrina.

CHAPTER 22

MAIN HIGHWAY
Trusting the Curve

Our wheels rolled onto Route 13, the main highway in Laos, but it differed from main highways in any other country. Occasionally, a long-haul truck or the odd scooter passed, but mostly it felt as if we had the winding road, the main transportation corridor of Laos, to ourselves.

We cycled higher and continued to rise into the mouth of the mountains until we were swallowed by jungle. Patchwork quilt patterns of vegetation cut into the steep hillsides and dropped off beneath the road in a chaotic labyrinth of greenery. Mike and I often thought we were alone until we heard singing that soared among the mountains. Barefoot Lao men and women walked off the road with machetes and disappeared into the thickets.

Compact villages precariously clung to the road, yet the road seemed to barely hang onto the mountain. Bamboo huts were anchored to the ground on one side, but stilts, often ten metres long, attached to the hillside below, supported the rest. It looked as if one big storm could tear whole villages apart.

We arrived soundlessly in villages with only the whisper of our rubber tires, although news of our entrance spread quickly through the woven bamboo of the shacks. By the time we passed the first few huts, kids poured out to wave at us. Young kids, only 4 or 5 years old, bore infants wrapped in swathes of cotton strapped onto their backs. Many children had distended bellies, a sign of malnutrition. It was the first time Mike and I had witnessed this level of poverty. Yet the children waved and danced up and down, laughing and running circles around us as we rode. During the day, the villages seemed to be populated by young kids. We realized that anyone older than 8 was working in the fields. In Laos, we learned it was possible to be 4 years old and look after a 6-month-old all day; that it was possible to laugh, even when in a constant state of hunger.

We came out the other side and I commented, "It's maddening how there's so much food and waste in other parts of the world, but here there's not enough."

"Have you noticed there's no litter?" Mike replied. There was no garbage because there was nothing to buy. Sometimes we found Chinese noodles, but we never saw a roadside food stall, no shake ladies or even rice stands.

One afternoon, as I hugged the side of the road, a bush beside me started to move. I recoiled. It took a few glances to realize there was a man attached to the walking bush. The bush towered over his head and out the sides. He realized he had frightened me and his body shook with laughter; his muscled calves held him up as the bundle teetered like the Leaning Tower of Pisa. Then I laughed too. As we rode on, many people came out of the jungle with loads on their backs: vegetables, fruit, firewood – bearing it all on foot back to their homes.

A mother and her children climbed out of the steep jungle to pile stacks of wood on the road. Five kilometres later, when Mike and I stopped for a break, the same family trudged passed. The mom wore a traditional flowered sarong, long top and a conical straw hat. Her basket of wood on her back must have been twice her weight. The two older kids, aged around 5 and 7, each had bags of wood on their backs, and the littlest one, probably 2 years old, walked on his own. We pulled ahead of them again three kilometres down the road. I couldn't believe they had to walk so far for their fuel. Amazed and sad, my head hung low as we cycled through the poverty of the next village, realizing how hard the people worked just to survive.

Families sat in front of their homes while their meals cooked outside. Fires burned in the bottom of a large clay bowl and a pot of food sat on top. Women and girls sat one in front of another, picking lice out of each other's hair, sometimes with tweezers but mostly with their fingers. It was a scene we'd see often in Laos.

A tiny girl stood in the road drying her long hair with a piece of a rag. She rubbed the rag through her hair so lovingly that I wanted to take out the big towel from my pannier and wrap her up in it. I wanted to. But I didn't. We cycled through the front yards of their lives, trod on their earth and rolled out the other side, but we might as well have been flying over in an airplane for all the use we were.

I was still wary. That one human being who stole the laptop also stole my trust. I was closed and cautious. But the poverty was overwhelming and it drew compassion from every pore I had – my tears came out in sweat. I should have wrapped the girl up in my towel. Maybe now she would still be tenderly massaging it through her hair or even her own child's hair, whereas I have since misplaced it.

We saw swollen bellies, rotten teeth and infected eyes, but all we heard was laughter and song that followed the curve of the mountains upward in a smile. The road climbed from 400 metres to 1000 metres, back down to 400, then up to 1400. Mike was strong. I tucked myself behind him as we climbed. At night, he helped me block the doors and then stroked my head to help me fall sleep. He told me again and again that everything was going to be okay. The resentment I had stored up inside me over the laptop began to fall away with every downhill.

Eight hours of pedalling brought us 80 kilometres to a guest house in a village we never did learn the name of. Six other cycle tourists, having come from the south, were there – the benefit of only one road. There were four riders from Thailand, Lawrence from England and Colin from Hungary. Lawrence played harmonica and the throat harp and throughout the evening we sang songs in all languages. Between songs, we asked each other lots of questions. What are you carrying? Where are you going? Where have you been? This curiosity in cyclist slang is known as "dog sniffing." We carried this into the next morning.

"Are you sure you want to go that way?" Colin asked as the sun still rose. He motioned south, where Mike and I were headed. Clearly, to him, we were biking in the wrong direction. "And why do you have so much gear? There's no way you're going to make it up all those mountain passes with all that stuff," he said.

Colin had his nose up in everyone's business like a Jack Russell in heat. I rolled my eyes at Mike. He laughed out loud and smirked at me. Colin didn't notice. "This is all you need," Colin said, patting two panniers on the back of his bike.

It did seem ridiculous to have as much stuff as we did, especially in this part of the world, surrounded by people with little to eat and little to own. Colin's comments made us analyze the differences between him and us, between what we carried and what Colin didn't. For example:

Runners: Maybe something to leave behind, but then we wouldn't have done aerobics or taken hikes or been as comfortable playing games at the school.

Cook set: When nothing else could be found, Mike and I made tea or soup and sat enjoying ourselves and taking in our surroundings.

Water filter: We stopped buying water. Not for cost savings, which were minimal, but because the amount of plastic waste was sickening.

A winter-weight sleeping bag: This was something we could certainly do without in Laos. But we *did* use it for the first four months and planned to again if we reached the Himalayas. I didn't want to ship it home only to have it shipped back to us.

Books: Yes, well. I could have given up a few books. But I liked them. And I was carrying them…doing all my own pedalling up the mountains, so really, *go ride your own bike*, I thought in my head. We all moved through this incredible world at a reduced pace, to explore, to learn and become better for it.

I actually liked Colin. If we learned nothing else in meeting other cyclists, it's that we're all individuals. There's no right or wrong way to go on a bike trip, in the same way there's no right or wrong way to be a couple. We can judge the way someone else is doing something, but, in the end, it's what works for them.

Lawrence was a prime example of taking a singular approach to cycling. He had a mop of white hair and crooked teeth that sunk into a smiling skinny face. He had cycled the world for 30 years on the same steel bike frame. His seat was made out of bike tubes twisted around like a cinnamon bun, which he inflated for comfort. His handlebars were also his own creation, and his water-bottle holders were made from plastic two-litre bottles, cut in half and then bolted to the frame. Bits of tarp and plastic sewn and taped served as panniers draped from the back. Lawrence was thrilled with himself because he had recently found the perfect stick for a kickstand. I doubt he'd spent much money since beginning this nomadic lifestyle. We all envied his knowledge and years on the road. Lawrence was the most "sniffed" by all of us, and Colin oozed puppy love, never leaving his side. Lawrence, with his tall narrow body, did not suit his name. I preferred to think of him as Rover Ramp, a name he had scrawled on his bike.

Everyone else was going north when Mike and I headed south. It was another tough day with a lot of vertical. Heavy weather moved in. Granite skies hid the sun and shaded the road into night. We turned on our rear blinking lights and pedalled into pouring rain. Clouds touched down and floated along the roofs of shacks as if they were on fire. We couldn't see far ahead and children ran out, reaching out to touch us as we rode by. Colin's voice would not leave my head. "Are you sure you want to go that way?" "What do you need to carry that for?" "You're too heavy!" "You won't make it up the pass."

But we did. We pushed through mist and fog until a massive downhill tested our brakes. We busted through the last of the mysterious clouds and into a sunny day that felt brand new.

Kids loaded to the limit with water jugs tried to wave at us. Their small bodies jiggled up and down. They walked together with jugs big or small, depending on the child's size, from the village's water source, often over 20 minutes away. The more fortunate villages had a waterfall in their village. A few times we saw a tap with kids bathing and playing beneath it with a World Vision sign prominently on display above. Women, washing up after their day in the fields, stood beneath water from the hills with their chests bare and yelled "*Sabadee*" (hello) as we passed. Their hard nipples indicated the temperature of the water. (Nudity was a common sight along the main highway in Laos.)

"Now this was worth the effort today," Mike said, as he admired our bungalow for the evening. A tiny wooden structure perched on the edge of a hot spring named Bor Nam Oom.

"I'll make tea." I fired up the stove on our private balcony to boil water we had filtered from a waterfall. Kids and adults stripped down and slid on smooth rocks into the warm pond. The sun set into an evening of gold, and we felt rich as we read our heavy books on the balcony. We went to bed together for a sleep that was not full of fear or sadness. The clasp on my emotions began to loosen. I was less terrified. I still insisted on moving the dresser to block the door, but I began to understand everything would be okay. Laos would take care of us if I opened my heart.

"How much money do we have left?" I asked Mike when I noticed him counting the last of our money the next morning.

"Not much. It was silly we forgot to take out money in Luang Prabang." He looked concerned.

We stopped in every little village we found. It turned out we didn't need much money because we found hardly anything to buy. As we came down in altitude, no more waterfalls fell from the mountains to filter from and we found no roadside taps with the World Vision sign. Our water bottles dried out. We rationed what we had left of our food, nibbling on a few dry cookies that tasted like chalk and went down like cardboard. The mountain hills stripped our strength away and our bodies were sore, ravenous and dehydrated. Late in the afternoon, we came upon a village and the only store, a tiny open-faced hut with a thatched roof.

But there was no water to buy. The only drink they sold was a slimy green liquid called "Miranda." We bought two each. The bottles were warm from the hot sun and it burned as the sugar slid down my throat. Five gulps and my veins filled with enough energy to look around. In the minute it took to acquire drinks, 30 people had circled and squatted around us. They were quiet, other than a few children who cried and alternated between staring at us and hiding in the cloth of their mothers' wraps. Ragged clothes that must have been worn year after year hung on dusty bodies. Matted hair covered their heads like stomped-on carpets. They observed us through eye infections that made pus swell out of the corners of eyes and oozed like gobs of toothpaste. They stared at us and we stared back at them. We smiled at the children, but they seemed afraid of us.

Water buffaloes splashed close by in a mud pool, but we couldn't figure out where the villagers got their water. We bought more dry cookies and finished off the second of our hot slimy green drinks, while those squatting around us never moved.

Days later the water came. Rain fell from the sky like it had held in its tears for months. We packed up in the rain and continued in the rain up and down rolling hills. Intense storm clouds blocked our view, but our blinking lights flashed in the back to help cars see us. When the sun came out, our view expanded to see jagged limestone karst formations poking up from the land. Towering jungle covered the lower half of the peaks, which were pitted with caves and underground rivers.

Sixty-five kilometres north of the city of Vientiane we found a guest house for 50,000 kip ($6) a night. Mike and I were wet, filthy and covered in mud, but we couldn't do anything about it since we had no other clothes to change into. We had done our laundry the day before in a town called Vang Vieng, but with all the rain the clothes had not dried. We packed them still damp and now hung them around the room. Those that didn't fit we slung in trees outside and spread on the grass.

"Look happy and clean," Mike said as the owner came close. The owner's face crumpled at the sight of us as if he wasn't sure he should let us stay.

He did, though – thankfully. The small room had a twin bed with a tiny window. There was just enough space between the wall and the bed to squeeze past a floor fan to get to the tiny bathroom, where we stuffed our bikes. In three minutes, the room reeked like dirty wet dog.

But that night I fell asleep easy. A thief would not have fit inside.

CHAPTER 23

SOUTHERN LAOS
Finding Forgiveness

Forgiveness typically comes easy for me. If someone apologized, I'd tell them, "no worries," and mean it. I never hold grudges. Yet forgiving the theft and forgiving myself for hurting Mike had not come quickly, and as I packed our dry clothes the next morning I questioned why. I knew there couldn't be total peace and happiness without forgiveness.

I was still thinking about this when I noticed the mountains melt away like ice cream, as if a spoon carved out the valley, and we were given a much easier road to ride on. Unfortunately, there was no ice cream. Instead, sticky rice grew alongside maize, beans and starchy roots – enough to make anyone hungry.

A teenage boy waved us over. We stopped our bikes in front of his one-storey home and tarps covered in peanuts. "Fundee," he said, pointing to himself. He was tall, skinny and standing proud in a bright red shirt. His arms moved rapidly as he explained to us about peanuts – in sign language.

Most Laotians are farmers. The major agricultural product is sticky rice, but, unlike in Thailand, the rice is not exported. Over half of the population grows just enough food to feed their families. Peanuts, on the other hand, are a cash crop.

Fundee took pictures with us before he presented Mike and me with a gift of a large bag of peanuts and a bag of hot peppers.

"What are we going to do with chili peppers?" Mike asked me once we were back on our bikes.

"Throw them at dogs," I joked. (Chances were the dogs were as used to the spice as the people.) I envisioned a pack of wild canines chasing us for pepper treats.

I got a flat tire shortly afterward; my fourth of the trip. Mike slipped the tire from the rim and pulled out the tube, sliding the tube through his fingers, searching for the hole. Instantly, Mike's hands were filthy – like he had just smeared them in a massive mound of water buffalo poo.

Which he had.

I'd biked through a poo pile because I was staring off into the rice fields instead of at the road.

"I'm sorry," I said, struggling to keep from giggling.

"I don't see you jumping in and helping," Mike said sarcastically.

"But you're so good at it now," I teased. I could change my own tire, but Mike had become an expert at it, and I was happy to let him be while I kept my hands clean.

Soon, we were surrounded. People came out of the fields and squatted near us and stared. I smiled and observed with them. Two older gentlemen approached from a hut, each carrying a glass of water for Mike and me. They grabbed the tube and disappeared behind the hut. We drank the water and then followed them to find my tube. They were dunking it in a large bucket of collected rainwater to locate the puncture. Bubbles surfaced where they found the hole. One of the men looked at Mike while he rubbed his hands fiercely together to show that Mike should also wash his poo hands in the bucket.

We gave them the chilies.

Our onward progress was slow, and we had no desire to rush to the city of Vientiane. Our legs were heavy from days of hard riding in the mountainous jungle, and I was beginning to not feel well. We stopped for the 20th time. This time at a fruit stand where a young girl sold us a pineapple. She took a long look at us then cut it up before handing it over. I didn't think it was typical service.

"I bet she's thinking, 'Stupid *farangs* (Westerners), don't even know how to cut up their own pineapple,'" Mike said jokingly.

It felt good to be taken care of.

In Vientiane, we chose a guest house for 90,000 kip (about $11). It included breakfast, coffee all day and a private toilet. The only downside was we weren't allowed to bring our bikes inside, so they were left outside with nothing but our flimsy cable lock to protect them. But I was done searching for another place. I walked into the room and sat straight on the toilet to let my insides out. I threw up and continued to experience diarrhea. When I wasn't on the toilet, I lay spread-eagle on top of our bed, sweating like a woman in labour beneath the ceiling fan.

I couldn't concentrate enough to read. I missed the laptop more and more, wishing I could watch a movie. I twisted and turned with the pain in my stomach. I stared at the walls and counted cobwebs and flies all night. Mike went out and bought antibacterial pills from a pharmacy in the morning.

"You have to drink a bit," he said, holding a water bottle to my mouth, making me take a few sips of water with vitamin C packages stirred in to help rehydrate.

"I'm off to the police station. You okay? I'll be back again soon," he promised.

I mumbled an okay.

Mike spent the day trying to obtain a police report in English for the laptop's insurance. He'd come back often, check on me and then head back to the station to wait some more.

"This is ridiculous," he said the fourth time he came into the room.

"Tell me about it," I replied, though I knew he wasn't commenting on my sickness. He held up the warm water bottle and told me to drink some more. I cautiously sipped.

"I've spent hours inside the police station! Now they want 50 US dollars before they'll write a police report. That's crazy! I'm going to get hold of our insurance and see what they say."

I groaned. I didn't care. I was too tired, sick and bored. Mike helped me to the washroom again.

"I'll be back soon." I listened to him leave and missed him instantly.

He came back an hour later.

"Good news this time," he said, bursting into the room. "We don't need an English police report. I'm going to send the Laotian one in to our insurance. I don't know if they have a translator or will just take our word for it, but it looks like we'll be covered for the loss."

"That's nice," I said, but I didn't really think about it. Instead, I thought, *I must have the cleanest insides in history and how can I possibly still be throwing up?* There was nothing left, I'd given everything I had to that disgusting Laotian toilet.

Two days later, I felt well enough, so we headed to the Vietnamese embassy to apply for a visa. Our plan was to continue cycling down Laos, through Cambodia, up Vietnam and into China. (We had a plan!)

After that process was sorted, we had a few days to wait, so I went to a sports doctor to see about the numbness in my hand. Mike had helped to reposition the tilt of my handlebars. He also took foam we found on the side of the road and taped it around the handle. This lifted the angle of my palm in an attempt to relieve pressure and the cause of the numbness. None of it worked. At this point, two of my fingers were completely desensitized.

At the hospital, I was given two hours of therapy that involved hot packs, then cooling packs, then back to hot, followed by a fantastic massage – all for the amazing price of 8,000 kip ($1)! The doctor then sternly advised me, "You need to go for a massage every day."

"That's the best doctor advice I've ever had!" I beamed. That evening, Mike joined me as I started my first "therapy" session. We turned our heads toward each other, smiling, while we lay on blue mats, wearing the loose cotton clothes that were provided.

Despite the massages, my hand was not getting better. I emailed my doctor friend in Canada and he wrote that hand numbness is a common occurrence in long-distance cyclists. His prognosis was it was likely a pinched nerve and should go away in two months. Two months seemed like a very long time. Mike fussed with my handlebars some more and made a fat cushion for my hand to rest on. It made me smile every time I looked at it.

Otherwise, I had very little to complain about. Close to where I went for therapy was a building called Cooperative Orthotic and Prosthetic Enterprise. They designed and manufactured prosthetic legs and custom-fit arms and hands for the people of Laos still being affected by the Vietnam War. Starting in 1964, America bombed Laos with a B-52 load every 8 minutes, 24 hours a day for 9 years. More bombs fell on Laos in this time period than during the whole of the Second World War. Laos is the most heavily bombed country, per capita, in the world. Millions of these bombs did not explode on impact, and now farmers and children accidentally detonate many of them. Those who survive the blasts are left wounded and without limbs.

It was hard to envision the war as we ate dinners sprawled out on a woven blanket on the banks of the Mekong River, watching fishermen in wooden canoes catch our meal in the fading sun. We ate our meal with a New Zealander named Nathan. Nathan was also cycle touring and an instant friend. He relaxed back in his chair and asked us, "What's the plan from here?" Mike and I both laughed.

"What's so funny?"

"Nothing," I said. "Actually, we do have a plan. We have dreams of making it to Kathmandu." Kathmandu, Nepal, was still a long way away – many border crossings away. Maybe it was just a dream. But it became an aspiration we began to cling to. As if, somehow, when we made it all the way there, everything would be right in our life.

Nathan smiled, "I'd like to go there too. Maybe we'll see each other again."

Nathan's voice was mellow and even-keeled, like nothing would ever phase him. Thankfully, this was the case, because the next day he was able to recover the photos from our camera's SD card, which had contracted a virus when we tried to download at an internet cafe.

"We need a new laptop," Mike said to me after Nathan saved our photos.

"But where will we get one?" I asked. I'd begun journaling again, but I missed reviewing our day and week in pictures and videos.

"I'm not sure, but I'll look into it," he replied.

When our visas were ready, we continued south. After 80 kilometres we turned onto a dirt road to the village of Ban Na. I hoped to see elephants. I had read the locals used to grow fruit and vegetables but then switched to sugar cane. At the same time, elephants had been pushed out of the highlands with the construction of a power generator. When they arrived in Ban Na, and tasted the sweet sugar cane, the elephants didn't want to leave! The villagers attempted to switch their fields back to fruit and vegetables, but the 50 elephants would not budge. The village gave in and a wooden tower was built where tourists could sleep and watch the sweet-toothed elephants.

It was late afternoon when we arrived, exhausted, in Ban Na. The village was small. There were no signs or advertisements about the elephants. I took a seat with Mike on a wooden bench, both our legs extended out in fatigue. "Come to think about it," I said, "I've no idea where I read about the elephants."

Mike turned to look at me, with a quizzical look on his face that seemed to say, *Well, what now?*

Too tired to do anything else, we sat. It was not long until a dozen people surrounded us. I looked at each of them, smiled and asked, "Elephants?" They all smiled back. A few minutes later, a guide came to talk to us. We were made to understand that the cost to stay a night in the tower was 70 dollars.

"For some reason, I expected it would cost around ten dollars," I frowned.

"That's a lot of money, Kat, and it's not even guaranteed we'll see any elephants," Mike replied. "We could last for a week on that amount."

Bummer. Well, now what?

I pulled out the map and draped it over my thighs. It was no help. I had no idea how far we'd have to ride before we would find a place to sleep, and I was nervous about pulling off the road to camp in Laos due to undetonated bombs.

"No elephants?" the guide asked us.

"Sorry, no elephants," I said. "Is there a place in Ban Na for us to sleep?" I pointed at myself, then Mike, and lay the side of my head on my hands.

219

"Stay here," the guide said by gesturing with his palms down. We were grateful to wait.

When the guide came back, he motioned for us to follow. We walked narrow trails woven among bamboo homes built on stilts. The dry earth, compacted by thousands of steps, wore away around trees and exposed large roots like snakes, a roller coaster for our bikes to navigate. Dogs barked. Young pups ran in circles and nipped at each other's hind legs. Roosters, chickens and chicks darted among the dogs, clucking at the ground and pecking in the dirt. Women sat on stools, their hands busy weaving baskets while men crouched in small circles.

We were led to a brick home and introduced to a man named Kai and his wife Laya. Three young children stood shyly by their side. I understood that it's typical for a new husband to move in with his wife's family, so we also met Laya's mother and father.

"*Khob chai, khob chai*" (thank you, thank you), we said with our hands cupped beneath our chins.

Kai wore bright flowered shorts and a red golf shirt. His hair was short and his smile welcoming. I thought to myself that he had to be at least five years younger than us. The red brick house stood out among the bamboo homes in the village. He led us inside to a large empty room with only a woven mat on the floor and a mattress in the corner. Chickens, roosters and cats were chased away through the door. My arms, heavy from carrying the panniers, dropped them beside the mattress. (Since they gave us the main room, I never did figure out where the family slept.)

Kai then grabbed a large wheelbarrow and placed his youngest toddler named Mali inside, inviting me to follow. Mike stayed behind as I accompanied Kai on the sand paths out of the village. The trail became wet and slippery and he worked to push through the red muck until we came upon a deep well. Kai made sure Mali was safe by my side then pushed aside the large stone lid. Again and again he tossed down a pail, pulling it back up until the wheelbarrow filled with water. Once it was full, he washed his face, arms and legs and had me to the same. We sloshed our way back, and this time Mali held my hand and led the way.

We found Mike sitting with three topless, shoeless men on a woven mat. The men waved me over as soon as I was noticed. Cigarettes dangled from stained fingers on one hand and large glasses of a locally made rice whisky, called Lao Lao, in the other. I smiled at their massive grins and continued with Mali. "*Tam Jook!*" (cheers!) they yelled, throwing back their heads to drink. The empty glasses crashed back onto the mat only to be filled again.

Mike came back to Kai's, claiming, "I thought they'd never let me leave!"

"That could've been trouble," I laughed. "I'm not sure if Grandma is impressed."

Grandma sat on a mat, weaving a basket, seeming to glare at us. She wore a brown sarong and a loose tank top with tiny red flowers. Her hair was tied back, brushed with streaks of grey, and her feet were bare. I guessed she might be around 50, my mother's age.

The cookhouse, which was a separate tiny bamboo structure, stood beside her. A fire burned in the corner and a metal tripod held a blackened pot over the flames. Baskets of spices and grains crowded each other on the only shelf, covered in soot from the fire. The late afternoon sun shone through the slats of the building and gave everything an orange smoky hue. Laya, the young skinny mom of three, would go inside every few minutes and stir the food in the pot.

I brought Mike around the back of the house to the barrel we had emptied the wheelbarrow into so he could wash up.

"Card game?" he asked me as he wiped his wet hands on his shorts.

"Absolutely."

Mike pulled out our deck of cards and soon the children and Kai encircled us. We sat on the mat and played for hours. First, we showed them the game memory and then go fish. Mike and I called out Lao numbers and we taught them the words for "jack," "queen" and "king."

Grandma and Grandpa watched through the open windows. Grandpa stripped apart lengths of bamboo that were then passed to Grandma to weave into baskets of all sizes. Grandma was a tough one to read. We couldn't tell if she minded our presence or was curious.

I grabbed the now standard pile of bananas stored on the back of my bike and shared the fruit with everyone. Later we were brought a huge meal of sticky rice, meat, vegetables and some sort of fish goo, all in Grandma's home-made baskets. Other than the fish goo (which we both forced down), the food tasted fantastic.

While the rest of us played cards again, Mali played with a tiny keychain of a small pink pig. It had been given to me months ago in a village in Thailand and hung on my handlebars since. This seemed like the right place to pass it on. She held it all evening long.

In the morning, the roosters woke us at five, pecking close to our mosquito net. I rolled over and heard through the open windows that the family was already into their day, cooking, cleaning and basket weaving.

We packed up and went outside. Mali and her brother took turns playing with the toy pig. Mike and I took the cups of coffee that were offered and sat on the stairs. Older women and naked kids as young as 4 years old smoked tobacco from a gigantic water pipe called *dieu kay*. It was made from a long piece of bamboo larger than the kids drawing from it. Pigs sat near us, their tiny tails swirling in the dirt. Mike got up and I watched while he played with the children, drawing pictures in the mud with a stick.

The love the family showed for each other sparkled in their eyes, their touch and soft voices, especially the children. As with many of the youth we met throughout Southeast Asia, the children never seemed to act out with sibling rivalry or jealousy.

I stood up and walked over to my bike. I gave the older brother a bag of popcorn we'd bought in Vientiane. Normally shy, he smiled so large that drool began to drip out his mouth like a big mastiff dog. We all started laughing as he wiped his face on his arm.

Mike and I were given more fish goo.

Grandma came over and took my hands in hers to say goodbye. As she held me, I thought about the beauty of Laos. Laos was the first county that presented us with some of the travails of travel: stolen laptop, days of vomit, numb fingers and corrupt police. As Grandma let go of my hand, I mused that I hadn't given the country a proper chance.

Mike had, of course. One of Mike's strengths is his ability to forgive. But not only that, he somehow let pain or bitterness go. While I had still been barricading doors, he'd already welcomed in trust. I watched him straddle his bike and I knew I needed to follow his lead.

My faith grew when Kai held up Mali, the pig toy clutched in her little hand. The popcorn had since been passed around to all of the kids, each taking turns to hold the bag and smile. It had not been opened.

It was still early as we made our way down the dirt road leading back to the main highway of Laos. The highway had been paved four years previous, but it seemed more like a pasture than a road. Goats, chickens, turkeys, ducks, pigs, cows and water buffalos sat on or walked down the road as we pedalled south.

A few days later, in the town of Paske, I had set the alarm for 5 a.m., though I didn't know why I bothered. Mike always ignored it, and I had begun to as well. Another great lesson from my husband: how to sleep in!

It was late morning by the time we left. Shortly after, we found a man stumbling on the side of the road, his scooter lying broken in the ditch. His hands were scraped raw from sliding, his forehead was cut and his chin had a massive gash. Blood poured down his face and neck, soaking his T-shirt.

I jumped off my bike and grabbed my first aid kit from the top of my front-left pannier. I gave him the roll of toilet paper Mike and I had just bought in the market and mimed how he should soak up the blood. He did as told, but his concerned dark eyes looked into mine with shock.

"Here, take this." I handed him a pad for his chin and told him to hold it there and not let go. Thankfully, another man stopped and took him on the back of his scooter.

"I hope they're going to a hospital," I said, watching them leave.

"I wonder when he arrives there if he'll realize the crazy *farang* gave him a huge maxi-pad to hold to his face," Mike smirked, clearly impressed with my first aid skills.

The road was quiet after that, the rice fields full with farmers and water buffalo. We yelled "*Sawadee*" hundreds of times before we stopped for lunch at an open shack. A family sat around the one table and a black stone cooker. We joined the only table and I asked if they had rice.

The father turned to his eldest daughter and said something. She stood up, accepted the money he handed her and took off on a scooter. Mike and I looked around again. There didn't seem to be napkins, hot sauce or advertisements on the wall. It took a few minutes for us to understand, but after we "ordered" our lunch we realized we were in a family's kitchen – not a restaurant.

I laughed and, thankfully, so did the father. He motioned for us to stay. In the meantime, the youngest daughter peeled an egg and offered us the chicken fetus inside. We said no as politely as we could. I tried not to scrunch up my face as she twisted off the tiny beak, threw it on the ground then munched on the slimy skin and bones. Thankfully, she was shy and didn't offer to share with us again.

The eldest came back after 20 minutes, presumably from a proper food stall, with a great lunch of rice, pork and greens. I caught her taking pictures of us with her cellphone. We smiled as two different worlds collided in her family kitchen. "Same same but different," as the common Asian saying goes.

They waved as we headed toward the Cambodian border.

The day was cooler than most – below 35 degrees. It would pour for a few minutes, then be sunny and then rain again. It was perfect and we made it 140 kilometres. In the evening, we came across a guest house. There had been no villages, so we were relieved to find a place to stay. The owner twirled her hands in the motion of a helicopter above her head.

"I've no idea what she's saying," I whispered to Mike, then continued to ask for a room. She responded by twirling and twisting her arms up high as if she were dancing uninhibited at a Bob Marley concert.

"No clue," Mike said, and copied her with his hands flying above his bike helmet, then gave a big shoulder shrug to show her we didn't understand. She took hold of my hand and dragged me to one of the rooms and pointed to the ceiling. *Oh, did we want a fan or air conditioning…* We were tired and horrible at charades. She laughed and we fell onto the hard bed beneath our welcome fan.

I cuddled Mike on top of our mattress. Finally, I felt at peace, as if a brooding cloud that had been smothering me blew away in the gentle wind. All of the good in Laos began to shine through. Realizing that, apart from the first night, our month had been incredible and filled with pleasantries from locals every day. Like children pumping their arms in two-handed waves to the farmers wanting to share their food with us. Big moments like Grandma from Bag Na finally giving us a smile and the amazing joy we were given from the kids doing a celebratory dance when they saw us, like they had waited so long for the two of us to ride through their country.

It had taken me time to forgive the person who broke into our room, the same way it took a long time to forgive myself. Our sins intertwined. We had both abused trust.

"I forgive you," I said out loud as we came toward the border. "You messed up, too, but I forgive you."

CHAPTER 24

CAMBODIA
Scuff Marks

A strong headwind pushed against us as we crawled from the Laos border further into Cambodia. Dusty fields dotted with sugar palms and small wooden huts sprawled toward the Mekong River.

We stopped at a roadside food stall and collapsed onto rickety wooden chairs to consume noodles on the deck. Chickens clucked beneath the floorboards. Finished, Mike disappeared into a shack in the back field.

"So how was it?" I asked when Mike came back. It was our third day in Cambodia and the fourth day since we had any toilet paper. I had used the last roll at the scooter accident. Mike looked at me like I had grown octopus tentacles.

"You seriously want to talk about this? You're ridiculous," he replied, pedalling off.

"Oh come on, how was it? It's not that bad, is it?" I pressed.

He shook his head at me. "You're right. It wasn't as awful as I thought it would be."

"I told you! Don't you feel more cultured?" I laughed and pumped my legs up and down on the pedals. "I hope you used your left hand!" I hassled him and moved to the front of his wheel.

"C'mon, let's jump on!" We raced to catch the draft of a slow-moving truck. Over a dozen Khmer farmers and their tools sat crammed into the back. I waved. They loved that we'd caught their tail, and smiled. With the truck's windbreak, I felt like an athlete again rather than a sloth riding an overweight bicycle.

One of the men opened a food package and threw the plastic wrapper off the truck as he took a bite. I rode close and jokingly scolded him for littering, shaking my head and finger. Cambodia was the most polluted country we saw on our trip. Garbage was everywhere. It flew in the wind, covered pastures in the countryside and filled gutters and lanes in the cities. Blue plastic bags by the millions sprinkled the country like a garnish. We'd been struggling with what to do with our own garbage, as there was rarely anywhere to put it, so I was carrying a growing bag of garbage attached to my back rack.

The truck made a right turn into a field and the men waved goodbye. We were back in the wind, fighting against the storm front. Graphite clouds rolled over top of each other like the running of the bulls, stampeding forward as if the devil himself galloped behind with a whip.

"We're in for it," Mike said. I smiled, up for the challenge. The gale wind plastered our shirts to our bodies, the fabric parachuting out behind us. We turned on our blinking red lights and put hats on beneath our helmets to prevent some of the rain blasting into our faces. We struggled like spiders up a drainpipe, only to lose our position and fall back. We pushed forward to the town of Kratie, arriving at the doorstep of Balcony Guesthouse a sopping mess.

"I can't believe they let us in," I said as we dripped half the monsoon inside.

"I can't believe how awesome this feels," Mike replied. We stripped off our wet clothes and piled them with our panniers. The rain continued to hammer on the window while we took warm showers. Once dry, we went to the top floor, which had a covered deck and restaurant.

"Whoa, you two can eat a lot," said Kathryn, a journalist from New Zealand who shared our table. We groaned in affirmation, our mouths filled with our second order. Meat juice dribbled down our chins in happiness. We had not eaten so well in weeks.

"It's my birthday on Monday. I work in Phnom Penh and it would be great to have you there," she said. "I want to eat bugs for my birthday."

We weren't sure what made us say yes.

A few days later, in the city of Phnom Penh, we found Kathryn in front of the Grand Palace. She had her journal in hand and a tight expression on her face as she tucked her mid-length brown hair behind her ears.

"Happy Birthday!" Mike and I greeted her.

"Ready?" she asked. She was all business. Kathryn had been hired to write an article on bugs for the *Phnom Penh Post,* and we were interested in learning more. "Bugs have been eaten in Cambodia for centuries for protein and nutrients," she explained as we walked over to our first bug vendor. "But some, like the big black hairy spiders, only became popular during the

Khmer Rouge genocide, when most of the country starved and anything became edible."

We warmed up with crispy frogs and crickets. Locals bought them by the bagful and ate them like popcorn. They tasted like salty oily popcorn, except with little legs that tickled the inside of my mouth. Otherwise, they were surprisingly enjoyable. I looked over at Mike. His face was scrunched up and he was digging into his mouth, pulling out pieces of cricket.

"Well, at least you tried," I told him.

Kathryn didn't look impressed with Mike's effort. We circled around a teenage girl who held a board with three baskets containing black beetles, crickets and larvae worms. My throat constricted and my giggles became frequent and high-pitched with nerves when Kathryn bought three beetles. Beetles the size of chicken eggs. I forced myself to smile at the girl helping us, not wanting to insult her culture. A small boy had attached himself to us in hopes of getting our leftovers. I smiled wryly at him too. The girl showed us how to pull off the greasy hard wings and chuck them on the ground. I put the body in my mouth and crunched down. I gagged but quickly recovered to swallow the rest of the beetle. Once it was choked back, we continued down the street to a cart piled high with termites, caterpillars, bees, wasps, grasshoppers, flies, silkworms, dragonflies and ants. Alleged delicacies, according to Kathryn.

"Let's try these spiders," she said.

"Those aren't spiders," I said. "Those are big, black, hairy tarantulas the size of golf balls."

Kathryn stared at me. I gave in. "Sure, let's do this."

Kathryn smiled. I felt she liked having me along. I certainly wouldn't have eaten bugs without her and she might not have continued without me. The hair from the spider was awful, like a thin carpet, softer and longer than a kiwi peel. The legs felt animated as if they were alive, jutting into my gums like a toothpick. I learned, after my first bite, to eat legs first, body second. It was not good.

Snakes were next. I held a ridiculously long barbecued orange snake skewered in multiple Ss on a stick. Tourists at the sidelines stared and commented loudly.

"What?"

"You're crazy!"

"Look at them!"

"I can't even watch."

After the spider, any nausea was replaced by a giddy toughness. "Do you want to share?" I asked, offering my snake skewer to an Irish man. He didn't. I laughed. The boy who had stayed with us caught my attention. His eyes were eager for a ration.

"What's your name?" I asked.

"Rotan."

"Rotan, do you want a snake? Will you teach me how to eat it?" Rotan nodded his head up and down. He looked to be about 8 years old and happily took the limbless reptile I handed him. I bit down on my snake and pulled its crunchy body into my mouth and chewed, copying Rotan. Not bad, actually. I kept my eyes closed. It tasted like chicken skin. I rather like chicken skin.

"I can't tell if I'm eating the head or the tail," I said to Mike.

"You ate the head," he told me, either amazed or horrified.

I didn't feel the need to ingest an entire snake, so I gave the rest to a happy Rotan.

The next arthropod looked innocent, a tiny larva worm half the size of my pinky. Easy-peasy compared to tarantula, beetle and snake. I pointed out the minuscule head and little legs to Mike and put the entire thing in my mouth.

"Oh! Oh!" My face screwed up and I hopped up and down as a fountain of innards erupted in my mouth. The sensation of a worm spewing in my mouth was more than I could handle. "That one spurted! I'm done!" I cried out.

"I admit defeat," I said to Kathryn, who looked up from her notebook, disappointed.

"The police are coming," Mike said. The women on the street picked up big trays of baskets filled with bugs and put them on top of their heads. They scooped up their plastic stools and headed toward the palace to give more space between them and the cops. Elephants meandered by. Time, for the moment, stood still.

The rules for street vendors are fuzzy. It's officially illegal to be a street vendor. There are fines and other repercussions, yet vendors are also charged taxes and fees collected by the police. Once the police left, the women came back to streetside and set up shop once more.

The next morning, Mike hailed us a tuk-tuk and it drove us to the Tuol Sleng Genocide Museum, a building that, in the early '70s, had been a high school before the Khmer Rouge converted it into a prison. Led by Pol Pot, the Khmer Rouge (*Khmer* meaning "person from Cambodia," *rouge* signalling communism) came to power in 1975. Pol Pot forced the urban population into the fields to produce foods that were then exported. Those who didn't leave towns and cities fast enough were executed: the sick, the elderly, the young. The Khmer Rouge also sought to create a classless society by killing "educated people." In five years, over two million Cambodians were killed, starved or died from disease and exhaustion. Some were interrogated in the school-turned-prison and were subjected to brutal treatment.

I clutched Mike's hand as we walked slowly into the courtyard. The building surrounds the yard on three sides and is three storeys high. We climbed the stairs to the top floor. Classrooms had been turned into torture rooms or small cells. We stood beside a metal-framed bed, a graphic picture behind it on the wall showed how emaciated the prisoners looked in their last minutes of life. My body shook. Mike turned to me and asked quietly, "Do you need to leave?"

I shook my head no and tears welled up in my eyes. Mike was concerned. He knows I can suffer from nightmares. He knows I won't watch movies above a PG-13 rating because I'm easily disturbed.

"I need to see this," I told him. The interrogation prison was one of 150 in Cambodia. Our footsteps dragged through a narrow hallway to another grey room. We didn't want to be there, but we forced ourselves to look at everything. Black and white images showed children, men and women. Horror and exhaustion filled their eyes and screamed deprivation. Each photo and every room showed different forms of torture used.

Once guards had been satisfied with prisoners' forced confessions, and there was no more space for bodies near the school, victims were sent to the Choeung Ek Killing Fields. Mike and I forced ourselves to go and stepped into a tuk-tuk for the 30-minute ride.

Guides stood outside the fields waiting for tourists. We nodded to one man and he came to our side and introduced himself as Phirum. His right leg dragged behind him as he walked, leaving a scuff mark in the brick-red sand. We followed him into the killing field. "I lost my brother and father to the Khmer Rouge. Now I have been guiding here since 1980." Phirum pulled his hat over his thin black hair. "I want to show people what happened here," he said solemnly. "There are 20,000 mass grave sites in Cambodia. This is only one."

Phirum picked up a skull from the ground and pointed out a crack. "The Khmer Rouge didn't use bullets because they cost too much money. Instead, shovels, hoes and bamboo spears killed people." He moved on slowly. "When I first visited the Killing Fields, the stench festering from decaying bodies was unbearable." There was no smell now. Just an eerie energy hovering over the grounds.

The rawness of the land struck me. Grass and trees have grown, but the mass graves became more evident with passing rainfalls. Mike tripped on what we thought was a stick.

"It's a bone," Phirum said. "Most likely a femur." Prisoners were forced to dig their own graves, he told us. They had been weak due to starvation and disease and could only dig shallow graves, so now bones, teeth and clothes were visible in what was once an orchard.

As we walked toward a glass stupa display of over 5,000 skulls, I wondered what it would be like to have so much of your country decimated, leaving only mass graves of bones? How could they possibly smell the flowers among the rotting corpses? I realized that in each country we travelled we came across the remnants of conflict. Battles over land, titles and religion. *Why do we have to suffer so much*? I asked myself.

Yet the people we met smiled and laughed. We left one mass killing site for another and, on the way, we heard more hellos (*Susa'day*) and saw more kids dancing than in any other country. The people opened their arms, homes and hearts to us. We mused, *Shouldn't it be the other way around*? Cambodians were strong and full of the will to live.

It was a full moon that night. Back in Phnom Penh, we walked in shock and sadness to Kathryn's friend Ivy's house. On the way, we found ourselves in a dark back lane. A man sniffed shoe glue from a plastic bag and a few women breastfed babies. Toddlers slept beside them on the hard pavement, their only comfort that they were with their parents. They lived in the open where nothing was hidden. I was careful not to step on anyone, but my emotions spiralled. We walked another hundred paces and disappeared up a set of stairs into luxury beyond the imagination of those we'd just trod over.

The smells from the street were left outside. Kids no longer grabbed for my water bottle. Walls and doors silenced the relentless thrum of tuk-tuks and moto drivers. We entered a suite with sparkling granite surfaces and polished stainless steel fixtures. A young woman skipped toward us wearing designer clothes and heels.

"I'm Ivy. Come in, come in," she sang. Ivy was an American on an internship writing for the *Phnom Penh Post*, but her passion was writing celebrity gossip. Her hair floated around her face and, for the rest of the night, I had to resist touching it.

"We just have to celebrate Kathryn's birthday." She danced over to the fridge and pulled on the door to grab a bottle of champagne. "I bought it at duty-free. It was only $50! Isn't that such a bargain? We'll have this and then I have lots more wine for later."

Ivy and Kathryn's friends came over, including two Cambodians who grew up in Phnom Penh but went to school in the United States. We roasted marshmallows over Ivy's gas stove and then left for an upscale rooftop restaurant.

Candles flickered in the moonlight. The illuminated city spread below. Mike pulled out a chair for me and helped slide me in. When he sat down, he rested his hand on my leg beneath the table and kept it there, a reassuring reminder of his love.

If I arched back, I could still see the back lane. As I laughed and enjoyed my evening, in the back of my mind I struggled with the unfairness.

The next morning, when we went shopping for a new laptop, my horror at the disparities stayed with me. We spent more money in ten minutes than the families in the back lane would see in a decade. I knew I'd never look at "stuff" the same way. I promised myself to remember how fortunate we are to have these luxuries in life, and I hoped we'd always be able to help others who needed some too.

CHAPTER 25

BAKONG
New Beginnings

With a new laptop packed in my back pannier, we pedalled west out of the city of Phnom Penh toward Siem Reap. Heavily laden scooters barely outpaced us. One scooter carried red crates, stacked as tall as a castle and out either side like wings. Another scooter transported carpets piled high as if they were a throne, with a woman perched on top like a princess. On the front handlebars, a knotted bandana swung a newborn baby. These scooters drove beside us, smiling and talking. I feared their loads would crash down and we'd never be found beneath the mounds of wood or plastic chairs.

"Just the way to go. With a load of long bamboo feather dusters taking me out," I laughed.

"Hello." Mike responded to yet another greeting from a friendly scooter driver.

"My throat's so sore. We'll have to take turns yelling hello," I suggested. Our mouths were dry from the dusty roads and our throats were raw from yelling greetings. Every villager called "*Susa'day*" multiple times and waved merrily. We loved it, but the hellos were so frequent that we began to limit ourselves to two hellos per family.

In the early afternoon, a boy passed me, quickly rotating his skinny legs on his single-speed bike until he caught up with Mike.

"Hello, sir," he said.

"Hello," Mike replied.

"I speak English. I practise. Where you from?" The boy stared intently at Mike instead of at the road in front of him. He looked to be around 15 years old. The basket on the front of his bike hung low, full of notebooks, and he wore the standard Cambodian school uniform of blue pants and a white dress shirt. The shirt looked dry. He obviously handled the weather much better than Mike.

"We're from Canada," Mike told him. Mike's own white cotton Thailand top that had billowed in the early morning breeze now stuck to his body with perspiration, caked with the red earth that blew from the dry fields.

"Canada?" The boy was puzzled.

"Do you know America?" asked Mike.

"Oh *yes*! I know America."

"It's near there," Mike told the boy. "Did you just finish school?"

"Yes. Now I go home. When do you go home?"

"We're not sure yet, maybe in six months."

"Six months! But what about your kids?"

"We don't have any kids."

"No kids?" the student said. The rotation of his pedals slowed. "But what about your ox?"

"We don't have any oxen."

"How do you plow your fields?"

"Well…" Mike began to answer, then looked around him at the torn-up land. Men worked the dusty terrain, holding thick leather straps attached to oxen. The large animals pulled at metal rakes plowing the parched ground behind them.

"I see! You have water buffalo!" the boy said excitedly, pumping on the pedals. He completely ignored upcoming traffic. His gaze never left Mike's face.

"No, we have no water buffalo. Actually, we don't have fields either. People that do have farms use tractors to plow their fields."

"Tractors. Yes. I have seen this somewhere once." The boy went quiet. I wonder if he believed we were the most poor and unfortunate people, to not own an ox or water buffalo, on top of having no children.

"Who is she?" He motioned behind to me.

"She's my wife."

"What does she do?"

"She's my personal assistant," Mike said in a serious tone, and then looked back at me with a smirk. He got me – he knew I wouldn't interrupt as it wasn't my conversation.

"Why do you have no children? You very old."

"My wife is barren."

"Barren? I don't know this word." I looked around, ready to grab a coconut from a tree to toss at Mike's head. Though I'm sure the boy would have noticed and would certainly have thought even less of me.

"Maybe we'll have a child soon," Mike said. This caused me to lurch forward in my seat. My legs forgot to pedal. We had only rarely talked about having a baby.

"Yes!" The boy stood up on his pedals and spun happily. "Yes! This is a very good idea. Otherwise, who will look after you and your no fields?"

The boy left. Mike and I rode on. The heat from the sun burned our faces and the tops of our hands. That evening, in our guest house, I asked, "Would you like to have a baby?" The bed had plastic sheets. We lay under a fan, still drenched in sweat.

"I wondered if you'd caught that," Mike replied. "I think we'd be great parents," he said, rolling toward me. "You?"

"Not right now." I laughed and pushed him away playfully. Wow. A baby. Here in Cambodia, it seemed so natural. I peeled my legs off the sheet and went to take another shower. The water dripped out of the faucet and I pondered over whether I would be a good mom. I had no doubts about Mike being a great dad, but I feared I was too anxious and not patient enough. Mike was right, though, we loved playing with all the children we had met.

The heat stayed over 40 degrees, and on our third morning of biking Mike had had enough.

"I'm frustrated today!" he said when we stopped at a stall to buy food but didn't find anything that looked edible.

"It's only 11:00 a.m. and we've gone over 80 kilometres already. You're doing awesome," I told him. "Here, have a banana." I grabbed one from the back of my bike and peeled it for him. Two cows came up to Mike and nosed the garbage beneath his chair. One chewed through a blue plastic bag and drooled on his leg.

I bought Mike a Coke that he gulped down. He didn't look well. His face was pale, but his sweaty skin held so much red dust that it looked like he had somersaulted the 80 kilometres rather than biked. Traffic had been heavy. Each vehicle honked and had become like a blaring horn shoved in our ears. Mike took off his helmet and squished the padding. Large drops of exertion landed on the sand. His usually bright blue eyes glazed with fatigue.

Even still, it was unlike Mike to complain.

"We can stop. We don't have to get there tonight," I sympathized. It was another 60 kilometres to a village where a Warmshowers host said we could camp.

"No. I'll go," he got up from his chair and walked back to his bike. "Let's push on."

Hours later we arrived at the property just minutes before the afternoon downpour. Our host came outside of an uncommon two-storey home to introduce himself as Jack. He was a big Scottish man with a bald head gleaming in the rain like a wet boulder. I guessed him to be in his late 40s.

The rain stopped and our footprints pressed long, bright green blades of grass to the ground.

"You can camp here." Jack pointed to a spot where wooden slats would spare our tent from the wet grass and coconut palms and mango trees would shield us from the rain. "And you have your own stove?" We nodded yes. "You can cook here." The side of the property had a covered tiled walkway.

"Come out front," he invited us. "The children will be home from school soon." We followed Jack to the front of the house. Puddles that were ankle-deep only moments before had vanished, soaked into the dehydrated ground. Behind us, the copper-red dirt road led to Bakong Temple, an ancient ruin. From there, it turned to the main road that continued 18 kilometres to Siem Reap.

"The track ahead leads to the kids' school and a community market," Jack explained.

Eight children approached. The boys wore blue shorts and white dress shirts and the girls wore navy skirts that hung to mid-calf and white short-sleeved blouses. They walked in plastic sandals.

"Are they all yours?" I asked.

"Nope," he laughed. "This is a foster home." I found myself intrigued by these children's lives and curious as to why Jack took care of them.

"This is Kiri. She's 10 years old, mute and deaf. Chea is 9, Sangha and Prak are 10, Leap is 12. Montha and Atith are both 13 years old."

They were tiny. *How could they be that old already?* I thought. They were like little dolls that would fit in an infant's bassinet. Jack stood like a friendly giant among them.

The children were mostly shy, but Kiri took hold of my hand. My soul softened when her palm pressed against mine. She pulled me into the house and showed me her bed. All the children followed and changed out of their school uniforms into light-cotton pajamas. They each had their own colour with matching tops and bottoms.

Mike had gone to get a deck of cards, and then the two of us sat on the orange tiled floor in the living space and spread out the cards face down. One by one, beautiful toothy grins surrounded us. They flipped up cards to match others, giggling out numbers in English while Mike and I practised our Khmer.

Days later, I poked my head out of the tent to watch the sun rise over the fields, casting an amber glow on the earth. I soon heard sweet voices filling the air like butterflies.

"Morning, Kat. Morning, Kat. Morning, Kat." I heard this eight times every morning and it filled my spirit more than 100 sun salutations. We had come for one night and had already stayed for six. We didn't want to leave. Jack had become a friend and his world had become ours.

I joined the kids on the outdoor patio where they played go fish.

"Good morning," I sang, and Kiri came over to give me a big hug. She loved to play the card games we'd taught her. We played go fish by holding up our fingers or by writing the numbers on paper. Although Kiri was deaf and mute, it didn't seem to limit her. She hadn't had the chance to learn official sign language, so she used a lot of her own, always making herself understood. And she clearly loved to learn. We saw this in the mornings as she skipped to school. She'd recently begun to say, "mum, muum." These were the first sounds Jack had heard from her.

Her smile was as large as all the other children's and her feet pranced in the mud when she spun around and around. She stopped spinning for a minute and grasped a short stick, pressing it into the dry clay of the ground to show off her written English skills to me. Her stick was short and delicate in her tiny hands as she pressed: *Kiri*. She pointed to her chest. "I am," I heard her silently trying to scream out. Crouched low, she shuffled her feet over to the right a little more to finish her next word with me: *Cambodia*.

I am Cambodia. She was right. Strong, determined and able to overcome major obstacles. Kiri liked to put her hand in mine. Her little palm cushioned me and my entire body relaxed to her touch. She tugged on my arm and I followed her around the yard. She pointed out a watermelon, proud of their small garden.

Kiri also idolized Mike. She made inaudible giggles when he came out of the tent in the morning and chased after him through the yard. With all the children we walked fields, jumped low fences and ran down dirt paths. We teased cows and played with ducks while dogs chased after us. Mike picked up Chea and held him upside down, dangling him over a mound of buffalo poo, pretending to dip his head in it. Chea squealed in delight and then all the other boys wanted turns.

I crawled into the tent that night, lying out on the sheet covering my sleeping pad, drenched in sweat and inspiration. Happiness filled my body to see Jack providing the kids with a safe place, good water, food and an education.

In the early morning, before Mike and the kids awoke, I joined Sothanya, a Khmer woman who worked with Jack, on her scooter to go to the market. She was tiny, with short black hair tucked behind her ears, and seemed as timid and gentle as a white-tailed deer. In the market, Sothanya settled at a stall and crouched on the ground. I stood beside her with a bird's eye view of what happened next. Now, like a cougar, she pounced on her prey, which in this instance happened to be a small fellow who sold coconuts. He squatted even lower, his grey shorts skimming the sand. The two of them screeched prices back and forth, while Sothanya shook, knocked and threw coconuts onto the ground, until finally they agreed on a price. We packed up five brown coconuts in a sack.

Further down the road, Sothanya dumped our coconuts onto a well-used tarp in front of an old woman. The woman's gnarled hands picked them up and halved them with one swipe of a machete – juice spilled and splashed my feet.

"The milk is only good in green coconuts. Once they're brown, the flesh is better, but the milk is bad," Sothanya explained to me. "This woman's coconuts are too expensive, but she shaves them for less than the other man." Coconuts were swallowed into a machine. The old woman cranked the handle and shaved coconut meat tumbled out the other side.

We continued around the market and I grinned as I watched her. Her bargaining skills were even better than Mike's. She bought snails at one, fish at another. While she was buying bread, I found a man on a bicycle selling iced coffee. The back of his cart held a large metal pot, from which sugary coffee was poured into a clear plastic bag that he knotted and poked a straw into.

I took a pleasing sip before I saw the tiger balm lady moving toward me. We had met her the day before, after Mike cracked his head on a low metal roof. Many in the market had heard the noise and the now dubbed "tiger balm lady" came to the rescue, layering spicy hot salve on Mike's forehead. Tiger balm is the answer to all maladies in Cambodia. It's the first thing applied at the scene of an accident – regardless of a gaping wound or a snapped limb. Mike escaped with his head on fire and tears streaming down his face.

I wasn't about to tell the tiger balm lady that, in the darkness that morning, I'd fallen off the squat toilet. The attempt to save myself resulted in hands full of poop, a sprained ankle and a large cut I was sure she'd have loved to heal.

Once the children left for school, we helped Jack with his community projects. Jack organized and built wells and huts for the villagers in the area. He employed locals, and volunteers from around the world, who paid to stay on the top floor of his home, provided the rest of the labour.

Jack brought us to a hut, where the owner, a skinny woman with a naked baby on her hip, had sadly lost her husband, who drowned while harvesting lotus flowers and lily stalks. Jack had recently built her a new hut on stilts, and she thanked him over and over before inviting us inside. The hut fit a small bed and a dresser.

Nearby, we visited new water wells and helped to dig holes for compost toilets. I struck my shovel into the ground and blisters formed on my palms within 30 minutes. I laughed. My palms, which in normal life bore callouses from lifting weights and paddling, were now as delicate as a princess's. Sweat poured down my face and soaked my T-shirt. I grunted with each shovelful of earth. Locals surrounded us, yet even with their encouragement, I had to give up the task when I could no longer hold the shovel.

Mike was still digging into the dry earth. His triceps bulged each time he picked up another shovel load. I gazed at him with a loving smile on my face, brimming with pride (and lust).

"You're not really needed," Jack interrupted my daydreams. I turned to him, tilting my head with curiosity.

"Look, there are lots of bodies here to help," he explained, motioning to all the people around. Many local men now picked up their own shovels. "Volunteers are needed for their money so supplies can be bought and permits paid for, not so they can dig holes."

I appreciated Jack's honesty. It suddenly made sense why it costs so much to volunteer in many parts of the world. Our value lay in our prosperity, not in our willingness to work. The real farmers took over and we became the spectators.

Five naked young boys were hanging around our tuk-tuk when we went to get our lunch bag. Mike ripped his peanut butter baguette in half and offered one half to the boys. There was no need to remind them to share with each other. The eldest patiently broke it into even sections. One of the boys held a baby girl whose tiny arms and legs were as skinny as straws, contrasted by an unnaturally round belly. The brother scooped peanut butter onto his index finger for the baby to suck on. They were very reserved but thankful, and we wished, as always, we had more to give.

Late in the week, we went to check in with Jack on how we could help. I felt tension radiating from him as we walked toward his desk. His large body had gone stiff and his eyebrows furrowed in frustration.

"I tried to bring a girl here to the foster home, but the woman who looks after her wouldn't let her come," he began. "I found out she's gone to live in Phnom Penh with her 14-year-old older sister," Jack paused. "So you know what that means." His hands shot up into the air and papers scattered from his desk. We didn't know what that meant, so Jack explained.

"It's sickening. Families are so poor they see no other way to pay off debt or buy food and young girls are sold. Some men will pay $3,000 for a virgin! The girls will be sewn back up so they'll rip again, until they're too shredded." He shook his head in despair. "They're worth less and less money each time."

Mike's body went rigid beside me and the colour drained from his face while Jack told us heart-wrenching stories. It was obvious that the years of trying to help people were hard. The struggle to transform a corrupt system that was unwilling to change had taken a toll on Jack. But still he kept fighting – I was awed by how strong he was.

We met the children on their way home from school that day. The rains came and they raced to the house to strip off their clothes and stand beneath the awnings and drain pipes to wash and giggle in Mother Earth's shower. Jack's eyes were still red from crying, but he smiled. It was a smile showing me his acceptance of the country he now called home. I could tell he knew he was doing all he could and it was the right thing, no matter how tough.

We left the foster home on a warm dark morning after placing two decks of cards on the table as gifts, and hopefully lasting memories of how to play the games we'd taught them. We gave Jack what money we could, but we knew it would never be enough. We moved slowly, our tires marking the road with imprints we knew would be gone by the afternoon.

On our way out of town, we stopped at Bakong Temple, the local shrine. We abandoned our bikes to climb it for the last time. Mike and I held hands on top of the ruin while the bright glow of the sun broke the earth's surface and filled the fields with golden light.

Cambodia changed me. It made me see the world anew: painful and sad, full of love and laughter. Mike wrapped his arms around me and I felt joyful tears slip down my cheeks.

"I'm so happy to be with you," I said, and rested my head on his shoulder. I could feel his heartbeat. I realized, with a smile, that after spending so much time with the children and realizing how tender Mike was with them, I was no longer terrified at the thought of having a child of our own.

New beginnings happen every day, I thought. Each day, each hour, each minute.

CHAPTER 26

VIETNAM
Zen and the Art
of Marital Maintenance

Vietnam is long and skinny, with a belly like a seahorse. Its eastern edge ends in the South China Sea, and Cambodia and Laos hug in from the west, as if holding on lest Vietnam swim away. We entered near the bottom of Vietnam and planned to cycle north. But, before we did, we had to navigate our way into Vietnam's largest city, Ho Chi Minh City.

Breathe, Kat, I told myself when I swung a right toward the city centre. Breathing wasn't easy, as we maneuvered among thousands of vehicles and toxic air. As I gulped for breath, my lungs filled with the fumes from buses, motorcycles and scooters. Drivers wore face masks to filter the smog. We had seen the masks for sale on the side of the road since the border. At first, I thought they were panties because they were folded in tiny packages, available in stripes, polka dots, cartoon characters, butterflies or skeletons.

"Mike, they have panties for sale!" I had exclaimed. I was quite excited since I'd been wearing the same three pairs for way too long. It wasn't until I opened the package that I realized they were face masks. Made sense really. *Who sells panties on the side of the highway?* The mask was lined with fleece. I slipped it onto my face and, within seconds, my exhales had me sweating at the mouth. It was too hot to wear fleece on my face.

I chanced a quick look back for Mike to make sure he was still behind me. I didn't want to lose him while navigating the roads in a city of nine million people. He was easy to spot, as he was the only person without a mask and wearing a tank top. The noise ascended beyond natural decibels with honks, beeps, yells and hellos. Motorists screeched and revved their machines in an ear-piercing current.

I ducked under a load of wood hanging off the scooter in front of me. *Anticipate every move, Kat. Just ride.*

I grinned, relaxed the tension in my shoulders and began to pretend I was snowboarding on a mountain slope with millions of other people, leaning into my turns as if carving on snow. I let everyone flow around me rather than getting pushed toward the gutters and curbs.

I kept my eyes ahead. I couldn't focus on all the blinking neon lights above the shops; they only provided the edges of a runway that I was to stay on. No one shoulder checked. I foresaw their movements as they deviated from their space and encroached on mine, their bodies so close I smelled their sweat.

A traffic light turned red ahead and I gently squeezed my brakes to match those of the person in front of me. Mike tucked his front wheel beside my back wheel and we stepped off our pedals.

"How are you doing?" Mike asked.

"It's kind of crazy fun," I admitted. "What do you think?"

"I thought you'd be having fun." Mike laughed. "I'm good."

The light turned green and we pulled into the frenzy again. A cloud moved over the sun and, a few minutes later, lightning lit up the streets. A crack of thunder followed and the clouds burst, sending down buckets of rain. I wiped my face to clear my eyes. The rain was cooling and welcome. Scooter drivers pulled off the street, hiding under the cover of awnings while the monsoon rushed down. We watched as hundreds of Vietnamese donned colourful plastic ponchos and the streets dazzled in a rainbow of reds, oranges, yellows and blues.

Puddles of water, soon knee-deep, swallowed our tires. Drivers who had pulled over yelled encouragement at us as we pushed through the next 30 minutes toward Pham Ngu Lao, the tourist street, and the chaos of District One.

The street was narrow and we dismounted to walk our bikes, negotiating a path through all the people. It was crowded with foreigners – eating rice and barbeque chicken, or walking in and out of shops. Lights from hostels, guest houses, businesses and restaurants blinked on and off. I tried to read them: Hotel Kim, ABC Laundry, Circle K, KFC. Hydro lines criss-crossed in every direction above our heads as if someone had taken an entire pot of spaghetti noodles and thrown them up, suspended in the air.

A tiny girl came to my side, reaching up to rest her elbow on my bike seat as she held up a stack of Lonely Planet books.

"Lonely Planet book. Good book," she called out.

"How much?" I asked.

"$10."

"$5," I countered.

"Yes," she answered and put down the stack on the wet pavement to hand me the Vietnam book.

"Thank you," she sang, and disappeared beneath the arms of another tourist.

Mike laughed. "Either your bargaining skills are improving or you just paid too much." I smiled. It didn't really matter to me. I was happy to have bought the book. There was still much I craved to learn about Vietnam.

We stopped outside a guest house. An older Vietnamese woman came to the front and shook her head at the look of our filthy bikes and drenched bodies. I cringed inside but kept a smile on my face, hoping she'd let us in.

"Clean, clean," she said while mimicking us to take off our dripping panniers. She picked up one from the front of my bike and brought it to the side of a wall. She turned on a hose and sprayed all the mud off our bags, soaking them even more than they already were, before she let us in. We took off our shoes and followed her up slippery tiled stairs to a room. She laid three towels on the floor, pointed at my entire body and told me to get into the shower.

I scrubbed my skin. Black oil came off in layers. Once I was clean, I decided my bike needed a scrub too.

I tended to ignore the maintenance of my bike, but it was time…which is how I found myself sitting in the middle of the floor with my legs splayed out and my front wheel laid over my thighs seeming to stare up at me, as if questioning me, what are you going to do now?

I opened up the hub, the centre of the wheel, and picked out the bearings. Bearings are small. They are steel balls, tinier than glass marbles. If you don't know about wheels then they may be thought of as insignificant. But these pieces matter. It's these small marbles that make a bike function. Make it run smooth.

I wiped each bearing with a cloth and degreaser until they were clean and then held them cupped in my hand. I brought them closer to my eyes and could see, now that they were polished, they bore battle scars. I saw life in their dimples, pitted and dented. It made me wonder about my own dents; chips that fell off a long time ago, scars to bear for all time.

I looked toward Mike, his body bent over and intent on making his own bike shine, and thought about our scars. He scrubbed it with a toothbrush that already had ten months of grease embedded in it, picking out pieces of grime from his chain. I rolled one of the bearings between two fingers on my left hand. My wedding ring sparkled from the sun's rays coming through the window. I thought how displaying scars doesn't necessarily have to be negative. They are signs of life.

I needed to carry my scars, never forget about them and digest their lessons. I had to put all the pieces back together and keep moving. It was necessary to learn how to glide after the dents (or, in our case, craters) were made. Forgiveness, love, communication and commitment: Are these our bearings? Can they help us keep rolling toward the future?

I put all my bike's dented bearings back into the cup, applied new grease and stuffed the wheel back together.

I came down the slippery tiles early the next morning to find our house mom, Biam, mopping the entrance. She wore a blue and green flowered shirt over loose beige pants. Her small feet were in gold sandals with a heel on them. I had no idea how she didn't slip on her waxed floors. Her hair, streaked with grey, fell to her shoulders. I guessed she would have been in her 20s when Saigon was captured by the North Vietnamese to end the war in 1975.

Before we arrived in Vietnam, we knew little about the country other than from watching *Forrest Gump* as he wades through the monsoon season in the Vietnam War. Of course, we knew about the war, but the first thing we learned from Biam was that many Vietnamese called it the American War. Our introduction was swift.

"You going to the Cu Chi Tunnels today?" she asked me. I knew what she was talking about because I had cracked open our new guidebook the night before. The Viet Cong, a communist guerrilla movement that fought against South Vietnam, had built the tunnels over a period of 25 years. It used the tunnels as supply chains or to hide in times of heavy American bombings. The tunnels are hundreds of kilometres long and, in spots, several storeys deep. The tunnels accessed a massive underground city with kitchens, hospitals and water supplies. They were a major frustration for the Americans and the South Vietnamese, who, even with their superior weapons, were still not able to infiltrate the tunnels with any major success.

"Yes," I told her, though I hardly looked forward to it. I knew it was something we needed to see, a part of Vietnam's own pitted history I wanted to understand, but I also knew the experience would be emotional. Mike came down shortly after and we hired a rickshaw driver to take us.

The Cu Chi Tunnels are now set up for tourists, and we followed a guide into a forest. "Can you find the tunnel?" he asked. Mike and I searched the ground but couldn't find it.

"Exactly," he said. This is what made these tunnels such a stronghold. He smiled, knowingly, then brushed aside leaves with the edge of his worn shoe and pulled off a lid covering the hole in the ground. It was so small. The size of my hips, maybe. I wanted to go in, and I did, for all of one second. But even though they had lit the walls with faint lanterns, darkness consumed me. I became claustrophobic and panicked. I couldn't do it and burst back up into the light.

"I'll try." Mike volunteered and slipped a headlamp on. I watched him crouch down and then slide his long legs into the hole, lowering his body to the floor below. He must have touched the bottom because he raised his arms over his head and squeezed his shoulders in and then the rest of him disappeared. I waited a few seconds and then a minute.

Mike finally came back up. "That's tight," he said while brushing the dirt off his body. "I had to crawl, and when I thought I should come back, there was no way to turn around so I had to back up."

"They've widened the holes here for big tourists," our guide told us and scanned Mike's body. "You would not have fit before." This tightness was a key strategy in preventing the bigger Americans from infiltrating the tunnel system. It wasn't until later in the war that the Americans set up a special force called the Tunnel Rats to attempt combat in the tunnels.

The Tunnel Rats not only navigated the tunnels but had to avoid the booby traps set by the Viet Cong. Our guide showed us hidden trap doors. "The enemy would fall onto bamboo spikes smeared in feces. If the traps didn't kill, severe cuts, infections or disease could." By the time the Americans were gaining ground in the tunnel war, it was too late. American casualties and costs were rising (and leaving Americans at home increasingly unhappy about the war), and they eventually withdrew, leaving the South Vietnamese to fend for themselves. They were soon defeated.

Mike went into another hole and stayed under even longer while I waited at the exit. When he emerged, I grabbed his hand to pull him up and didn't let go. At the end of the tour, we sat at the edge of an outdoor restaurant and listened to other tourists take turns at shooting AK-47s.

"Barbaric, wasn't it?" Mike commented.

"Yes, I just read that the Viet Cong, who essentially had the upper hand in the war, still lost over a million people. The South Vietnamese lost over 200,000 and 58,000 Americans died, over 10 per cent of them from the booby traps," I told him. "I can't believe you went down there."

"I couldn't have for long," Mike said.

On the way north from Ho Chi Minh City, yet again we were stuck in grid-locked traffic as horns honked from buses and semis while scooters drove within an inch of us, spewing clouds of exhaust. By the time we were on the outskirts of Ho Chi Minh City, with grey skin moist from sweat and pollution, I was again thinking of the resiliency of people, the Cambodians, the Vietnamese, us. How we as a species can learn how to thrive after such devastation.

I repositioned my right hand, which was still numb from the pinched nerve. The grips on the handlebars were sticky from the heat, the rubber melting into a gooey substance that rubbed onto our hands and gloves. By now, all our gear was weathered. Our fingerless bike gloves were faded, tattered at the edges and now ended just above our knuckles. The cleats on our shoes were worn smooth and popped out of the pedals often. Our bikes were caked in dust, the lettering scraped and peeled off. My bright red panniers, bleached from the sun, had faded to pink. Once waterproof, each seam was now held together by multiple strips of duct tape. I patched them more times than I remember. Our helmets, clothes, bags – everything – was disintegrating stitch by stitch.

Yet I was proud of our dirt and our tattered clothes. They showed how committed we were. I was pleased with how thin our fabrics had become. Their stories were our story. Besides, our spirits were soaring. The road had gone from bumpy and rough to level and smooth.

We were happy, laughing and talking, and we never ran out of things to say. I could ramble on and on (even at the worst of times), and Mike talked too. He told me about building tunnels of snow as a kid, and I told him that, even as a child, I could never go in them. He told me about learning to scuba dive from his dad, and I retold him stories about getting lost in the forest when I was younger. We talked about food. We talked about the future and where we wanted to live. We talked about other trips we'd like to take. It was as if each month, each country, we scrubbed off more skin, peeled away layers until we saw each other's core. We couldn't have known each other more.

It dawned on me that I finally felt in control. I wasn't bombarded anymore by shameful thoughts and feelings. I respected who I was and who I was becoming. I smiled to myself and enjoyed this pleasantness in my body and my mind. Finally, I was comfortable in my own skin! Relaxed even, which was good because the road began to twist and incline sharply toward crisp blue skies. Pine forests encircled large, emerald lakes near the highland village of Dalat. We breathed clean air again.

"It reminds me of home," Mike said, and pointed toward three children at play, all bundled in down jackets with woolen hats pulled over their ears. The temperature had dropped to 25 degrees Celsius, not exactly cold. We felt right at home and explored waterfalls in the area for a few days, but didn't linger longer because Zach and Elise, the couple we'd first met in New Zealand, were waiting for us at the coast.

Before we left Dalat, I asked the guest house owner to write "new road to Nha Trang" in Vietnamese on a piece of paper. Zach and Elise had told us about the new road, but it wasn't on any maps yet.

We stopped early to ask directions from a woman wearing a traditional conical hat woven from palm leaves and standing barefoot beneath a banana plant. I showed her the piece of paper, but she waved it away with a flick of her hand. Her smile grew into a bright red grin, stained red from years of chewing the leaf of the betel nut.

"Nha Trang?" I tried. She didn't read, and our pronunciation of Nha Trang must have sounded like we had a mouthful of betel nut ourselves.

"Nha Trang?" Mike said it a few times until he got the pronunciation close enough and she understood what we were asking and showed us the way, saving us hours of heading off in the wrong direction.

There was no traffic on the brand new road. Our tires glided on the smooth perfect pavement. I felt like an eagle flying. We flew over cliffs and beneath hills covered in coffee plants, dropping toward the sea.

At an overlook, we pulled out our picnic of baguettes, cheese and berries. I took a seat beside Mike. Our legs hung over the edge and we marvelled at the endless view of rolling hills and a patchwork of fields below us.

"I feel free and happy," I told Mike. He had a full bite of sandwich in his mouth, but I could tell he was smiling.

I continued, "Today's ride reminds me of when I was a young girl. Our dad would tie Michelle's and my leggings together at the feet and then hang us upside down from the closet coat hook in our front foyer." I laughed. "It was hilarious. My sister and I would have to grip the waist of our leggings and hold on upside down, laughing until our heads turned red."

"Life was easy." Mike smiled.

"It was," I answered. "But I feel like it's easier now, too, and I'm really loving it."

As soon as Mike finished his last bite, I jumped up, grabbed my bike and Mike quickly followed, chasing me around turns.

Life is great, I thought to myself as I pushed the pace, pumping my legs whenever there was a slight roll in the terrain. Mike stayed close.

Our life had been recreated on the bike. Sweat streamed along my cheek-bones and down the back of my knees, and I felt pure joy. I didn't relent and pedalled hard until my pace matched the beating of my heart. My quads began to throb. Mike was right there behind me.

As the terrain levelled, we slowed down to our normal, plodding pace to match the sticky heat.

"Hey! We've gone over 130 kilometres and you haven't had a flat yet!" I exclaimed.

"Now you've done it," Mike joked.

Wouldn't you know it, only minutes later his tire took on a huge screw and leaked out all the air.

I could smell the sea before we saw it. Salt wafted through the air and tickled my nose. The sun set swiftly as if it had been knocked down from the sky with a racket, and darkness came before we were in the centre of Nha Trang.

As we pulled up to the 24 Hour Hotel to meet Zach and Elise, I realized Mike and I would be losing our alone time together. I wasn't scared to lose what we had, but I was nervous about the change and how it would be to travel with others. The two of us were used to our own company. We learned to thrive in it. We knew how we would react to certain scenarios like hot weather, no water, lack of food or dirty rooms. I was proud that I was no longer frustrated when Mike couldn't find something in his pannier or was slower in getting ready. Along with patience and understanding came a new appreciation for how thorough he was in tasks I normally passed over. For example, his mind constantly thought about matters at home, like calculating our expenditures, mortgage, insurance, banking – things I didn't pay much heed to. Travelling with him had become easy, habitual and lovely.

At the same time, I was a little giddy to bike with friends. We bounded up the slippery stairs of the hotel and banged on Zach and Elise's door. They opened it immediately and Zach's skinny, strong frame wrapped me in a big embrace and Elise went in for one from Mike before we switched. I squealed. Another cyclist, Steve from New Zealand, was also there. He walked right over and welcomed us with a handshake to Nha Trang.

Once settled, all five of us circled around a blue plastic table at a nearby restaurant. Chicken bones and dirty napkins covered the cement floor. Slurping sounds echoed from nearby tables. The noisy eating was a sign of respect, telling us the food would be delicious. Mike sat to my left and wore the same dark grey T-shirt that had been commonplace since we left home. He ordered rice with chicken, exactly as I thought he would. (He had already eaten *pho* that day, his favourite Vietnamese soup.) I knew him. Mike was reliable and predictable.

Then Mike surprised me. Conversation circled around the table and it differed from our usual discussions. He expressed opinions on topics including the Vietnam War, politics and world affairs. I leaned back in my chair and I just listened. Being with others gave him the opportunity to engage in conversation so different from our own.

It brought me back to the very beginning: the first time I heard Mike's voice. We were 18 years old and I thought he was truly exotic because of his unique accent. (He had told me jokingly it was from travelling the world, but, really, it's a speech impediment. He doesn't fully pronounce the letter *R*.) I remembered how it seemed as if everything he said in those first months of our relationship I had never heard before. He mesmerized me. I found myself in love with him very early on. In fact, for years before we were married, I felt I loved him more than he loved me. And, perhaps, I had become insecure with that feeling. Of course, I wanted to be someone's everything too.

What I now grasped, listening to Mike engage with our friends in a noisy restaurant, was that Mike had always been in love with me. He simply showed it differently than I did. Whereas I would clasp him in a spontaneous hug, he would set my alarm because he knew I wanted to wake up early. I give and want physical attention, yet he makes sure to order the book I had mentioned.

Slowly, I was giving up the idea that he needed to show me love in the same way I showed it. I hoped, when this trip was over, I could continue to recognize the way he gives love, as I could see now it was thoughtful, generous and ultimately great.

I turned to look directly at Mike. His stubble had grown long and his face lit up as he laughed over something I'd missed. His blue eyes sparkled in the dimly lit room. Heat stirred low in my belly and I was excited to get back to the hotel.

I must have had a goofy smile on my face because, all of a sudden, Elise gave me a look that said, *What are you thinking about?* I tucked my head in closer to hers and welcomed the conversation with another female. Something I'd missed.

One morning later on, Elise and I walked along the shore, watching waves rhythmically rush in before calmly backing out. She shared with me one of the best pieces of wisdom I had ever heard regarding relationships: "I promise to never get to know Zach."

I picked up a flat rock and skipped it along the water. The mellow light of the early day reflected off the back of the stone until it sank. I stared at the ripples it created, expanding circles of current, thinking about what she had said.

It took three skipped stones before I caught on to what she meant. As much as I thought Mike and I knew everything about each other, I didn't *want* to know everything. I wanted the chance to get to know him each and every day. I shouldn't correct his thoughts or his memory just because they were, or would be, different from mine. (I was realizing I did this all the time.) Rather, I should like that he had his own opinions, and though we had blended into one current, we didn't have to agree on everything or sacrifice our individuality. There was no reason for Mike and I to be exactly alike as long as we appreciated our differences and found the balance between being independent and being a couple.

Elise continued. "There should always be space in a relationship where we both can have our own freedom to recreate who we are every day. Otherwise, how boring would that be, if, years from now, we were the exact same person as we are now?"

I hugged her and smiled all the way back to Mike. How did she sum up so easily what I had needed years to discover?

CHAPTER 27

COASTAL VIETNAM
Tied Together

The road along the coast of Vietnam appears straightforward. On the map, the line is thick and red, running south to north. We followed it. Mike and I didn't know all the turns ahead, or when the road we were on would end. Or, as often happens on long trips, when we would want a change of scenery. What we did know was whatever route we were on, we were on it together and we'd take care of each other. We were in love again. And when in love it seems simple to stay on course.

Yet there were five of us now: Zach, Elise, Steve, Mike and me. I knew welcoming others into our space was a part of the progression to eventually going home one day. It made me uneasy though. I welcomed the company but worried it would break the connection Mike and I had developed.

Steve woke us up early – before dawn. And he woke us with boundless energy and enthusiasm. I blamed it on the New Zealand time difference, but I knew he wanted to ride before the hottest time of the day. I began to think of him as our morning rooster, and, as the days passed, I felt my trepidation about our expanded group dissipate. Finally, I wasn't the only one persuading Mike to wake up early.

Steve was tall and slim, with light skin and short, curly, ginger hair. His hair was thinning in the front, like Mike's, which made me believe he was close to our age. He had a lopsided grin and a carefree demeanour that put me at ease right away. Instead of being loaded down with racks and panniers, Steve pulled a yellow trailer behind his bike.

We left Nha Trang together, pedalling north toward Hanoi, with Steve or Zach usually in the lead. Both were strong riders.

During our second meal together, Steve leaned over and eyed the pig's snout and ear in my bowl of noodles. "Are you going to eat that?" he asked with a wide smile that overtook his face. I smiled back at him and shook my head no. I didn't know how to eat those bits (or if you should). Ordering food in Vietnam was proving difficult. There were not as many roadside stalls as in the previous Asian countries we had visited. We soon discovered it was easier to order meals if other customers were already eating. If we liked the looks of theirs, we'd point at their food and order the same dish.

This day, no customers were in the garage-sized restaurant. Mike and the others took a seat beside a whirring fan, while I walked to the kitchen with the woman who welcomed us. The kitchen was at the back of the restaurant, behind a low wooden door and a faded orange curtain. A metal table took up most of the space in the kitchen, and displayed on top was the pig's head.

"We will have pork for lunch," I said to the chef, pointing to it. On the wall, I spotted long greens hanging from a nail. "And a salad!" Yum, a salad, I thought. The woman nodded her agreement. As per usual, we didn't know what would be served. My Vietnamese was pitiful.

Thirty minutes later, Steve expertly worked his chopsticks around my bowl. He pinched out the pig's nose and then went to work on Mike's leftovers. Steve's appetite was endless and my excess often ended up in his bowl. I had no idea where he put it. He was as skinny as an aspen tree.

After lunch, we rode by fields of green as if in slow motion. Way too slow.

"Does my tire look okay?" I asked Elise, who was riding behind me.

"Nope, you're flat," she said.

"Argh." I pulled over to the edge. It was my second flat of the day. The tires we'd bought in Thailand were too thin and not designed for what we put them through. I pulled off the panniers and threw them into a pile. A truck passed, the driver pressing down on his horn as he and his passenger waved heartily. The drivers always seemed excited to see us, but I always worried about the little attention they gave the road.

I brought my hands to my temples and rubbed them fiercely. The noise was relentless. The air was so thick and humid. I wiped my brow on my T-shirt, adding another dark stain of sweat across the fabric. There was no respite. Between the heat, pollution and noise, my head felt like it might explode. I imagined the others felt the same.

I told Zach, Elise and Steve, "We'll fix this. You all go on and Mike and I will catch up to you."

I didn't want them to go, which was why I was frustrated about the flat tire. Mike had already put down his bike, ready to help me. I knew Mike and I would be okay on our own, but it hadn't taken long before we got used to the daily companionship of others. Camaraderie and friendship come naturally to me. I wanted to share our relationship with others, but we couldn't keep having flats and slowing them down.

"No way. We're a fellowship now," stressed Zach, who started pulling out his ample supply of bike tools.

"Here," Steve said, holding out a brand new rolled-up tire. "Put this one on and we'll keep the one you take off as our spare if we need it." I took hold of the tire and my entire body relaxed. I knew then it was no longer just Mike and me. And these three had a plan.

We finished fixing the tire and I thought about the upcoming plans. Elise had a week to bike with Zach until she would go solo, west into Laos and Thailand, toward a teaching program. Steve still had another month and wanted to stay with us until we reached Northern Vietnam. Zach's plan involved riding with Mike and me into China, and from there we were hoping to bike through Tibet together. But that was still months away.

In the meantime, we had Mike's birthday to celebrate. On July 16, before the sun was breaking over the earth, Mike emerged from our hotel still wiping sleep from his eyes. "Never in my life have I woken up this early on my birthday," he said.

"Don't blame me," I smiled, standing near his bike. Elise and I had bought a large helium-filled balloon shaped like a Power Ranger. It was the largest one we could find. We tied it to the back of his bike and it floated back and forth in the subtle breeze.

"Golfing. I should be golfing. With a beer. Golf cart and beer," mumbled Mike.

"Happy Birthday, babe!" I wrapped my arms around him in an embrace. "We decided you definitely deserve Power Ranger status." His pretense at grumpiness made me smile, as I knew he loved biking too. I kissed him and hugged him again.

"Good morning, Kat." A man ran over to us while I let go of Mike. It was Lael, a middle-aged man with a basketball-sized tummy and a wonderful smile. I had met him the night before, when we arrived in the town of Quang Ngai. He didn't work at our hotel, and I never did figure out where he worked, but he was curious about us and couldn't understand how we found food without help.

"How was the cake I brought you?" he asked. The day before, when Lael discovered it was Mike's 30th birthday, he bounced down the street and came back with a large cake layered with white icing.

"It was delicious. We ate it all," I told him. "Lael, what are you doing awake?" (Only Steve woke up this early.)

"I want to make sure you eat," he said. "I go order you breakfast now." He turned to run away before saying, "You want eggs for five? Please tell me and I take care of it." Lael placed his palm on his chest. "It's easier for me," he insisted.

I nodded my head up and down. I watched him navigate his way across the street and talk to a woman at her food stall. I took hold of Mike's hand.

"Amazing," Mike said.

"What's up?" I heard Steve come up from behind us.

"Lael just ordered us breakfast. He's incredible. This country is incredible." Lael wasn't the only person to help. Many people along the way ordered us food and found us places to stay.

"Great! Let's go wake Zach and Elise," said Steve. I laughed because I knew how happy he was to be able to start biking so early.

Lael had spoken to multiple stalls on the street, and when the five of us folded our legs around the small blue plastic table on the curb, food was quickly laid out. We were given fried eggs, warm baguettes with shaved meat and vegetables and tall cups of Vietnamese coffee.

"Do you need anything else?" Lael asked. His face went solemn and I thought he pitied us for not being able to speak the language.

"It's all perfect," Mike laughed. "Please join us." Lael grabbed another stool, but he only had time for a quick photo before standing up to leave. "Everything is all paid for," he stressed as he bounded away, "so don't pay again or you'll be paying twice."

After breakfast, we went to grab our bikes and Mike found he had a flat tire. "It's my birthday and I have a flat. I should be golfing," he said out loud but smiled as he grumbled.

Zach led the way after breakfast. He cranked down on his single speed as the road we followed slithered its way up another pass. I pedalled behind Mike, watching his strong calves strain under each push to keep up. Once we all reached the pass, we paused to admire the view. The South China Sea sparkled below us and Vietnamese men fished from traditional boats called *thung chai*. They looked like large baskets woven from bamboo. The swell was light and the baskets floated like the leaves of lotus flowers on the turquoise water.

We rolled down the other side of the hill as the road carved a slit through rice fields. Bright green grass grew only centimetres tall like a shaggy carpet. Bicycles lined the fields, held up by kickstands and with their baskets full of lunch and water. Their owners bent over the crops, tending food.

"Kat, don't look!" Mike called out. There was a disturbance on our right and, before I could process Mike's words, I had turned my head. A man's limp body lay half beneath a truck. Dead. A dozen people stood nearby as we came up. There was nothing we could do. It wasn't the first accident I had seen in Vietnam. My stomach rose in my throat and I keeled over my handlebars. I could feel my heart thumping in my chest. *Life can be so easily taken away.*

Silent in our own thoughts, we cycled off the red line of our map to visit the site of the My Lai Massacre. In 1968, hundreds of innocent men, women and children lost their lives there, in what was later recognized as a war crime. We parked our bikes near a large white stone monument depicting a defiant mother punching her fist upwards while her family takes their last breaths at her feet. We entered a museum and read the horrible accounts of what happened when American soldiers had wrongly been ordered to kill. Mike took my hand and we walked outside, speechless, along dirt pathways and past remnants of homes. We knelt at gravesites beneath the Bodhi trees in the empty village. The sun penetrated the thick foliage and warmed our chilled skin.

Riding again, we stayed on sandy trails far from the main road we'd eventually have to find. The track petered out into sand dunes at the sea, where we stopped to watch fishermen. They wore loose white tank tops and sat cross-legged beside each other on the shore. Fishing nets spread out over their laps as they sewed holes. Life must go on. That was a constant reminder in Vietnam. Fighting was not the answer, but persevering was.

The ponds we passed were filled with splashes of red lotus flowers. The lotus flower sinks into muddy water at night and then rises above to open again at dawn. The Vietnamese consider it a symbol of health, purity, commitment and optimism for the future.

As early mornings with the group continued, I bugged Steve that he woke us even before the lotus flower opened. Mike didn't appreciate Steve's optimistic commitment to early mornings, but I loved it.

Optimism was something the people in Vietnam excelled at. We were never far from being reminded of the greatness of life, even right after death. Over the next days, the sombre silence of the My Lai Massacre site had been replaced with laughter. Laughter flew in from behind us like birds taking flight. Children leaving school met us on the outskirts of their villages and chatted amicably about everything: our bikes, our journey, why we were here on this earth and what we were doing in their country. I could only guess the words they were saying, but their smiles and laughter we shared.

Mike's shoulders visibly relaxed and his own laughter pealed through the air as he mimicked biking with only one leg. Kids often shared a bike in

Vietnam. One child sat on the seat and the other sat on the top tube, but each of them pedalled with one leg rotating up and down and the other held in the air, giggling the entire way. I slowed my pedal strokes so they could keep up and share their happiness with us.

Watching our group of cycling friends play with the kids, I shook my head in amazement once again at Vietnam. I had begun to think of the country as an elder, ready to teach us life lessons but too stubborn to learn new things like how to drive safely or not constantly honk. As with my own grandfather, I wanted to absorb his knowledge and be shown my innocence – but, at the same time, I was frustrated at his unwillingness to adapt.

In a small village, Elise and I went for a walk in the market. We dipped under worn tarpaulins and wound our way around dozens of women tucked in a squat. The area smelled of fresh fish, salt and fruit. Countless colourful baskets, piled neatly with mangosteens, lychees, star apples, papayas and jackfruit, were laid out on tarps. I stopped to purchase apples. When I was handed the bag and took a step away, I noticed a handful of ladies nearby. When we walked, they walked. When we stopped, they stopped. I looked at Elise, and her normal smile was now strained.

Elise was beautiful, with short, cropped hair framing her round face, broad shoulders and a flat stomach. Neither of us had much of a rack. The difference was her bra still worked, whereas mine was so thin it left nothing to the imagination. We were constantly being touched by people – and by touched, I mean grabbed. Mostly by women, but by a few men as well. We had been riding on back roads, through small villages where locals probably didn't see white women often. Especially ones who had been on bikes for months, wore dirty clothes and smelled like pigs. Even so, it was tiring.

Elise walked back to the restaurant. Then it was my turn to be the women's main interest. Most women were curious about my legs. I wore tight bike shorts and had inherited my dad's big Dutch thighs. (Which I love, by the way.) But the Vietnamese women were enthralled with them! They would grab, pinch and knead them like dough, many indicating they liked them. I didn't understand it, their need to touch me. From what I understood of their culture, I shouldn't lean in for a hug unless invited. As the weeks went on, and I had more butt grabs, I began to find the entire situation hilarious (I had to or I would have gone crazy). When I stayed long enough, and tried to answer their questions, the women opened up like lotus flowers themselves. They gave us compassion and welcomed us to their country, usually by making us more food. It took time to process all of these experiences, and we fell into bed exhausted every night.

The next morning, I told myself that all the brightest colours in the world were discovered in Vietnam. Everything was so vibrant, from the brightest pink, purple and red flowers to the brilliant green rice paddies ending at the sparkling blue sea.

The bike is the best mode of transportation, I thought. We were so immersed in the land, the weather, the people. Which was also exactly the reason why biking could be the worst. I failed to concentrate on the beauty as the grey road became cracked, potholed and ridiculously busy. The noise was deafening, and we all baked under a vicious, persistent sun. Energy seeped out of me as if my body had a leak of its own. *I shouldn't be this tired, even after 125 kilometres.* Soon waves of nausea swept over me and I realized I was getting sick.

Pssssssssst. My tire was flat again. *Argh! We don't have time for this*, I fretted. The sun was nearly down and we had 35 kilometres until Hoi An. I pulled over and paid a villager to fix my tube. This usually cost 30 cents, but I handed over the equivalent of a dollar and we all sat on the curb, melting, hungry and exhausted.

We stopped in a small village called Tam Ky, and, as the others ate, I went to the toilet. It was a cement block with no hole in it. Later, at the table, I slumped back into my chair, feeding my lunch of strange things to Steve, and tried to have a few spoonfuls of plain rice.

Riding again, I moved my legs forward but stared sideways into the fields. Not the ideal place for an emergency. Every rice paddy, small bush and ditch called to me to drop my pants.

The final two hours to Hoi An took every ounce of strength I had. I mentally scanned my body. My stomach gurgled and would catch me unawares. My legs pushed, and the pedals rotated, but my legs felt like limp noodles. The traffic was busy again and the shrill honking felt like punches to my head.

"Are you okay?" Mike yelled up to me. I couldn't answer and shook my head no. We missed the turnoff. Thankfully, Steve and Zach were able to find the correct road. I could no longer think straight. By the time we arrived in Hoi An, I straddled my bike, choking down deep breaths and staring at the broken pavement in front of me. The others looked at the map, deciphering where to go.

"Can you drink water?" Mike asked. His voice came in quietly and I had to concentrate on what he was saying. I shook my head no again and willed myself to stay upright.

"Keep your eyes on me," I managed to say. "I might pass out." My body swayed. I concentrated on standing but felt my legs buckle. Mike caught me.

My vision blurred and I shook my head to bring it back for a few seconds before I lost it again.

"Stay with it, Kat," Mike coached me. He held me around my waist and when the others found a place to go, we walked our bikes behind them.

The first hotel room cost $15. It was much more than we normally spent. I slowly lifted my head to smile at Mike, thanking him for not trying to find something cheaper. He leaned my bike against the yellow washed wall and walked me to our beautiful room, where I collapsed on the bed.

When I was healthy enough to venture out the next evening, we walked hand in hand down peaceful alleyways. Colourful, handcrafted silk lanterns lit up the sky and palm trees swayed in the light breeze. Hoi An was left nearly untouched during the Vietnam War, and centuries-old buildings, temples and pagodas were left for us to explore. We walked across a Japanese-style bridge and marvelled at the incredible architecture around every bend. In the evenings, lights from lanterns and temples reflected in the calm water of Thu Bon River.

Continuing north, my sickness diminished, but, unfortunately, Mike then got sick. After leaving the town of Danang, the five of us began the 21-kilometre climb up to Hai Van Pass. Zach rode fast, with Elise close behind him. Steve, who also wasn't feeling well, still climbed past me and disappeared around the curves ahead. I stopped and waited for Mike. I hadn't realized I was so far ahead. When he came closer, he looked skinnier than I'd ever seen him. His arms were long and thin, with muscles taut from gripping the handlebars. Despite his heavy tan, his face seemed gaunt and deathly pale.

"Are you all right?" I cried out, instantly concerned about him. He pulled up beside me and stood over his bike. His breathing was laboured and his back rose excessively with each inhale.

"My head is spinning," he admitted. Mike had been cursing his black T-shirt ever since we set off in Asia, and this morning it was already drenched in sweat. I looked down at my wrist. It was only 7:30 a.m.

"Take it easy. There's no rush," I said.

"I think I feel a bit better when I'm moving." He tried again, but he barely moved. A minute later, I told him to stop.

"Take off your helmet," I instructed. He leaned forward and I poured water on his head and watched it splash onto the pavement and evaporate. I fanned his body and wished a breeze would blow in. Mike took off his sunglasses and his glassy eyes stared obliviously into the horizon.

I looked in the same direction. The sea didn't have a ripple. It calmly lapped into secluded beaches nestled among rock coves kilometres below us. They were within view, yet out of reach. We still had a way to go to the top of the pass and Mike's body drooped as if he'd given up.

I went into survivor mode.

I dug into the pannier storing our fix-it gear and found a bungee cord to make a tow line. I had never towed Mike before, yet in adventure racing my teammates and I often towed each other. I knotted a loop in each end of the bungee. On one end I attached a carabiner and clipped it onto the back of my rack. On the other, I hooked the loop onto Mike's handlebars. When pulled tight, it would stay in place but could also pop off in an instant in case Mike needed to quickly separate.

Mike glanced my way when I began to unhook his back panniers to drape them over top of mine.

"I'm going to tow you," I told him. He didn't respond and just stood motionless, staring into space. "Mike!" I called him back. "If you need to release the bungee, slip your finger under this loop and it'll come off." I took his hand and showed him how. *Perhaps it would be better to wait or give him a longer rest.* I looked around again. We were alone on a quiet paved road in burning heat. Our friends were out of sight, but I knew they'd be waiting for us at the top of the pass. We still had a lot of climbing to do. *I have to keep him moving with frequent stops.*

"You can pedal if you want to," I said to Mike. "But, otherwise, just keep your bike upright and stay awake. Okay?" Mike nodded yes and my gut wrenched watching him suffer. I took a deep breath and kept talking the entire way. I wasn't sure if he was making sense of anything I said. I was only trying to keep him awake. I could tell when he helped pedal and when he didn't. If he stopped pedalling and let his lower body rest, I knew sleep would soon follow. Not caring if I was annoying or not, I kept up a constant stream of chatter.

"We've gone 25 kilometres since Steve woke us up," I told him. "We should be at the top in under an hour, then we'll have a break. I'm sure someone will be selling cold Coke up there." Many hilltops had drink stalls. I sure loved Asia for that. I chanced a look behind me to see if that garnered a smile from Mike. Not quite. But he wasn't passed out, so I kept going. "Did you know the top is the dividing contour between South and North Vietnam? I read there's an American bunker there. We could go and check it out. It's probably dark and cool and will have a great view." *We just won't think about what it was originally built for,* I thought.

Even though words continued to escape my mouth, I had a lot of time to think on that hill. I was proud of Mike for letting me tow him. It's not easy to admit when you need help. (That might have crippled some men.) On the other hand, perhaps some women wouldn't believe they had the towing ability. But I knew I was strong, physically and mentally, and Mike understood it didn't make him weaker because he let me help him.

Having that bungee cord attached to each other made me love him even more. It was like a physical representation of our relationship. Sometimes I was towing. Sometimes he was. Yet, most of the time, we were side by side together, through good and bad. How I wished I had let him help me when I was suffering in our marriage. I put my head down and pushed as hard as I could on the pedals. I stood up and, though the pedals barely moved, I stayed on them and kept pushing. Sweat dripped from my face and covered my handlebars. I promised in the future I'd tell him when I needed him more.

We inched our way together to the top of the pass.

"Is everything okay, Kat?" Zach asked when he saw us. "Can we help?"

"Can you buy Mike a drink? We need to cool him off."

I walked Mike over to the makeshift stall and he collapsed on the ground. I stayed with him. A Vietnamese woman came over and started fanning him with her conical hat. She reached over and grabbed my quads and smiled, chattering away. I pretended she was impressed with my effort, but perhaps she was telling me to put on more clothes.

When Mike was feeling a little better, I handed him a new shirt to put on so he could begin again in a lighter, dry one.

"It's beautiful isn't it?" Mike said. The words sounded as if they took so much effort to say, but he couldn't go on without commenting on his surroundings. I took that as a good sign. The panoramic view of cloudless sky and sea was endless, stretching in each direction along the sea cliffs.

When Mike was ready, he got back on his bike and was able to ride the winding road down from the top of the pass. Once on the flats, we moved slowly as the heat seared our skin and cooked us thoroughly. I put the tow line back on, and Zach and Steve tied Mike's panniers on top of their own gear. When I stopped because I was afraid Mike would pass out, they stopped too.

On one of our last breaks, Zach brought Mike another freshly squeezed sugar cane drink and Elise fanned him. Mike's eyes rolled to the back of his head as I grabbed him to stop him from falling off his chair. I changed his shirt again and he fell asleep for an hour with his head on the table. It was a massive group effort moving toward the city of Hue. Many times Mike was too dizzy to hold the bike up. I questioned my decision to continue, but when we passed another small village and I pulled Mike out the other side, I knew we were helping the best way we could. In Hue, Mike would have an easier recovery. More food options would be available, and, if we splurged, there would be a clean place with air conditioning and a bath.

Our friends didn't falter in helping us. In Hue, I stripped Mike's wet clothes off and cooled him down with a cloth before he lay down in bed. An hour later, Zach and Elise knocked on our door and, when I opened it, they handed us food. I hugged them both hard, grateful for their friendship, and learned, once again, we cannot do everything alone.

I sat on the bed beside Mike while he slept and thought about our friends at home. I realized how much I missed them. I looked forward to sharing what I had learned and wanted to thank them for how much they had helped me before we left on the trip. I knew I had leaned on a few of my friends hard. I couldn't have made it through that dark time if I hadn't. I lost some good friends too. And though I wish I hadn't, I knew they had the right to lose faith in me. Since I had forgiven myself, I wondered if perhaps one day they would forgive me too. As for the friends who stuck with me, that night I thought about how I would be forever grateful.

Mike's breathing came back to normal and colour returned to his face. I stood up to angle the fan perfectly over his body. I watched him fall into a deep sleep, fanning him long into the night, then lay down beside him and fell into my own peaceful sleep.

CHAPTER 28

NORTHERN VIETNAM
On a Mission

Hanoi's congested narrow streets overflowed with food vendors. Smells and sights collided with our bikes as we swayed among a sea of scooters. Rain poured down, locals barely paused to don bright ponchos. Our wheels spun in mud-caked puddles, rear brakes clenched as we skidded into the chaos of squealing tires, honking motorists and calling vendors.

We ignored it all. We were on a mission: I needed a new bra.

The situation was drastic – my old bra was officially ranked useless. If I reached my hands up, my brassiere popped over my nipples and coddled my neck, elasticity a distant memory. After ten months of handwashing, the worn spandex smelled like a mix of durian fruit, dead animals and a college dorm room. It wasn't even fit for cleaning bike chains.

Before resigning myself to the bra's fate, I tried embracing my inner hippie, but given that my shirt had also disintegrated, its thin material left nothing to the imagination. As I tested my new free-spiritedness, Mike raised his eyebrows and simply said, "It isn't proper."

The metal cleats of our bike shoes tapped along the shop's cement floor as we shook off the warm rain. My wet, worn shirt clung to me, and my hard nipples greeted the sales staff, right at eye level. "You need?" she asked. She was striking, less than five feet tall with a hard jaw line and beautiful straight black hair. My panniers surely weighed more than her.

I explained my plight using an array of hand gestures, pushing the limit of recognizable sign language. She seemed to understand what I was saying.

"You, NO!" Her arms spread in wide semicircles in front of her tiny frame, imitating a large woman's bosom; her English only laudable enough to insult me. "Oh, nooo. You too big!"

Mike laughed. I jabbed him in the ribs and threatened to go braless. The woman walked to a rack and returned with a T-shirt, thrusting me toward the change room.

"Men's XXXL?" I asked as I glanced at the shirt's tag. "I'm not *that* big!" Okay, maybe I towered over the majority of people in Vietnam, but triple-letter large? My attempt at self-preservation was lost on the petite woman.

"I think this fit," she said happily, as though she had solved the world's hunger problem, squeezing my seemingly monstrous build into a Vietnamese-sized garment. Unsatisfied, I crept like an elephant to a distant rack in the store. Water dripped down my bare legs, creating pools wherever I stepped. Then I found it: an XL sports bra. "Oh NOOO, won't fit!" she insisted. I tried a new approach. I took the palm of her hand in mine, patted the top and we became friends. I wasn't a monster after all.

In the end, I, her most corpulent client, managed to purchase a workable sports bra, a Vietnamese XL, three times my regular size by North American standards. (Victoria's Secret beware.) "I love your persistence," Mike said, smiling at me as we got back on the bikes.

For a few days, my hands kept absently wandering up to snap my bra. After ten months, it felt foreign to wear a new piece of clothing.

"Are you going to be doing that all the time now?" Steve asked after I did it again.

"It has elastic!" I said, amazed. "Do you even remember what it feels like?" Steve smirked at my answer. All of his clothes were worn as well. We stood outside of our hotel waiting for Zach. I tucked our passports with their new Chinese visas in the security pocket of my front handlebar bag.

"What do you think of the new tires?" Mike asked, probably to change the topic. Not only had I shopped for an undergarment but Mike had shopped for new tires online and shipped them to the Canadian embassy in Hanoi. I ran my hand along my new front tire, still a shiny black colour with a diamond pattern cut into the centre and grips that ran along each side.

"These tires deserve to be ridden," I answered. I looked forward to heading back into the country, riding again on quiet roads.

"And we won't have to wait for you two to fix your flats all the time!" Steve joked.

I was ready to go, even though I'd enjoyed the city for the few days until our Chinese visas were ready. We'd eaten a lot, went to a Vietnamese water-puppet show, visited the Ho Chi Minh Mausoleum to walk by its namesake's entombed body. Zach had taught us a card game called rummy 3-13 and we played countless rounds while drinking pots of coffee. In the few weeks we had been riding with Zach, I realized he was one of the nicest people I'd ever met. His presence was soothing. Spending time with him was like walking into a yoga studio or going for a massage. I felt better just being near him.

"There's Zach now," Mike said. I looked and saw him coming up the street. He walked quickly. His head was down and his hands were curled up in fists beside his long black shorts. I could tell by the way his shoulders slumped that something was wrong. He lifted his head and we could now see his eyes brimming with tears.

"I can't go," Zach said. "I didn't get the Chinese visa. Instead, they found the dates wrong on my Vietnam visa and I have to leave the country immediately."

"Oh man, that sucks," Steve said.

"Can we do anything to help?" Mike asked.

"No, I'm not sure what I'll do yet, but most likely I'll head to Laos to see if I can catch Elise. She should be there by now." Elise had left a week earlier to ride toward Thailand, where she was going to teach English for the two months that Zach was to ride with us. Zach rested his hand on my handlebar. He stood as tall as he could. I imagined it was an effort to not show how upset he must have been. I was devastated. It was as if I had been told my closest friend couldn't come to my birthday party – which, side note, was only a week away.

"Laos is a great place to apply for a Chinese visa. Then you can still meet up with us to ride through Tibet," I told him.

"That gives me hope," Zach said. "You should all get going." Zach hugged Mike and Steve goodbye, and then me. I squeezed him.

"I'm really going to miss you," I told him. While travelling, I found we said goodbye to people every day. It was harder this time though. It was unexpected and too sudden to leave a good friend. I felt him watching us as we pedalled away.

The city seemed busier than normal. The skies were dark and heavy with clouds. Potholes were full of water from the most recent torrential downpour. We kept getting lost. I slid to a stop in front of a woman who was manually pulling a gate across the road. She kept a small part of the barricade open for scooters until the very last second when a train chugged past.

I stood in a puddle up to my mid-calf, shaking the rain from the rest of my body like a dog, starting with my head and ending with my tail. I took a deep breath and expelled some of the sadness of leaving Zach.

Mike was just behind me and Steve pulled up on my left, splashing me with water. I flinched, turned my head to the right and glimpsed large, soiled pots filled with burning coal. Above the pots were small dogs roasting on metal rods. "Same same but different." I cringed.

Cars and scooters poured in, jockeying for the best spots but ultimately blocking both sides of the road. The train guard slid back, drivers pressed down on their horns, but traffic was at a standstill. I shook my head and laughed. We followed Mike through the gridlock, resting our hands on cars and pushing away scooters that came too close. We eventually found our way out of the city.

For the first day out of Hanoi, the road was flat. We pedalled northwest along the Red River Delta. The Song Hong (Red River) begins in southern China, 1000 kilometres away, and filters into this huge expanse of land, carpeted with rice fields irrigated from the river.

We biked 85 kilometres and found a guest house in a town called Lam Thao. The young girl working there offered to show us a restaurant. She skipped beside Mike until the end of the street, stopping outside of a large building. I assumed it was the town's banquet hall. Steve pushed on the heavy wooden door and we entered a large quiet room with vacant tables. A man came in beyond another door.

"*Ba lúa và gà*" (three rice and chicken), our order echoed against the walls. The man nodded his head, spun around on one foot and disappeared into the kitchen.

"Our Vietnamese is getting better," Mike commented as we took a seat at one of the long tables. My stomach growled and I patted it. We waited. Thirty minutes later, the man placed three plates on the table, each one yielding one piece of deep-fried chicken. We stared at the plates, but there was nothing more. No rice.

"*Bao nhiêu*" (how much), Mike asked as soon as we finished.

"150,000 dong," the man said. Mike peeled out the bills from his wallet.

"He must be too hungry to argue," I whispered to Steve. This equalled $10 and was the most we had ever spent for a meal in Vietnam. Our sandals scuffed up the dirt road back toward our guest house. Thankfully, we found a small store to buy packaged noodles along the way.

In our room, I dug out our pot and filled it with water from a sink down the hall. When I returned, I was hit with the humidity and heat of our small room. Standing in the middle and stretching my arms, I could nearly touch both walls. Mike had taken off his shirt and put it with the rest of our wet clothes, hung from every part of our bikes. He was now stretched out under the single bed, searching for an outlet to plug in our water heater. The heater was an electric element that, when placed inside a pot of water, would boil water within minutes. I'd never seen one in North America. It was probably not the safest device, although it had become the easiest way for us to purify drinking water or to boil noodles. A glass-top nightstand sat in the corner of the room. I folded up a towel to insulate the pot from the glass and then placed our water heater in it.

Crack.

I quickly lifted the pot and towel and found the glass cracked in half. It reminded me of setting off the fire alarm most times when I cook at home… but worse.

"I didn't marry you for your cooking skills," Mike smirked, and took hold of the pot and finished the noodles on the floor.

I felt guilty for breaking the glass. I tossed and turned all night, nearly pushing Mike off the sticky bed.

In the morning, Steve woke us up early as per usual. I found the guest house owner, still asleep. Her sandals were kicked below her cot. I bent over to wake her. I managed to use enough hand gestures to coax her up to our room to show her the broken glass. Considering it was still five in the morning, she was quieter than I had expected. She sighed and went back downstairs. I grabbed my money and found her back in her room. I handed her 100,000 dong (just under $7 and the same price as our room). She held my hand while I apologized, and seemed to appreciate the payment, giving me a hug and a tap on the bum before we left.

Steve met us outside and we discovered that Lam Thao was actually on a road we hadn't meant to go down, so our first pedal strokes of the day were to backtrack. When we arrived on the right road, Steve pedalled ahead for the first hour and Mike and I were able to bike beside each other.

"So why did you marry me?" I asked. We were coming up on the date of our anniversary.

"Because you used to let me sleep in!" he laughed. "Remember you would exercise on your own in the morning! Those were the good old days," he joked.

"I'll order dinner tonight," I told him, to make up for waking him. (It was the equivalent of cooking in my opinion.)

We crossed the river frequently and eventually it rose above a large, long reservoir dotted with bright green islands and sailboats. The weather alternated between extreme heat and refreshing torrential rain. We arrived in the late afternoon in the town of Yai Bai. I was exhausted. The ride had been hot and hard and we hadn't had enough food. Now I felt like my stomach was a black hole. Steve's bottomless stomach was probably gnawing on his organs.

The restaurant we found was empty and I walked right into the kitchen. The woman inside was sitting on a dusty blue crate, flipping through a magazine. She stood up and said hello. She wore a loose yellow blouse, blue cotton pants and green plastic flip-flops. I spotted the rice pot in the corner, a large white container with pink flowers. I pointed to it. She smiled and then scooped up vegetables from the floor, including one similar to a cucumber (but not), cassava, lettuce, mint and sage. She grabbed a chicken by its foot, sliding it across the metal table.

"Vâng làm ơn" (yes, please), I said. I left to the sounds of a knife chopping up the chicken. I sat down beside Mike, across from Steve, and rested my head on the table.

"Tired?" Mike asked. I lifted my head slightly, nodded yes and plopped it back down. I felt Mike's hand begin to rub my neck. I melted.

"Me next," Steve quipped, and Mike laughed.

"How much for the meal?" Mike asked. Darn, I forgot to check. I regretfully raised my head, slipping his hand off, and went to follow through on my promise to make dinner.

"250,000," the woman said. I assumed she was joking and I laughed. She began to yell. I jumped back as her large knife slammed into the chopping board, angrily dicing the vegetables. Perhaps she wasn't fibbing? I didn't love the bargaining process like Mike did. Especially as we moved each day, how could we know if what we were being asked was a reasonable price or if we were being taken advantage of?

"100,000," I countered in Vietnamese. Her face scrunched up in disgust. The entire time, she banged around the kitchen, adding sweet and peppery spices to two tall metal pots and a large wok. I realized everything was being made from scratch. I leaned against the wall. I was so hungry and the aroma wafting from all the pots made it worse. I cringed as she yelled. For a tiny woman, she stomped like a giant. The wooden floor reverberated beneath her bare feet. Billows of steam moved out of her way. I eventually figured out she was cooking us an entire chicken.

I imagined she yelled, "But you came into my kitchen! You asked for a whole chicken! Even the best bits of the legs, beak and neck, and NOW WHAT? It is not good enough for this price?" She and I discussed prices and portions back and forth for 15 minutes before Mike ducked under the doorway and peeked into the kitchen.

"You okay?" he asked. "It sounds as if she's tearing a strip off of you. I was getting worried about the sounds of the slamming knives."

I smiled weakly. "I'm okay," I told him.

"Thanks for cooking, hon! It smells delicious," he said, and then added, "*thơm ngon*" (delicious), to the woman. After a few more minutes, we agreed on a price of 150,000 dong for half a chicken. Once we began to eat, it turned out Mike was right. It was the most delicious meal yet.

Our hostess beamed. Her entire face and posture relaxed while she watched us eat. She grabbed hold of my arms, stroked me and patted me on the head. I decided she was happy with the price we ended up paying. Before we left, she gave my bottom a good whack.

"Why don't I get any bum slapping attention?" Steve pouted. I had no idea. The women of Vietnam seemed to hate and love me all at the same time.

We stepped outside. Rain came down like hail, hammering our bodies. Whatever happened to the soft rain? Lightning flashed, lighting up the dark road, followed a moment later by a crack of thunder. We ran through the rain with our hands over our heads to our guest house. As we rushed up the stairs toward our room, a waterfall flowed down.

"Oh no!" I yelled, worried about our laptop. Mike opened the door to our room. It had turned into a kids' wading pool. I sloshed my way in and bent over to look under the bed. The laptop was missing. My heart raced.

"I put it under the pillow before we left," Mike said. I ripped the pillow from the bed. Our laptop was there, high and dry. I took a deep breath and calmed down. The rest of our stuff was soaked. But this was normal. Our bags were used to being wet, as well as all of our clothes. The rain continued to pour in through the roof. I stacked everything on the dry part of the bed and began the process of moving rooms.

In the morning, the rain stopped and the heat kept rising. Mike's white cotton shirt clung to his back, soaked with sweat. We began to see entire thatched huts wrapped in corn, drying in the sun. Bunches of green bananas hung from tall banana plants and batches of laundry baked on lines. In the huts, the bamboo screens designed to cover glassless windows were perched open and children giggled and waved from inside. The girls wore white beaded necklaces and looked as sweet as sugar cane.

When we couldn't take the heat any longer, we stopped at a sugar cane and tea stall. Right behind the stall, a group of men swung pickaxes above their heads and slammed them into large rocks, breaking them to pieces. They never stopped. Not once.

Mike took off his shirt, twirling it into a coil to wring out the results of the morning's effort.

"I should have my towel handy," he said.

"Don't you mean a mop?" said Steve. I burst out laughing and it took me a few more seconds than normal to open a package of Oreo cookies we had bought in the city. My mouth was full when a woman came over. Without asking, she poured us each a cup of tea. She looked about five feet tall and wore a loose blouse with splashes of pink, blue and green flowers. Silver diamond buttons decorated her blouse and her sleeves ended at the elbows. Her black hair was knotted in a bun like mine, showing off her circular face, a dimpled left cheek and laughing eyes.

She pointed at the Oreo. I handed her one. She held it, looked at it, tipped it over to see the other side and then finally took a bite. Her smile twisted into something resembling a bulldog, and she began spitting the Oreo on the ground, emitting barking sounds in between. She wiped her face with the top of her shirt sleeve and thrust the unfinished Oreo back at me. I giggled and reached into my pannier for some chocolate-covered candy. She popped them into her mouth and then quickly spat them out again. She pushed on my shoulder and I tipped to the side of the bench, reaching for Mike so I didn't fall over. She was strong and grabbed my pannier to dig into our food bag. Her voice pierced the air, drowning out the sound of the pickaxes. She found our jar of peanut butter, twisted off the lid and stuck her nose inside. I pulled out a squashed baguette and smeared peanut butter on it for her.

She took a large bite of the sandwich. Her mouth opened and closed as she contemplated peanut butter. She brought her hands up to her throat and proceeded to pretend (I hoped) that she was choking, and then began spitting it out again. She yelled at me the entire time. Mike and Steve giggled like junior high school girls at a slumber party.

The woman snatched the teacup she had filled for me and drank the entire cup before continuing to spit out peanut butter. I guess trying peanut butter for the first time in the heat was pretty awful. I was now laughing too. She then squealed and grabbed a hold of my thighs, shaking them and smacking them.

"You can be insulted anytime now," smirked Steve. I didn't feel insulted because I didn't know what was happening. Was she calling me fat, strong, brave or awesome? Either way, she was thoroughly bashing me up and everyone laughed hysterically. My front handlebar bag was open on the table and she noticed the pictures of Isabelle and Anthony, my niece and nephew. I assumed she thought they were our kids, as she smacked me on the arm and yelled as if to say, "Why the hell would you leave your kids behind?" In between yelling, she poured more tea. Regardless, I knew we were providing great entertainment for Mike and Steve.

A medium-sized dog, missing tufts of orange hair, sauntered over, gave a weak snarl and stole Mike's shirt that he'd hung over his bike to dry. The salt must have tasted fantastic. The woman, Steve and I all laughed hard as Mike jumped up and ran after the dog to get his shirt back. The woman pushed me over to make room for her on the red bench. The red paint on the bench was faded and chipped, like her painted toenails scrunched up in her flip-flops. She wrapped her arm around my body and we pinched each other for the next 30 minutes. When we departed the stall, the woman smacked my head, grabbed my butt twice and held my hand. I hadn't been sure what to think of all this attention. Oddly, it felt like love.

Despite the fact that we were having a great time on our trip, all three of us were somewhat falling apart. My hands were still numb, and now my right knee had started to hurt. It throbbed on every pedal stroke, making my rotations slower and slower as the afternoon waned. Mike was constantly wet and changing shirts. The wet shirts and the vibrations from riding rough roads made his nipples chafe and they had begun to bleed. I tried to attach bandages and athletic tape to his chest, but nothing would stick in the oppressive heat. Steve also suffered from numb hands and, as we cycled further north, his back was now totally giving out.

We found a thatched hut we presumed was a restaurant. The woman who ran the stall helped us get cold water from a waterfall and then served up coconut popsicles. She looked at Steve and must have seen the agony on his face, because she motioned him to follow her to a single bed at the back of the hut. It was made from plywood and had a simple straw mat, which had a sleeping man on it. She whipped the man on the shoulder to wake up and then told Steve to lie down. The man who was woken didn't seem to be bothered. He sauntered out with rumpled shiny black hair and an open shirt, taking a seat on a small plastic stool beside us. He began to pack tobacco into the communal bamboo pipe. The pipe gurgled as he inhaled, and his exhales filled the hot air with the sweet smell of tobacco. A small puppy sauntered over, but even he was too hot and tired to play and passed out by my feet. Mike was wringing out his shirt again.

"Well, at least if we ever get too thirsty, you can have a drink from my shirt," Mike said. Even Steve laughed through his suffering on the bed. I was glad Mike could still joke around.

Nothing was easy. Finding places to sleep, ordering food, managing the storms and the heat. We were tested all of the time. We weren't the craziest of adventure travellers – many people do more, push harder and go further – but I knew not everyone could do what we were doing. And, certainly, not all couples could have done it together.

When Steve was ready, we continued upwards into the mountainous region of Lao Cai. Barefoot children moved water buffalo on the road using a thin piece of bamboo. A boy of about 8 years walked in front, holding a thick brown rope. The other end was looped through the pudgy nose of the buffalo. Another child, about 4 years old, sat on top riding bareback.

The views changed constantly between lush palm rainforests, cornfields and vibrant green rice terraces leading to the top of mountains. We entered the highlands and met people of different tribes. The colourful dresses seemed to change around each corner. We met the Red Dzao women (also known as Yao or Dao) who wore bright red triangular headdresses and who shaved their eyebrows. The Black H'mong became more frequent as we neared the town of Lao Cai. Their calves were swathed in scarves, hiding what I imagined were strong muscles. Their clothing was made from hemp, dyed a deep indigo blue. Bright pink, green and yellow embroidery decorated the sleeves of their long blouses, complementing knee-high dresses and shorts. Many of the girls had long hair tied back in ponytails reaching their waists. Their hair always looked clean and brushed, again unlike mine, which was sweaty, oily and turning into dreadlocks. Every woman seemed to have a woven basket strapped to her back.

The Flower H'mong women wore bright red scarves tied around their hair like a turban, and we stopped often to buy lychees from them. We would sit for an hour peeling away at the small fleshy fruit before pedalling again. They tasted different from previous lychees. They were sweet and sour. I was quite proud of myself. I knew in the past I would never have had the patience to sit and peel.

It took an entire day to cover the 38 kilometres from Lao Cai to the village of Sapa. We climbed the entire time. The rice fields wrapped the hillside in long loops as if they tied the mountain in green ribbon. Every rotation of our tires pushed us further up the mountain on our right, and on the left the earth dropped away. It was like looking out the window of an airplane. Waves of clouds, with lofty peaks poking up far below us.

Sapa sat on the edge of Mount Fan Si Pan, Indochina's highest mountain. Mist rolled from its spine and shrouded the alpine village in a dream-like quality. We biked to the town centre and stopped outside a large, white, stone church. There were stained glass windows along its length and a high bell tower above the front doors. The church was on an elevated platform and looked down onto the main square. The sounds of flute hung in the mist.

This area was filled with women, children and babies of the H'mong, Dao and Dai. They had converged in the square to sell their wares. The men and boys, we realized, would still be tending to their crops. An elderly H'mong woman came toward me. She stood only as tall as the handlebars on my bike, and she held an instrument that looked like a mini-harp. The wrinkles on her face, especially when she smiled, looked as etched as the valleys and mountains we had just crossed. I asked her about her instrument.

"Đàn môi," she said, and then put the metal to her lips. The sound vibrated with a deep guttural richness. Her numerous large-hooped earrings clanged lightly together as her head moved in time with the music of the jaw harp.

We applauded when she was done and she seemed so touched that she forgot she was trying to sell us something. I asked her to show me a place where I could buy fruit and bread. Steve and I left Mike with the bikes. When we came back, he was surrounded by a group of teenage girls. They were all dressed in the traditional H'mong dress. All of their heads were thrown back in laughter, hoop earrings swaying against their shoulders.

"Guess how old she is?" Mike asked me, pointing to a young girl.

"Sixteen," I ventured.

"No," laughed the girl. "I'm 21 and I have a baby in my tummy." All of the other girls laughed too.

"He said it's your birthday tomorrow and he is going to buy all of our crafts," one of the girls said to me.

"No, I didn't. I told her we don't have room." Mike said.

"Yes, you do. Right here." One of the others pretended to push a few purses into Mike's back pannier.

"It's too heavy! Did you see those hills?" Mike said.

"You're strong. And it is all downhill from here." All of the girls spoke incredible English. Sapa is a base camp for travellers preparing to hike among the rice terraces and to visit the hill tribes. It was the first week of August and the town was bustling with tourists – the first foreigners we'd seen since leaving Hanoi. I sat on the steps and ate a peach, handing some to Mike and the girls. Mike was in his element, bantering back and forth with the locals.

The next morning, I woke up early. It was my 30th birthday. The streets were quiet. There was not a person in sight. Even the dogs were curled up under awnings. The women and children had not yet returned to the town from their homes; for some, their villages were hours away. I found an internet cafe whose door was unlocked. I went inside and convinced another early riser to make coffee – and, because such things exist in a tourist town, I bought a piece of cheesecake. (It was my birthday after all!) I took a seat beside the window and savoured my first bite. I thought of my sister Michelle and of her love for cooking and baking, totally the opposite of me. If I had been near her, she would've made my birthday cake from scratch.

I opened up my laptop, punched in my passcode and then phoned Michelle on Skype. I wiggled my legs back and forth, hoping she would answer.

She did, singing, "Happy birthday to you! Happy birthday to you!" The reception was crystal clear. I smiled and listened to her sing the entire song. I remembered the beautiful sounds of the harp from the day before. Michelle's voice attracted the attention of the owner of the cafe and he came over to listen too. I couldn't believe it was only a year ago when I was desperately trying to make a change in my life. Mike had only just said yes to the bike trip, and we were rushed to pack our panniers. The shift that had happened in my heart and my soul, within one year of hearing that song being sung to me, was remarkable.

When Michelle finished singing, even the part about, "You look like a monkey, and act like one too," she asked how we were.

"Great!" I told her. "It's our last full day in Vietnam. We've been travelling with this guy named Steve, but tomorrow Mike and I will be on our own again and will enter China."

"I can't believe it's been so long! When are you coming home?"

"We don't know yet," I said. The word "home" echoed in my head. The meaning of that word was so fluid. I'd come to think of home as where we parked our bikes for the night or where we set up our tent. Home was no longer the city I had run away from. I didn't think we would ever live there again.

And, yet, I didn't know if that was because we were still seeking change, or because I feared going back to Canada. We didn't have jobs and had nowhere to live. Then I decided to not worry about it yet; we were having way too much fun to go home now.

"Don't forget to get it on with Mike tonight! It's your birthday!" Michelle said, blunt as always.

"Speaking of Mike," I said. Mike had just walked in the door and came right over.

"I thought I'd find you here." He draped his arm over my shoulder and leaned in for a kiss, "Happy birthday."

Michelle coughed.

"Hi Michelle," Mike waved at her through the screen. "I found the best birthday present!" he told us both.

"What is it?"

"We can get our laundry done! In a real washing machine and a *real* dryer." The speaker cackled with Michelle's laughter.

"Hey, we haven't had that for, like, seven or eight months!" Mike tried to defend himself.

"Laundry! That sounds like Mike!" Michelle said. I started laughing too.

We said goodbye to Michelle and left the cafe to walk to our guest house to pick up our dirty laundry.

"Kat, Kat!" we heard. We turned around and the same girls from the day before were running toward me. They encircled me and began to sing "Happy Birthday." Their voices rose in unison and the melody lingered in the street long after they finished.

"We were looking for you," the eldest said, taking my hands. They each gave me handcrafted gifts: bracelets, colourful pillows and a purse. "They're small for biking," I was told.

I felt like I was bursting with happiness. Their hands and arms wrapped around me, their heads rested on my stomach and chest. I felt so completely loved. My head and shoulders soared above their tiny bodies. The fog lifted and the mountains reappeared, rising behind the village. I gazed into the distance before finding Mike standing nearby. We stared into each other's eyes. His blue eyes lingered and I felt right where I belonged: at home.

"Hey! Me next!" We heard Steve yell from down the block. "Why does she get all the loving?"

CHAPTER 29

CHINA

Bouncing along the "Potato-Rock Road"

The thing about cycling every day is there is a ridiculous amount of time to think. Hours to ponder happiness. Days to think about being present wherever life takes you. Weeks to reflect on your relationships. Months to plan your future. If I added up all the time we sat on the bike contemplating life, my guess is it would equal 2,000 hours.

That's a lot of therapy.

It was August 7: our fifth wedding anniversary. We were no longer newlyweds and certainly no longer innocent about the challenges of marriage. We had grown and had gained strength and wisdom. Most importantly, we had learned how to forgive.

As we neared China, I knew we were one border closer to finding the end of this trip and to creating a new home for ourselves. China would be the tenth country we'd visited on this cycle tour and the 28th we'd travelled together.

We said goodbye to Steve. He was, of course, awake to see us off. I would miss his early morning energy and quick wit. "Be good you two!" he called out as Mike and I rode away from Sapa. We wore thin jackets as the road dropped down the mountain and the cool air whipped against us.

Before we entered the town of Lao Coi, at the boundary with China, we sat on the ground and rested against the trunk of a solid tree. I gazed up into the umbrella of foliage and sighed. I felt reluctant to leave Vietnam and still needed a few minutes to process the change we were about to experience. Another country. Together, we had crossed many borders and leaned against a good many trees too. The bark on the trunk was scratchy through my thin jacket. Older leaves had fallen off and lay strewn around us. It reminded me that when something, someone or even a situation is left behind, it will be replaced by something new.

"Happy anniversary, hon," Mike said, and linked his arm through mine. I leaned in, resting my helmet and head on his shoulder. It was nice how comfortable it was to be just the two of us.

"Happy anniversary." I smiled. Snippets from our wedding came to mind. We were married in his parents' backyard. His mom, a gardener, had designed the yard. Orange tiger lilies, pink roses, hydrangeas and soft purple clematis were in full bloom. Different-coloured paper lanterns and twinkling lights decorated a large white tent.

When it was just about time for me to walk down the aisle, I peeked from the corner of the house to see Mike, standing confidently in front of 200 guests. He wore a silver dress shirt. A calla lily was pinned to his black suit pocket to match the bouquet I clenched in my fist.

My sister had made my beautiful dress. It was fitted and long, made with soft white satin, and hung off my shoulders with an open back held together with laces. Our family and friends sat on white folding chairs, while munching popcorn from bags decorated with a stamp of Mike and I snowboarding. My dad's arm, linked into mine, held me back from running down the aisle toward my husband-to-be. I felt like the luckiest woman ever.

As we signed the marriage certificate, Mike's sister Nicole played the violin beside my new brother-in-law, Dave, who strummed a guitar. The music was uplifting and powerful. Perfume from the flowers intermingled with the murmurs of guests. When evening came, bowls of sweet strawberries sat on the tables. A large canoe filled with beer overtook the centre of the yard. The cake, made by my mom, was a delicious replica of the Colosseum, representing our love of travel. We danced with our friends and family until the sun rose, marking our first day of "In sickness and in health, till death do us part." (I was never a big fan of the last part of that sentence.)

"My favourite part of our wedding was the Slurpee machine," Mike said. I opened my eyes and was back to leaning against him and the tree.

"That's funny. I was just thinking about our wedding too. Are you only saying that because you're hot and want a Slurpee?" I snuggled further into him.

"Yes. My favourite part was you, of course."

"Why didn't we write our own vows?" I asked.

"We were busy. You were working and adventuring a lot. I organized a lot of the wedding myself. I loved doing the registry, but I'm not a writer."

"A year ago, I didn't think we'd make it to celebrate another anniversary. Especially being this happy," I admitted.

"I'm glad you stayed."

"Me too." I lifted my head to kiss him. Our relationship was no longer like a neglected, brittle houseplant. We had given ourselves nourishment and were starting to flourish as a couple. Like the rugged tree behind us, I started to think there wasn't much that could blow us over.

"Let's get to it," I said, standing up and brushing off my shorts. At the border, Mike took the lead. I followed him onto the bridge spanning the Red River and we pedalled into Yunnan, China.

"More tea?"

"*Shì de, qǐng*" (yes, please).

The porcelain teacups were tiny. They reminded me of playing tea party as a young girl, each cup holding only two sips. Mike's hands looked like a giant's, holding the little porcelain cup in his palm. I'd already had my cup filled a dozen times and hoped I was not insulting my hosts, two teenage sisters who were teaching us Chinese.

"*Qǐng, qǐng*" (please, please). The eldest demonstrated again, pushing the word through her bottom teeth to make the *ch* sound, similar to "chicken." We sat on mismatched stools, a bench and a chair. Furniture surrounded us, all of which was for sale. Every sign was written in Chinese characters and we hadn't learned to read any yet. We wouldn't have known that the furniture store had a guest house above it, but the two girls had been outside and waved us in.

They studied English in school and were excited to practise.

"Can you teach us how to count to ten?" Mike asked.

"*Shí*" (yes), they said together like twins and began to count, using their fingers. It looked familiar until number six, when, still using the same hand, they made a sign with their little finger and thumb extended and their other fingers closed. It reminded me of the shaka sign from Hawaii. For number eight, their hand took the shape of a gun, and for number ten, they held a fist.

"What is that?" I asked.

"We are counting," one said.

"But why with your hand like that?"

"That's how we count. How do you count?"

Mike counted to ten, adding one finger each number.

"But what do you do after ten?"

"Well, that's it, I guess…?" I answered. The girls went on to explain how, with only one hand, they can count as high as they would like. I laughed and suggested it would be easier if we just learned hand signals rather than trying to speak. By the time we left the next day, the girls had taught us to count, say common greetings and say "thank you" and had written down many sentences asking for food, water, lodging and to explain we were on our bikes travelling from Canada. We left the border town of Hekou feeling quite confident.

Within an hour, we were completely lost.

I straddled my bike, staring at the map. Mike, I knew, wouldn't be able to help. Not because he didn't want to but because maps and compasses weren't his strength. Most of the time I was okay with that. I turned left.

"If we follow the Red River north, we'll be going in the right direction. We can change course in a few days to go more inland," I told Mike.

"Is this the road?" Mike asked. I grinned eagerly. The road was ancient and looked as if it was about to fall into the river.

Mike and I twisted around the mountains in what I imagined was still old China. Heavily laden donkeys were travelling at nearly the same pace as us. I caught Mike staring longingly at a new road, a smooth fast expressway that wound through the jungle above us, appearing to barely touch the mountainside. At times, it looked like the entire expressway was built on pillars, or it disappeared into tunnels. The old trail we travelled on allowed us to feel every bump, dip and ridge in the mountains, and we wound around every corner of the river. Donkeys, horses and women carrying woven baskets filled with colourful produce greeted us. Babies and toddlers wore toilet training pants with slits at the bum, which I thought was genius. The day was very peaceful. Drivers didn't honk like they had in Vietnam. The only loud sound was men hacking and spitting.

It took two days to reach the town of Yuanyang. When we arrived, we biked up and down the main street, trying to decipher where we could stay, when a young man chased us down and invited us to his family's hotel. It turned out that waiting for someone to find *us* was the easiest way to find somewhere to sleep in China.

"Welcome, I am Feng," he said while leading us inside a three-storey building. Feng had a round face, with long straight black hair ending below his ears, and wore wire-rimmed glasses. Dressed in a polo shirt tucked into a pair of jeans, he looked to be about 18 years old. We rolled our bikes right into our room, which cost 40 yuan ($6.50). The walls were freshly painted light pink. A flowered bed sheet matched them, and a small window allowed light into the room.

"This is great," Mike enthused. I laughed out loud. Feng tilted his head to the side and slid his glasses down his nose, questioning my laughter. The night before, the only room we could find came with complementary cigarette butts in the bed and condoms beneath it. Showering involved straddling a squat toilet. I had to put lavender under my nose so I could smell something other than urine. Mike, on the other hand, didn't seem to notice it wasn't clean. In fact, I'm pretty sure he thought that room was great too.

"It's perfect," I told Feng.

"Thank you, I'll leave you now." Feng shut the door behind him.

Mike flopped onto the bed. "Ooh, it's luxury. There are no plastic sheets," he said, sprawling around like he was making a snow angel.

"As if you would notice," I bugged him.

Knock, knock. I opened the door to find Feng again.

"Would you like to have dinner with my parents?" he asked.

"Of course," we said, and followed Feng down the hall and into his family's kitchen. Five bowls of soup were set on a red tablecloth, covering a short round table. Feng's dad was already seated on a low stool and nodded to us. Feng explained he was the only child – the norm in China – and that he studied English in school.

"Please sit," Feng said. Once our soup was done, his mom brought out a large bowl of rice, another of cabbage, onion and eggplant, and one of thinly sliced meat, which I assumed was pork but wasn't certain. Feng's mom scooped rice into my bowl, adding greens and the meat on top. Feng's parents' questions were translated through Feng, but mostly we sat in comfortable silence and listened to the sounds of slurping.

I wasn't sure if slurping and eating loudly was a sign of respect for the food, but if it was, I thought I should participate. I made a circle with my lips and drew in a deep breath to try to create the right sound. Instead, I inhaled a piece of rice that lodged in the back of my throat. I coughed it out and laughed at the same time. Mike reached over and pounded on my back.

When I had finished embarrassing myself, Feng asked me where we were going.

"We're going to Jianshui," I told him.

"Which way will you go there?"

"We'll cross the river and go uphill."

"You're taking the broken road to Jianshui?" Feng asked, sitting up in his chair and pulling his neck back in shock as if I'd just spit my dinner on him.

"It looks like it will be quiet, and a nice ride," I said.

"It is quiet. It's broken," Feng confirmed. He then scooped another bite into his mouth, managing the perfect amount of noise. Mike gave me a look that said, *Where are you taking me*? He had totally given up on looking at maps.

"It will be beautiful," Feng said after thinking about it for a few minutes. *That's the spirit*! I thought to myself.

In the early morning, we said goodbye to Feng and crossed the Red River. In a series of switchbacks, the broken road rose above the valley up into the morning fog. All sounds of town faded away until we heard only our own breath. The road, once paved, was now cracked and potholed. It was perfect for our new tires and for keeping cars away.

My bike rolled beneath me as if the wheels were my wings and I was the bird. We rose steadily, soaring above the fog. We felt independent and free. I realized I trusted Mike entirely to take care of us if something happened. (I figured he could even learn how to navigate if needed.) It was pleasant, being there with Mike and experiencing the remote roads. I imagined riding alongside him in the back roads of China until the end of time.

We stopped, taking in the view, sitting on the fringe of a cliff. We overlooked hills and rice terraces while nibbling on pieces of bread. *How will we bring this sense of freedom, adventure and discovery into our lives when we won't be moving every day*? I wondered. Travelling couldn't go on forever. One day, we'll have full-time jobs and spend less time just being with each other. Would I find Mike's contentment with living a simple life boring or exasperating? Even though I knew being content was an incredible quality he possessed, I also understood it frustrated me. I wanted to make sure I wouldn't misinterpret his serenity as laziness. His calm demeanour was, in fact, a great part of who he was and something I had come to more fully appreciate after these months of travel. It was one of the reasons why I loved him.

We got up and meandered higher among rice terraces sculpted into the side of the mountain. Each set of terraces was splashed in a different shade of green: emerald, shamrock, sage, seafoam. The splendour of hard work was laid out before us. I had no idea how anyone could have thought this mountain was fertile centuries ago, but they had figured out what they needed to do to thrive. I knew we would too.

For three days before our arrival in the city of Kunming, our approach was heralded by the appearance of McDonald's fast-food garbage on the side of the road. We hadn't seen a McDonald's since Bangkok, four months earlier.

Our first stop in Kunming was to wash our bikes to free them of filth from mud bogs, dirt tracks and from horse and donkey poop. Our second stop was the golden arches. We propped our bikes up against the window and skipped inside. (Oh, the smell!) I shut my eyes, breathed in the oil and fries and was instantly transported. I opened my eyes and, even though this was the same food chain, the experience was entirely different. There was no resemblance of a lineup. I thought I'd picked a line and then felt an elbow in my gut, which made me stumble, and my spot was taken. I retreated back to the door. A small older man with a black cap and a limp came through the front door, shoved a younger man aside and squeezed into the middle of the crowd. Cutting seemed natural, expected even. I had no idea how to work the system.

"Oh no, don't stand between her and her fries," Mike said, laughing. I must have had a determined look on my face. I jumped in and minutes later we were sitting on the curb, sucking on the largest of Cokes and biting into burgers.

"I don't feel guilty at all eating this," I mumbled with my mouth full. After months of noodle soup, rice, stir-fries and thousands of kilometres, it was perfect.

Everything *was* perfect until we tried to leave Kunming. We wanted to head north toward the city of Chengdu, where we were due in a week to meet the friends we'd bike through Tibet with, but I couldn't find the way out of the city. We covered our mouths to escape the pollution and biked in circles for hours. Skyscrapers stood in the way of pasture land, vehicles instead of terraces. My stomach felt empty. I was starving but ignored it. *We're lost.* I stopped, pulled out the compass and held it in my shaky palm. I spun around, pointing northeast.

"I'm pretty sure it's that way," Mike said, pointing a different direction. I glared at him. *How would he know?* I was the one attempting to match up railway tracks on the ground to those marked on the map. I was the one who spent an hour planning a route the night before. The noise and pollution of the city filled my head, and hunger dulled my senses. The patience I had worked so hard on for the past year evaporated.

"Fine, you navigate!" I thrust the map into Mike's hands. *It would be so much easier if he could just do it,* I told myself. Alex could navigate. I dropped my bike on the ground and slumped down beside it.

Damn it, Kat, don't bring Alex into this.

I took my helmet off and covered my eyes with my hands, hoping Mike couldn't read my mind.

"You're hangry," Mike said, his voice even and composed. "We're not going anywhere else until you eat something. Stay right here; I'll be back." I sat on the dirty pavement beside my bike feeling crushed. Motorcycles rushed past. It was noisy, but I felt invisible and homeless. Tears slid down my cheeks. It was our first argument in a long time. Well, not even a proper argument, but it was the first time I'd gotten angry.

Alex would have yelled back at me, I realized.

Mike was gone for 20 minutes and returned with noodle soup. We slurped in silence. Mike would never bring it up again, never even look for an apology from me. I knew that, to him, the disagreement was already over.

"I'm sorry," I apologized. "You were right. I was just bothered and hungry. Sometimes it's difficult when I don't know the way or when we'll get to where we're going." I chewed on my bottom lip and wiped my hands on my shorts. "I'm good now," I said. "It makes me happy you know me so well."

"It'll be okay, Kat. We'll keep asking for help and we'll figure out the way." We did. Numerous people helped with directions out of the city and, eventually, we found a quiet road. Pomegranates grew in the ditches. They were bright pink and beautiful. Mike broke one open for us and we scooped out the sweet seeds. Our hands became stained with red, and I wondered if our future would always be this way: perfection and then frustration, impatience and then devotion. I decided it would be. And taking the lesson Mike had imparted earlier in our day, I also decided that everything would be okay.

The next morning, we went to breakfast at a noodle shop. Large blackened pots rested over coal fires. Containers filled with chopsticks hung over the pots to be sanitized with the rising steam. There was a chill in the morning air and I yearned to warm my hands in the heat. We stood in a fast-moving line and chose from four options of noodles. I decided on the widest ones and Mike picked the skinniest. A woman scooped noodles into two deep bowls, covering them in broth, green onions, pork and bok choy. We also helped ourselves to dough dumplings to dip in hot soybean milk. Mike sat across from me, and we relaxed amid the noise of water gurgling from the pots and slurps from satisfied customers. Businessmen reclined, enjoying breakfast and cigarettes while their shoes were being shined. Children smiled at us between large mouthfuls of noodles. A tiny woman filled our tea every time we took a sip.

Once we were full, Mike asked, "Where do you have us going today?"

"Another broken road," I said happily.

"Seriously?"

"Once in a while it gets close to the expressway that goes to Chengdu, but otherwise it'll be remote. It looks nice."

"Sounds good. Camping tonight?"

"I hope so. It's probably too far to make it to the next town."

"I still can't find where all my warm clothes went," Mike said. "I wrote to your mom again yesterday." Mike was sure he'd sent home a bag of clothes after New Zealand to store at my parents' house. But no one knew where the bag was. "I'd really like to have them for Tibet. I'm pretty sure it'll be cold."

"You might have to buy some in Chengdu," I said.

"Another shopping experience." Mike laughed and finished off the rest of his soup by bringing the bowl to his mouth. He slurped loudly and didn't choke.

We ensured our panniers were on tight and made our way to the back road. It was instantly quiet. The road disappeared into the hills and we rose up and down like we were on a teeter-totter. Our conversations circled around Mike's clothes, returning home, our upcoming ride through Tibet and the scenery. Rice and potato fields pockmarked the land. By the afternoon, the road surface changed to cobblestone. I gripped my handlebars tighter and smiled wider. I loved it. The fields had been scoured by hand. Any stone too large had been brought to the road and pounded down by hooves and wagons over the centuries. It took a lot of effort to maneuver our wheels over the potato-sized rocks, but the road to me was fun – my perfect playground. It was challenging and my giggles erupted in spurts and jumps. We climbed higher and higher into the clouds.

The front end of Mike's bike wobbled and I watched his arms strain to hold the bike straight. "Something isn't right with my wheel," he said as he pulled to a stop. Stopping was quick, since we were hardly moving anyway. Our pace had diminished and I knew I could run faster.

Mike removed his panniers from the racks and then lifted the front end of his bike to spin the wheel. It rotated, but the wobble in it spun off kilter like space saucers at an amusement park. It was enough to make one dizzy. I dug through the fix-it pannier, found the spoke wrench and handed it to Mike. Sitting down on the stones and stretching my arms to grasp my toes, I watched him tighten and loosen spokes, straightening his rim. It was a constant exercise of give and take.

"We haven't made it very far today," I commented, though I wasn't concerned. I looked forward to sleeping in our tent. Once Mike's rim was straighter, we rode for a few more hours. Our speed decreased further and in six hours of pedalling we only travelled 30 kilometres.

"We'll have to find water before we can camp," I said to Mike.

"I know, I've been keeping my eye out for anything, but no one has even passed us for hours." The hills were parched and looked like they could use a drink themselves. The clouds taunted us, but no moisture fell. The sun began its descent and the skies darkened. Moments before everything turned black, Mike spotted a goat farmer moving his animals to another pasture. We rode toward him and, thankfully, he filled our bottles from a large drum of water.

Further up around the corner the ground levelled, if only for a minute, and off to our left was enough shrubbery to hide our tent.

I helped Mike set up the tent before I lit the stove. A cold breeze picked up. A shiver ran through my body and I slipped on my puffy jacket. I hadn't used it for months. After a few minutes, I even dug into the depths of my cold weather bag for my toque. Mike was in the tent, spreading out our mats and clipping them together. I stared upwards; the clouds had dispersed and faint stars sparkled across the night sky. *Home is where we zip our sleeping bags together*, I thought.

"Do you want to use my fleece jacket?" I called out to Mike. I didn't have many extra clothes, but I at least had this to help keep him warm.

"I'm sure I have another long-sleeve. Can you toss me that pannier?" he asked while pointing to the grey pannier still attached to the front of his bike.

"Sure," I got up from where I had started the stove.

"Here you go," I said, tossing it through the open door of the tent.

Back in front of the stove, I opened two packages of noodles, dumping them into the pot. Mike began to laugh.

"What's so funny?" I asked. His laughter was now echoing through the hills. I imagined all the farmer's goats running down the valley, away from Mike's bellowing laugh.

"I found all of the clothes I thought I sent home to your mom. They've been here the entire time! My long underwear, thick socks, black long-sleeve and my jacket! I haven't dug to the bottom of this pannier in six months, but here it all is!"

Mike continued to laugh. I just shook my head. As much as I had come to understand how Mike's mind worked, I couldn't fathom how he found it impossible to remember what was in his panniers – especially when he could remember what the price of cauliflower was in 1998! Mike came out of the tent wearing his red puffy jacket and blue toque. He walked over to me and wrapped his arms around my shoulders.

"See, I'm organized," he gloated, and planted a kiss on my cheek.

In the morning, we woke up in a cloud. We could only see each other and the rocks right beneath our bikes. It was like being in our own bubble. After an hour, a faint orange glow brightened the sky as, little by little, the fog dispersed. Biking on the "potato-rock road" (as we began to call it) was an incredibly slow process. Mountains rolled out in the distance, ridges outlined in hues of purples, blues and greys. We rode past fields of golden corn and jade-coloured rice. Brilliant yellow flowers carpeted the edge of the road.

My mouth was parched. We had drastically rationed our water. We hadn't brushed our teeth or made coffee, the most significant sacrifice (the coffee, not the clean teeth). We munched on crackers. After another hour, a home revealed itself in the distance and we sped up. A giant bee buzzed passed me. And then another. Soon bees were hitting my cheeks.

"Kat, it's a beekeeper. I can't stop!" Mike yelled. The last time Mike was stung on his hand, the swelling extended to his neck. He bounced past me and took off his helmet, releasing bees that had flown into the vents. I closed my mouth and willed my legs to go faster. I didn't want to think what could happen way out here. We made it clear of the bees a few minutes later. I took a deep breath. Mike hadn't been stung and we were alone again. Our bikes rattled. The adrenaline made me thirstier.

Several thousand jolts later, we came across another home. A brick fence encircled the little house made out of orange brick and mud. It had a tiled roof and holes for a window and door, through which I could see a fire burning and a kettle. I pulled out our pot, two packages of noodles and opened the fence. Chickens, cows and pigs all stopped eating and stared at me. An elderly couple busied themselves in the kitchen, but they didn't hear me until I was standing in their doorway. The woman wore a purple blouse with a black vest. Her hair was pinned up and hidden under a light blue cap. She noticed me first and had a sharp intake of breath. I held out our pot and noodles. The motion she then made would have been mistaken for being shooed away in North America, but I'd begun to recognize that perhaps it was a form of welcoming. I wasn't sure, but Mike and I needed water.

"*Shooie?*" (water), I asked. The man reached over to his kettle, wrapped a cloth around the handle and then walked to me to pour water in our pot.

"*Xièxiè*" (thank you), I whispered. My entire body relaxed. The couple came with me as I walked back to Mike and the bikes. I handed the pot to Mike and I grabbed our water bladder. The man brought over a large bucket of water and filled every container we had. When he finished, the couple seemed more comfortable with us two dirty, ragged, starving cyclists and invited us into their yard. The man disappeared and came back with a low wooden stool and placed it in the middle of the tiny yard. Mike took a seat. I then saw the woman walking toward us with each hand wrapped around shorter stools. "Mike, you're sitting on the table!" I said quickly. The woman noticed Mike jump up and began to chuckle.

When we settled onto the proper stools, the couple, seemingly now at ease with our presence, invited us inside. To the right of the door was the pigpen and to the left was the kitchen, complete with a coal fire. Only a tiny amount of light came through the one window and door. I blinked as my eyes adjusted to being indoors.

The home was small and had no electricity. The floor was bare ground swept clean. Mike helped carry the table and stools inside and we sat down again with our pot of noodles. The woman took our forks right from our hands and handed us chopsticks instead. She offered up four large bowls of rice and, within minutes, covered the table with massive dishes of salted fried pork, stewed vegetables, boiled potatoes and chilies (which we managed to avoid). The food was spicy and delicious and all four of us ate and ate. Mike offered our pot of noodles to the woman. Her face shrivelled into a look of disgust, which could have meant, "That is peasant food, and I do not intend to try it." Every time we managed to make a dent in our bowls, they were quickly filled again.

It was peaceful inside. We made soft murmurs of contentment, but no extra effort was made to converse. All we needed were smiles and slurps. I felt they would have shared anything to make sure we were happy. I imagined Mike and I 30 years from now, taking in people from the street to feed with the same generosity we were given by the couple. I realized, of course, I didn't know anything about their lives. I was just a Westerner ducking through their front door. Yet we were invited in, and for that I felt grateful.

Half an hour of gorging ourselves later, I stood to help clean up. The leftover food, including our noodles, went into a big bucket in the corner. The woman and I lifted the bucket together, walked it out to the pigs and dumped the slop over their wall. She showed me a different water bucket to wash our pot with while she made tea. We sat back down. The pigs rustled and burped as we sipped in silence. It was serene. When it was time for us to go, the two of them stood at their gate and waved goodbye.

In the late afternoon, our potato-rock road crossed beneath an expressway.

"Kat, we're going to have to get off of here, or we're not going to make it anywhere," Mike said.

"But we're not allowed on the expressway," I pointed out. There was an undeniable sign that said no bikes.

"I think we should give it a go."

"I like the potato-rock road."

"We've gone only 70 kilometres in two days!" Mike said. "Our bikes are rattled, and I swear my teeth are going to fall out if we get tossed around anymore. Plus, we're running out of food." Food. That was a good point. I followed Mike up the ramp heading to the expressway. Even going uphill, the pavement felt fast. We flew past the toll booth, the barricade and then the second sign with a bike and a slash through it. We smiled and waved at the men manning the gate. They stood up and waved back. I was nervous to break the rules and bike on the freeway.

"Mike, look ahead!" I spotted a police car and officers standing outside of it. I slowed down, ready to turn around. Mike did the opposite. He sped ahead. (Anything to not go back to the potato-rock road.)

"Come on, Kat," he encouraged me. It was a brake-test zone for trucks. Over a dozen police officers were there. My heart sped, and then I heard them calling us. I listened.

"Are they cheering us on?" I asked.

"Sounds like it!" We biked past the cheering officers and onto the main highway.

"Whew, just made it through that one Kat," Mike said sarcastically, wiping his hand across his brow to stress my ridiculousness. *Humph.* Apparently, no one cared where we rode.

The expressway was much faster. The road took the straightest line possible, even tunnelling through a mountain.

When we made it to the town of Daibu, Mike chose the third guest house he looked at. I found a post to lean the bikes against, then grabbed our lock and crouched down to slip the cable between the spokes of the back tires. Mike's bike was on the outside, and my eyes locked in on long cracks between his spokes.

"Mike, come have a look at this!" I called. I then looked at my bike and found the same thing. Three spider cracks had appeared in the middle of the rim with the potential that the spoke needles would pull through or the rim could split altogether.

"We certainly won't be getting back on the potato-rock road," Mike said.

"I don't think we're going anywhere," I answered.

"Let's see if a bus comes here." We walked to the main street in town in search of an internet cafe. The sky was already dark. A man saw us and invited us into his house to use his computer. Mike brought up Babel Fish, an online language translator, and we learned the man's name was Wang. Mike asked Wang if a bus stopped nearby by typing the question in English and then having it translated into Mandarin. The computer-generated translations didn't always make sense. Wang typed back and what popped up was, "You still have to spend the night tomorrow, now go away."

Mike's brow furrowed in concentration. "I think he's asking if we're leaving now or if we have time for dinner," he said.

"Charades is much easier than Babel Fish," I laughed. Mike and Wang seemed to be enjoying themselves, so I settled in to read my book while they conversed for an hour. I wasn't anxious about the bikes. I knew we'd figure something out. Any concerns were set aside when Wang brought us down the street to a restaurant and ordered large amounts of food. Rice, greens, what seemed like half a cow and six large potatoes each. Wang sat with us, smiling the entire time, but would not eat himself. Mike and I clutched our bulging stomachs on the way out.

In the morning, we caused all work to stop in town as many people attempted to help find us a ride. Pigs and chickens explored the pile of panniers while we hung out. Three taxi-vans were waved down, but the drivers seemed shy or maybe thought we were too much trouble. Two buses stopped but would not take our bikes. The third bus tried, but the storage underneath was too small and we weren't allowed to bring them inside.

"Let's try to hitchhike," I said to Mike. He was already sweating and dusty from the effort of trying to get our bikes into multiple vehicles.

"Where are we going to hitchhike to?"

"It doesn't matter. If we go north, we'll get to Chengdu. If we go south, we'll go back to Kunming. Both places have great bike shops where we can get new wheels made."

We waved goodbye to everyone who tried to help. I didn't know if they knew we were going to try and hitchhike.

Close to Daibu on the side of the expressway was a gas station. We pulled into the parking lot. I stood near the exit and waved down the first vehicle I saw. It was a minivan. The driver was probably in his early 30s and a beautiful woman of similar age sat in the passenger seat.

"Kunming?" I asked while pointing to the Chinese characters naming the city on my map. The couple's head movements seemed like a yes. I pointed toward Mike and the bikes. The driver's face lit up as soon as he saw the bikes and he quickly backed up. I ran after him and by the time I arrived he had the trunk open. Mike and I pulled off both sets of wheels. I held up Mike's back wheel and showed him the cracks. He nodded again. *Good, I didn't want him to think we were just lazy.* We stuffed our bike frames, wheels and panniers inside.

I gripped the side of my seat as he peeled out of the parking lot. The wheels on the minivan squealed. He held a cellphone to his ear with one hand while the other pinched a cigarette and casually rested on the steering wheel between puffs and changing gears. We sped around blind corners, and every other second he honked the horn. We drove past a landslide. The van's wheels slid beneath us as we slipped sideways across the road.

"My name is Katrina," I said, tapping my chest, pulling my eyes away from the drop into the canyon down below and onto the young woman up front. "We are from Cha-na-da." She seemed calm, unruffled. Her skin was smooth and she had shy brown eyes.

"No English, no English," she said.

"Your boyfriend drives like a maniac," I said, smiling, while he slipped onto the shoulder and suddenly we were three abreast around another corner.

"No English, no English," she said again.

"I think his driving is normal for here," Mike said. "Plus, we'll get there faster."

"It would have been safer riding broken bikes on the potato-rock road." I looked longingly into the hills where I knew our road had zigzagged. It had been a long time since we'd been in a vehicle. Our speed over the past few days had maxed out at six kilometres an hour. There were no seat belts in the vehicle and I bounced back and forth between being terrified and grateful for the ride. My head was dizzy when the driver swerved to the right and came to a dramatic stop in front of a restaurant.

They brought us inside. We sat down around a red circular table and the driver ordered for us. Soon bowls of vegetables, potatoes and an entire barbecued chicken was placed in the centre of the table. The amount of food was staggering. The woman lost all of her shyness as she dug in first, scooping out the chicken feet, sucking on the bones and nails before spitting chunks onto the floor. I reached for a wing. Chewing, sucking, spitting. It tasted amazing.

When we finished, Mike reached into his wallet to pay, but, instead, we heard the only English word they knew: "No."

It took three hours to make it back to Kunming. We tried to explain they could drop us off at the edge of the city, but they insisted on bringing us the entire way, to the same hostel we'd stayed at before. They must have gone out of their way. I was so happy not to have to navigate through Kunming again. Mike held out some yuan to pay for gas. But they said no again. I was thankful to be alive and even more grateful to be shown generosity by so many people who had never even learnt our names.

"*Xièxiè*" (thank you), we said over and over, and the couple lit up with smiles.

I missed the couple and their erratic driving the next day when we realized we would have to catch a bus to Chengdu. There were only a few days left until we had planned to meet the rest of our group to ride through Tibet. We had heard about a man named Fink who lived in Chengdu and ran a bike shop. We were able to email him and he said he could fix everything for us, so we decided to get there as soon as we could.

The bus station was crowded and loud. Street merchants stuck to our side, trying to sell us water and Chinese magazines. We found the correct bus, but the driver wouldn't take our bikes, giving us hand signals for the amount we would have to pay. He pushed Mike's bike away when Mike attempted to haggle down his asking price of 200 yuan. Mike eventually paid the full price. The underbelly doors opened and snakes slithered out from the bus onto the concrete. I jumped back and slipped, my bike falling on top of me. Mike picked me up as the driver grabbed the snakes and tossed them back into the storage and our bikes followed.

The bus was packed. There were three single bunk beds across the width of the bus. Our tickets gave us a bunk bed right at the very back, the furthest away from the toilet. We piled the panniers on one bed and squished beside each other on the other. Five hours into the ride, the stench of urine made its way to the back of the bus. My new deodorant came in handy as I glided it beneath my nose. Just after midnight, I heard a massive explosion and smelled burning rubber. I woke up Mike and everyone around me and pointed out the window until they finally yelled to the driver to stop. I thought for sure they would let us out of the bus because of the smoke and burning tire, but they never did. *Riding a bike is way easier than taking a bus*, I mused. The squat toilet overflowed and its contents sloshed down the aisle.

Sleep eluded me. The driver who had picked us up hitchhiking seemed geriatric in comparison to the bus driver. Instead, I wrote in my journal and thought a lot about home. Friends of ours would be getting married soon. Craig and Sarah. As we spun around the countryside of China in the black night, I thought a lot about marriage.

I cracked open the curtains on the window. The sky went from black to dark burgundy to rose until I caught the exact instant when the sun broke over the horizon. From then on, each second the sky changed, expanding into brilliant oranges then yellows. Clouds swirled softly. I took hold of Mike's hand and he mumbled in his sleep.

I couldn't recall the promises I'd made to Mike or those he'd given me on our wedding day. I remembered being thrilled to stand with him in front of our friends and family and have a big outdoor party. But, as I watched the sun soar upward, I now understood I hadn't taken the time to believe in what I was promising. I imagined our friends saying their vows to each other and hoped they knew in their hearts what they were offering and promising.

When our 18-hour bus ride was over, and our new wheels were ordered, we sat in a courtyard in a quiet space of Chengdu. A fresh breeze blew in. Mike had the laptop on the table and I sat close beside him with my journal, holding down the fluttering pages.

"I want to tell Sarah and Craig in this letter that being married won't be easy," I said.

"But it's worth it." Mike flashed me a cheesy smile, standing up to change the angle on the umbrella.

"Exactly! But it'll be hard." It took me too many years to learn that marriage takes work, commitment and even sacrifice.

"But it'll be awesome."

I smiled. For our wedding five years ago, Sarah gave me something blue. It was a pair of panties with a Canadian maple leaf emblazoned on the front. Funnily enough, I had brought them on this bike trip and happened to be wearing them as I wrote my letter to Sarah and Craig:

> Bringing two lives together is filled with pushing each other to be the best in whatever that may be. You will realize how much you depend on the other. But in particular aspects, there is still independence. Support your spouse. Grow from one another. And when you grow apart, which will happen, never forget to pull each other back in to rediscover the love that you have on this day. If you do this always, your love will be forever.

I looked up at Mike after sharing it with him. "Babe, anything else you would like to say?"

"Mazel tov!" Mike yelled – so loud a group of birds squawked and flew away from the tree. I laughed, remembering all of the wedding speeches he has interrupted over the years. I leaned over and wrapped my arms around him, kissing him long and deep.

And then I got back to work. I decided I had my own vows to write.

CHAPTER 30

TIBET

Pedals and Prayer Wheels

Tibet has a smell to it. The sweet and salty fragrance of yak butter tea. The pungent aroma of meat suspended from stained wooden structures. The honeyed perfume of butter lamps.

Scented candles with long-burning wicks lit our way as Mike and I meandered Lhasa's narrow, early morning streets. We had arrived in Lhasa the day before and now found ourselves outside the Potala Palace, high on top of Marpo Ri (Red Hill). It presided like a fortress over the rest of Tibet as if it were its own Everest. I hadn't been there long, but I instantly felt its energy, its strength, like a mountain. *It's no wonder the Dalai Lama's residence in India doesn't have the same ambiance as his home once had in Lhasa, Tibet*, I thought.

We stood in place to watch the sky shift from black, to deep blue, to gold. Then we moved to the entrance of the palace, where a Chinese guard asked for our permit. I handed him our paperwork. Tibet, once an independent nation, is now occupied by China. The Potala Palace, formerly the political and Buddhist heart of Tibet, is now a historical tourist site. History had not been kind: battles fought, contents stolen and burned. Still, the palace stood. If it ever crumbled to the red earth, reduced to flecks of white-walled dust, I think it would yell defiantly, "Is that all you got? You can't take me!"

I pressed my hand against one of the thick, milk-coloured walls and dragged my arm slowly behind me while I followed Mike up the stone-washed stairs. I knew we were somewhere worth savouring. I inhaled first through my mouth, bringing oxygen down to my belly before releasing it, then took a deep breath through my nose. Smelling Tibet the entire time.

Breathing, it turned out, wasn't easy.

Lhasa sits at 3490 metres above sea level. The city acts as the lungs of the Tibetan Plateau, exchanging oxygen for karma and purity. We had only walked one storey into the palace before we needed to rest.

"This is a lot of work!" Mike exclaimed. "My head is pounding from the altitude!"

"I never expected it would be this hard to breathe," I said, bent at the waist. I was fighting my own headache and felt as if I'd just completed a double marathon. Mike started to cough, a deep and consuming cough. His shoulders shook as he tried to clear his throat. When we caught our breath, we pushed off the wall to explore the halls, stupas and scriptures, taking frequent breaks. I couldn't imagine biking at this altitude.

We were in Tibet to bike, though, and for three days we prepared for our ride by buying food and trying to acclimatize. On our final evening, Mike and I paused in front of the Jokhang Temple on Barkhor Square. The last rays of light gleamed on the golden roof. The temple was four storeys high and took up an entire block. Buddhism was first introduced to Tibet here. It is one of the most sacred temples. Dozens of pilgrims surrounded the square, murmuring mantras and chanting.

Mike lifted his arm to spin a large prayer wheel, one of hundreds lined along a red railing. Sanskrit writing was etched on each wheel like art engraved into gold. Prayer wheels are used to accumulate wisdom and merit (good karma) and to purify negatives (bad karma). Mike's touch was tender, and the wheel spun smoothly clockwise.

I had read it was best to turn the prayer wheels using a gentle rhythm. Smooth instead of frantic. It made me think about how wound up I had been at the beginning of our trip. How desperate I was to pedal my bike. Yet it was the constant, easy rotations of our tires that moved us through our emotions. Spinning away negativity, confusion and doubt. Every revolution of our wheels was a plea for patience, forgiveness and love.

At the end of the row, I grasped Mike's hand and together we finished our walk to a restaurant. A heavy tapestry, thick with dust from the streets and grease from cooking, covered the door. Mike pushed it aside to let me through. The restaurant was 300 years old and it was rumoured that the sixth Dalai Lama used to dine there. I blinked to adjust to the dimly lit room.

"There's everyone," Mike said, and grabbed my hand to lead me toward our friends. It was illegal to travel through Tibet independently, and so Mike and I had organized permits and a guide and invited others to meet us in Chengdu, China.

"We're doing it!" I said to Zach as I wrapped him in a hug. We had loved riding in Vietnam with Zach and were excited he got his Chinese visa approved.

He was a great riding partner – calm, knowledgeable, loved to play cards and was an incredible bike mechanic.

Billy, our longtime friend we hadn't seen since Bangkok, was also back. His large camera was slung over his plaid button-up shirt and he lit up the dim room with his smile.

"Hey, you two," Nathan said, lifting his hand in greeting while still leaning against the back of the booth. Since we had met Nathan in Laos, he had tried to bike into Tibet by himself but was escorted back across the border by authorities. Unfazed, he contacted Mike and me to say he would join us.

"Ya! This is great!" Bob exclaimed in his thick Dutch accent, raising his beer. "We made it!" His voice reminded me of my extended family and I loved his easy laugh. Bob's curly blond hair sprung out from an army-green ball cap. Only days earlier, he had arrived in China with no plan other than to buy a bike and try to ride through Tibet. We met by chance at the hostel in Chengdu. I enjoyed his enthusiasm and was happy he accepted the invitation to join us. I finished my round of the table by locking eyes with Mike.

With the help of a local woman, and ignoring the rule "no bikes on the train," we had managed to stuff all of us and our panniers, wheels and frames into a cabin for the journey from Chengdu into Tibet. The bike ride we were about to embark on would be over 1100 kilometres. We would ascend multiple 5000-metre passes and stay at Everest base camp. This portion of our adventure would end in Kathmandu, Nepal. The three-week journey cost us each $460, which included a guide and vehicle. The truck would lead and we'd have to ride as a group across military checkpoints. It was the only way to get permission to enter Tibet.

That night, I jolted awake. I reached for my headlamp and turned to Mike. His face looked pale. His breathing was rapid and shallow, aching for more oxygen. I got up and walked to the window to pull open both of the heavy wooden shutters – anything to help him get more air. I shivered on my way back to the bed and crawled under the heavy blankets and listened to Mike struggling to breathe. I didn't fall back asleep.

At breakfast, Mike cradled his head in his hands. His lips were deep purple and his eyes rimmed dark blue. The rest of him was chalky white, as if he had been drained of life. I'd never seen anything like it. But I knew what it was: acute mountain sickness. It can occur when the body has trouble adjusting to lower amounts of oxygen at high altitude. Symptoms can include loss of appetite, headache, fatigue, flu and dizziness. Kind of like the worst hangover ever. Exertion is not recommended.

"Rest, honey," I told him. I ate what I could and then packed our gear. Tears streamed down my face. I wiped them often on the back of my hand while Billy looked on, concerned. I was scared. Oxygen is the prime source of life and my husband wasn't breathing well. I knew adjusting to the altitude would take time. *But how much time?*

"Can you keep an eye on Mike?" I asked Billy. I went down the street and bought three oxygen bottles. Cycling the Friendship Highway had been a dream of mine for years. We had worked through a lot of bureaucracy to get here. Now that it was time, I didn't want to start. Had we been on our own, without the restrictions that came with a group and a guide, we would have stayed put. Instead, I helped Mike onto his bike and we joined our friends in front of the Potala Palace.

I felt tortured watching Mike suffer. My gut turned to mush as if I'd been kicked over and over. When our guide arrived with a truck that couldn't transport passengers, I panicked. A proper support vehicle was included in our contract. Again, I wiped away tears, pretended I was stronger than I was and fought for a different vehicle. A few hours later, a massive army truck with five seats and an enormous green canvas canopy rumbled toward us. By the time it arrived, it was late morning and Mike had regained some colour.

I walked up to Kunchen, our Tibetan guide, to thank him. He wore a faded brown T-shirt and a large black backpack. I bowed my head when we met and Kunchen wrapped a white silk scarf around my neck. I brushed my hand along the fabric as he rested another one on Mike's shoulders. The scarf was part of the custom known as Khata and is a token of sincerity, purity and compassion.

"Welcome," Kunchen said. At that moment, I knew he was welcoming us to this place and all places. The palace hovered majestically in the background and I imagined Kunchen was congratulating us on everything we had done to make it to this point.

I turned to gaze at the palace, but an old man with pieces of wood strapped to his palms grabbed my attention. I watched him as his hands touched in prayer. He raised them to his forehead, mouth and chest before sinking onto worn knees, sliding his wooden palms forward to stretch his body out, tipping his palms to the sky. He gracefully stood back up and repeated the action. We watched him for a long time and his movements never faltered.

"In doing hundreds of prostrations," Kunchen began, "they purify negative thoughts and generate spiritual merit." I turned to smile at Kunchen and he smiled back. His burgundy cheeks rose into the corners of his eyes. Thin whiskers outlined the shadow of a goatee, while thick black hair swept the top of his shoulders. He looked to be in his early 30s and his easy presence calmed my hesitations.

Kunchen had never guided cyclists before, but he thought he'd try biking as well. He gave up on the first hill and we never saw him ride again. He was surprised we didn't need much from him. We carried our own panniers, set up our tents and cooked our own food. Fact was, we needed him for the permit. But as our trip progressed, Kunchen's insight into what it was like to be Tibetan under Chinese rule was invaluable. I knew from the moment he offered me the white scarf that we were privileged to have him share his home with us.

Soon the city turned to countryside. Massive mountains formed in the distance, their tops decorated with snow. The smoky blue Kyi River flowed beside us, off to somewhere in more of a hurry than we were. The air was thin, dry and hard to breathe. I slipped my bandana over my mouth to filter the harsh air.

Colourful prayer flags fluttered in the breeze atop homes and cliffs. Bronze barley, ready to harvest, and yellowing poplars gave away the change of season. We had been on the road for nearly one year.

"We're cycling in Tibet!" I yelled to Mike. We high-fived each other as we pedalled. A small boy waved excitedly from outside his home. As the kilometres ticked past, Mike began to feel better. We lagged behind the others, but I was proud of him for being on the bike.

After 80 kilometres, we found our camp for the night. The hiss of five small stoves took over as we cooked potatoes, broccoli and edamame beans. Kunchen relaxed on a mat and watched us cook dinner with an amused smile on his face. The others were still chatting around the fire when I snuggled up to Mike in our sleeping bags. Sleep came easy.

In the morning, I peeled myself away from Mike, sat up and rested my hand on his forehead. It was hot, but his body was clammy and chilled from sweating.

"I'll be okay," he said.

"Are you sure?" I croaked. In the night, my throat had closed and I was fighting my own sickness and headache. Every time I swallowed, my throat ached like it was lined with grains of sand. Mike nodded yes and I got up to make our coffee.

We had camped at an elevation of 3608 metres and now we had to climb to our first 5000-metre pass. For 27 kilometres the road crept up a steep incline through dozens of switchbacks. The air was crisp and clear, making everything appear closer than it was. Mike and I both struggled, persuading ourselves to ride for five more minutes before we'd stop and slouch over our handlebars to suck in air. Billy was still far below us on the road.

"I think he's taking pictures," Mike said. "I'm going to wait for him a bit." I nodded and worked to move up another switchback. It was one of the few times on the entire trip I rode alone. Everything was quiet except the grind of my chain and the wheeze in my chest. The slopes were steep, but big burly yaks still scoured them for food. Around yet another corner, a yak herder ran toward the road and me. (*Running!*) The switchback was short and, when I turned uphill, I lost sight of him, but I could still hear his footsteps. When he reached me, he slowed to a walk to match the pokey rotation of my legs.

I pulled down my bandana to smile. He grinned back. His yellow teeth were crooked and his cheeks chapped red. He put one hand on my handlebar and one on my back rack and began pushing me on my bike.

"Wow," I laughed. "The altitude certainly doesn't affect you!" It felt great to let someone else do my work. He pushed me to the next switchback, waved goodbye and crossed to the other side of the road. I tried to go faster, I really did, but my top speed still matched his walking pace. He came back to push me again. Then he began to run. I glanced at my speedometer. It was the fastest I'd gone all day!

When he stopped for a break, I opened my handlebar bag and pulled out the Skor chocolate bar my family had mailed from Canada that I'd been saving for a special occasion. I handed it to the yak herder. I wondered if he'd eaten chocolate before. He gulped it down, licking his tongue around his mouth and through the holes in his teeth. I took hold of his calloused hand and thanked the man for pushing me.

As I arrived at the top of the pass, Bob strode over to take my bike and lean it on a railing. I looked back down toward the valley and saw the Yarlung Tsangpo, the highest altitude river in the world, raging below.

"Stunning!" I exclaimed.

"That's nothing," said Bob. "Look over the other side." I walked over the crest of the pass, ducking beneath a string of colourful prayer flags. Yamdrok Yumtso, the most beautiful lake I'd ever seen, was far below. Long arms of piercing blue water extended into valleys, making the lake look like a scorpion. I felt it stare back at me, as if it searched my soul to see if I was worthy of witnessing its beauty. Barren dry mountains reflected on its mirrored surface. Snow-peaked summits rose behind: *the Himalayas.* I grinned. I stared at the lake for a long time, thinking about its future. Yamdrok Yumtso was the largest freshwater lake in Tibet and a sacred place for Tibetans. I knew the lake had become an environmental concern as it had been recently taken over by a Chinese hydropower plant. If development continued, this lake would disappear in 20 years. I didn't want to imagine it.

"Zach is sick," Bob said, interrupting my thoughts. I spun around to find Zach hanging his legs over the edge and holding his head in his hands. A pile of puke lay nearby. I grabbed him a water bottle and put my arm around him.

"My head is pounding," Zach admitted.

"You're too good of a climber," I replied, making fun of his athleticism and his ability to gain altitude too quickly. But I was worried about him. And about Mike and Billy, who hadn't yet arrived at the pass.

Curious yak herders, including many women, surrounded us. One woman filled my mug with steamy tea. I took a big swig and, before I could stop myself, spat it out, splattering the dusty road. My lips puckered. "There must be a cup of salt in this tea!" I exclaimed. Mike and Billy arrived to a silent cheer from the rest of us. Mike took hold of the mug for a sip. He agreed. It tasted horrible. The Tibetans didn't seem to mind and enjoyed looking at the pictures of home that decorated my mug.

"How was your climb?" I asked Mike.

"It was hard, but I'm good," he said. "Billy took a lot of photos." Billy was already striding over to check out the view on the other side and slipped his camera in front of his eye.

The descent was fantastic but over too fast. Our overall pace was slow.

"I feel awful," I told Mike. Everything hurt, and between my own cough and the altitude, I figured I was only able to access a tenth of the oxygen I usually could. It seemed as if the effort to get to Tibet had been keeping my body together, and now that we were here, it collapsed.

We rode past the truck and Kunchen stood on the side of the road. "We'll camp just around the corner," he said. The corner took hours to arrive. The sun let out its last exhale when we finally crawled into camp. I craved sleep but, once I was tucked into my sleeping bag, it wouldn't come.

After a few hours, I got up. I zipped the tent door closed behind me and stared into the darkness. Millions of beautiful stars penetrated the black sky. The moon began to rise beyond the mountain and moonlight flooded the field. When I got my bearings, I walked to the left and squatted in the grass. A creek flowed beside me. The same stream from which I had watched women and children fill their buckets to carry back to their home.

We were camped at 4500 metres and my body hurt more than I'd ever known. I couldn't breathe through my nose, and my throat was as rough as the dry grass I grasped in my grip. When shadows took on the shape of giant Tibetan monsters, I went back to the tent and sat beside Mike. Thankfully, his fever had broken and his breath was even. To entertain myself, I used the last few Q-tips to clean my ears. I found our clippers and cut my nails. I coughed up wads of phlegm and, through a slit in our tent zipper, made a huge pile of snot on the ground. It was not my favourite night of camping.

"Kat, just stay in the middle of the road."

Mike's voice barely registered, but I did as he said. I was like a stumbling drunk attempting to ride home after too many beers, unsuccessfully staying out of the ditches. This while we were still on the flats. We were about to ride through the narrow gorge at the start of the climb up to Karo La Pass.

Reality replaced any fantasies I had about the beauty and serenity of Tibet. Everyone had noses with mucus hardened onto raw sun-chapped faces. I threw another lozenge in my mouth. Thankfully, Nathan had brought an entire rainbow spectrum of them. They only helped for a minute. My throat was too dry and I couldn't stop coughing.

Kunchen and the truck were well ahead, *but if he comes back, I will get in,* I told myself. I had stopped caring how I compared to others in our cycling pack. I couldn't remember who was ahead and who was behind. I missed being alone with Mike. Missed stopping when we were sick and pushing hard when we felt good. I was not in a good headspace.

I can't do this, I thought. *You're never going to make it,* I told myself. But I stayed silent. To voice my self-doubts would have been too much effort. But I felt tortured. It wasn't the flu, the cold or the altitude. It was losing belief in myself. My will power is usually strong, but now all I wished was that Kunchen would turn around and come back for me. I was dizzy and kept setting myself goals; "just pedal for three minutes, Kat," I told myself. But I'd only make it one minute, failing to make my mental targets. A fierce cold wind blew off the glaciers and threatened to push me over. An enormous mountain on our left featured a glacier shaped like the ace of spades. I stopped and leaned over my handlebars, having another coughing fit. Finally, I lifted my head, searching for an answer to the question: What was I even doing here?

I got off my bike to walk. *Why am I doing this when it's not fun?* My head needed to be sorted out. I had to find my inner strength. *Not everything can come easy, Kat. There will be hardships.* Who was I to complain? I'd been on holiday for a year. I got to exercise every day, try new food and experience meditative therapy while riding my bike. My life was awesome. *It's fricken awesome,* I told myself, and got back on the bike to put a little more road behind me. *Well, pardon me if you're going to have to work a little harder. I'm not giving in to you that easy. But why not?* I wondered. Surely I had put in my time, done my due diligence. Why couldn't things just be easy?

"You okay?" Mike asked, probably in reaction to my sporadic activity.

"Not really," I admitted. "I'm not having fun."

"I never have fun," Mike joked. It caught me off guard and made me smile. We were going to have to work at this every day, whether we were zipping downhill or striving to move uphill. Even in all this beauty, there was pain.

It was at that moment I realized this – Mike and I – was not going to be easy either. After everything we had been through, and all we had learned, biking through Tibet was going to test us physically and mentally. More than we ever thought possible. *In sickness and in health,* I remembered.

Mike rode in front of me acting as a windbreak, keeping the pace as slow as I needed. I concentrated on the back wheel of his bike and forced myself to move my legs at the same speed as his. Right, left, right, left.

Because I was staring downwards, I missed the prayer flags signalling the top of the Karo La Pass at 5020 metres. Mike stopped and when I looked up Kunchen was there. His hands were tucked into the pockets of his black cargo pants, and his T-shirt, which he hadn't changed since we met him, billowed from the wind. He brushed aside his long, thick, black hair as it blew in front of his eyes, seemingly oblivious to the effort we had put in, acting like he knew we would make it all along.

"That's Nojin Kangsang," he said, pointing to a mountain on our right. The largest glacier in Tibet poured toward us in thick white chunks. Prayer flags fluttered in the wind, slapping against the cold air. The flags are made of vibrant, colourful, rectangle cloths and were strung at most high points in Tibet. I had come to understand that each piece of fabric had its own mantra printed on it, which, when moved through the wind, blessed the surroundings, spreading goodwill and compassion.

"The blue represents sky and space," Kunchen told us. "White represents the wind and air, red is for fire, green is water and yellow the earth. Balancing these five key elements is the basis for achieving health and harmony. Tibetans believe that if all of the five elements are balanced, they will achieve unity with the environment. Internally, if one can make balance, it will bring health to the body and mind."

I closed my eyes and listened to the flags flap in the wind. My heart seemed to pound to the same beat as the flags and I strived to gain strength from being present. We were higher than any mountaintop in the Rockies. I felt Mike's hand on my back, checking to see if I was all right. I opened my eyes and smiled at him, noticing how half of the prayer flags were faded from exposure, their mantras no longer visible. New flags had been strung right alongside the old, symbolizing an ongoing cycle. New life replaces old.

Perhaps it was my part of the journey to feel awful. Maybe I was sacrificing my body and health to spiritually connect with this land and to experience its depth and wonder. *Perhaps each breath I could take cleansed me, got rid of damaged cells and replaced them with compassionate ones,* I thought. Perhaps this was a final test for purification.

"The flags give everyone peace, wisdom and strength," Kunchen explained.

I hoped he was right.

"We'll camp just around the corner," Kunchen told us.

"You said that yesterday!" I teased.

"You're slower than a truck," he said, and began to laugh. Kunchen's laugh shook his entire upper body. He always seemed to follow up his laugh with shyness. This time was no different. He looked away and dug his foot into the side of the road, complete with a smile on this face. Though Kunchen was still figuring out the daily pace of a biker, I got the sense he was enjoying guiding us.

Nathan, Zach and Bob had already set up their tents by the time Mike, Billy and I arrived at camp. The wind cut through the valley. It took four of us to hold our tent in place before we could secure it into the dry ground. Kids from a nearby village stared as I pulled out my warmest jacket and toque and crawled into the tent. For the next hour, many heads peeked into our vestibule. I didn't have the breath, never mind the energy, to talk to the Tibetans. The kids were quiet. I relaxed while allowing them to satisfy their curiosity.

"Let's go cook," Mike suggested after an hour. I opened my eyes to three children's heads in our vestibule. They danced away as we emerged.

"Kat, let's use your tarp to make a windbreak," Nathan recommended. He picked a spot between the two tents and, as we stretched it out, I found myself crouched on the ground needing a break. Nathan came to finish tying up the tarp near me. I dropped my head into my hands. I never knew altitude could be so challenging.

Previously, I had wanted to climb Everest. I had dreams of great mountaineering adventures. I had read countless books based in the Himalayas, of trekkers, climbers and cyclists, and whenever I read how hard exercise at elevation was, how much effort it took to put one foot in front of the other, I thought, *suck it up, it cannot possibly be that hard.*

I was a fool. It was that hard.

With the tarp finally up, I joined the group in making a meal of rice, broccoli and ginger. Kids sat with us, watching our every move. I noticed their windblown faces, their dry, cracked skin. Snot ran freely, and their hair was so caked with dust, it stood straight up. As we got closer, we could see head lice munching on their scalps. Their clothes fell off them in tatters, worn, torn and either too big or too small.

"Kunchen, can we give them food?" I asked.

"You could try, but they'll probably be too shy to take it," Kunchen replied, and left to walk up a narrow valley to their village. We placed two bowls of food in front of the kids and they dug right in.

When Kunchen came back an hour later, he said, "They're starving. Four hundred Tibetans live here. They only own this piece of land we are camping on and that hill." He pointed to the brown hill that rose up from the creek. "The village owns some sheep, but there's not enough land for the sheep to feed on. Every year, more babies are born and the village grows. They don't have enough food."

I wished I could do something. Anything.

I stared wistfully at the kids. Since they finished eating, they'd been spinning each other around and taking turns giving piggyback rides. The camp was heartbreakingly beautiful and the view dramatic, but I had no stamina to play. My body begged me to retreat to the tent. I was upset I couldn't garner the energy to engage with the kids. When Mike zipped closed our vestibule door, the sounds of giggling filled my ears. I surrendered into the sleeping bags we had zipped together for more warmth – and romance, if we'd had the energy.

Four days later, my flu subsided and I could finally call "*Tashi delek*" (hello) to a farmer plowing a field. He stood on a massive wooden rake being pulled by a large yak, surfing it as it dug into the ground. The land, parched from the harsh sun, was fractured with thirst. It was amazing that anything grew in this environment. The man sang in a rich, throaty voice that accompanied us as we moved up the road. I looked upwards as I listened. The brightest blue sky went on forever. It was like innocent young eyes: pure, honest and clear.

We arrived at a large grass field that would host our camp for the night. Zach, Billy and Nathan were already snacking and were surrounded by a group of Tibetans and a lot of goats. A huge vehicle, parked near ours, made our green army truck look like a toy. Mike and I put down our bikes and Kunchen walked over.

"They're on a pilgrimage," he explained, pointing to the other group. "Going on a pilgrimage is about finding enlightenment. It's an act of devotion to find a source of healing."

Three women squatted around a yak-dung fire, taking turns pumping a set of bellows. The Tibetan Plateau is bare of trees, and all meals were cooked on dried dung fires. I had learned that sheep dung was a fast burner and yak dung was slower and perfect for a pot of butter tea. A huge pot bubbled on the flames.

I walked over and knelt beside them. They wore long robes and colourful striped aprons to signify they were married. On their heads, they had square felt hats, each in a different colour: turquoise, purple and grey. They smelled of smoke and smiled shyly. I noticed the eldest had calloused fingers, worn from a lifetime of rolling prayer beads between her thumb and index finger. She reached for the pot and poured me a cup of tea.

"Thank you," I said. I brought the warm mug to my lips and took a sip. It was delicious. Salt-free. I asked them to show me how to pump the pig stomach bellow. Fanning the flames took constant attention and required a finesse I did not yet have. A young boy, no more than 4 years old, laughed and twirled around playfully while I tried. He then took the bellows from me, wrapping the handles in one tiny hand to show me what to do. I cheered him on while Zach handed me our titanium pot. The women built a rock stand for my pot and ripped up more pieces of dung. And I wondered why, when we left home, we felt like we needed the most technical gear to experience a simple, wonderful existence.

The afternoon was long and enjoyable. When Mike and Nathan got hungry, they lit our stoves, and the noise attracted the Tibetans from their smoking dung fires to our instant fires.

When the pilgrims' meal was ready, they gathered together and sat in a large circle. I was motioned over to join them and sat cross-legged beside the eldest woman. She handed me *tsampa*, roasted barley flour mixed with tea and rolled into small balls. They tasted dry but were a good source of energy and could be made anywhere in this area and so were a staple of a Tibetan's diet. A man cut off a considerable chunk of yak meat and smiled a toothless grin as he pushed it into my dirty hands. It was the leg bone. *An honourable piece of meat*, I thought. Yak hair was still attached, and I did my best at making a good go of it.

It was quite a feast, but, put off by the thought of more hairy yak meat, I started to get up. The man beside me pulled me back down. He said something to the group and many started talking. I looked around the circle and saw the smallest child being passed through everyone's arms until she settled in the lap of the man. He tilted his hat up to look me in the eyes and then brought his attention back to the little girl. He began undoing her jacket. She was entirely at peace in this man's hands. He released many layers until he freed a thin chain with a locket from around her neck.

Everyone shuffled in closer. He opened the locket to reveal a faded picture of the Dalai Lama. My eyes opened with surprise and wonder. In Tibet, the Chinese government forbid photos of the Dalai Lama. I was honoured the pilgrims felt comfortable enough to share a photo of their spiritual leader. They prayed, cupping their hands in front of their chests. I imitated their movements.

From what I understood, a pilgrimage is about stepping out of oneself and seeking purity. It always involves a journey with risk. In accepting that risk, whether it is through penance, devotion or hard travel, pilgrims find the renewal they seek.

I caught Mike's eye and thought about our journey, searching for our own moral and spiritual significance, and how we had transformed this year. How devoted to one another we had become.

CHAPTER 31

MOUNT EVEREST
Soaring on an Air Current

Nathan always started his stove first, its roar waking us one by one. I, always eager for coffee, was usually the first to join him. Today, Nathan still lay under his bright orange tarp, coated with frost. He was tucked deep into his sleeping bag – an attempt to stay as warm as possible as he stared into the stove's flame.

"Morning," I said when I sat down, wrapping my jacket around me.

"Morning," Nathan replied with an easy smile.

Billy, Bob, Zach and Kunchen soon circled Nathan's tarp. Everyone seemed relaxed and not rushed to start riding. I reached for one of the Thermoses and emptied it into our pot, thankful it was already filtered. The process of purifying enough water for all of us was tedious. Zach had taken on this chore with pride and was often found down by a creek or stream pumping the water filter.

I felt fortunate to be part of such a great group. During the days, Mike and I often cycled on our own, but at camp we grouped back up for meals. In the evenings, we played cards, with Mike and I hosting others in our tent, as it was the largest. The night before I had even won!

The boys had started calling me "Camp Mother," which I didn't like, so I told them I renamed myself "Sexy Hot Camp Chick." The new nickname didn't catch on, and when I saw myself in the mirror of my compass I knew why. Bags of skin hung beneath my eyes, my hair was matted with dust and my clothes were stained and full of holes. I was definitely not a sexy goddess.

Unless eating like a champion is sexy. I was starving! My appetite was back. Overnight, I had eaten every crumb in every food bag close to our tent. I emptied Mike's handlebar bag of all cookies and crackers, including the squishy Tibetan candies. I even devoured the gross, hard PowerBars he had carried for far too long.

Mike sauntered over last with a sleepy smile, dragging his mat with him. He laid it down on the grass beside me and rested his head in my lap.

"It's one year today," I whispered as I stroked his head. He flipped around and fixed his eyes on mine. The moment lasted for all of two seconds. We both realized the significance of this anniversary. One year ago, we had left home without a plan. When given the chance, would we fall back in love?

"We did it," Mike said.

"French toast?" Nathan asked. We answered with a resounding yes. It was a treat and a change from our usual oatmeal. I handed Nathan my plate. It sported a long crack. With a year of abuse, most of our gear had done well. We had begun 365 days earlier with two bowls, two plates, two forks, three spoons and one knife. Now we had one spoon, one fork, one bowl and one cracked plate.

It's like we had become one!

Our frying pan was nearing the end of its life, however, and the tent zipper was always split open. Even so, I thought everything had held up amazingly well. Including us. I snuggled in under Mike's arm. After being battered, broken and sick, I had never felt closer to Mike.

The frost melted and once again I gaped in awe at the brilliant blue sky. We took a 50-kilometre detour to visit Sakya Monastery. The monastery, built in 1073, dominated the grey landscape. Some of the buildings lay in ruins from the Cultural Revolution that destroyed the area in the 1960s, but many had been restored and religious teachings continued again. I learned that, in 2003, 84,000 gold-bound scrolls of literature were found hidden in a wall; scriptures and recorded history untouched for hundreds of years were uncovered.

Our group walked inside where two monks greeted us. We wandered the halls and then sat on the steps in the main square, watching an elderly woman as she prostrated herself in front of a golden statue. She ignored us. Her hands, placed carefully on the grey earth in front of her brown, beaded prayer necklace, were calloused and worn. She slowly pushed with one hand and then the other, raising one knee up first and then into a standing position. I caught a view of her face, weathered with waves of wrinkles rolling over one another, creating sandbars out of brown eyes. Her back was rounded from hard work. She looked like she had been doing prostrations for a hundred years. Her devotion was inspiring.

"Kat, want coffee?" Zach asked as I walked out of the monastery. I laughed. I knew I was devoted to coffee. Mike powered up the stove and Zach pulled out a pair of brand new socks and began to cut them up so we could use one as a coffee filter. Zach's mom had mailed a dozen white cotton socks to him in China. He didn't need 12 new pairs, so we had each been given a few. It was fantastic to slip my feet into clean new socks. The remaining socks were being used as chain cleaners, mug cozies and mitts on frosty mornings. Now one of the last pairs was being turned into a coffee filter. We watched the thick brew drip into our mugs. Mike and I shared a cup and I raised it on our behalf, toasting to one year on the road.

One year. It seemed magical to me. A lot can happen in one year. I had found everything my heart and mind needed. Now not only did I love Mike unconditionally, I also loved myself. Loving oneself is tricky business. But I had learned that if we're not filled with self-love, we can't share that love with others. I had been so emotionally frail in the beginning and now I was as strong as Mike. I understood how lucky we were to be here together.

Gyatso La Pass, at 5248 metres, was a long ride up. The wind whipped up the tight valley and we didn't make it to the top on the first day. We found relief in a yak pen made out of flat rocks piled up like stacks of pancakes. The large animals were curious and wandered around, knocking their heads against the fabric of the tent and spooking themselves.

In the morning, Mike and I put on all of our layers, including our mitts and toques, to pack up and start riding. Zach, Nathan, Bob and Billy were already riding and Mike and I made our way alone. I shivered long after we began biking. Mike and I stopped for a second breakfast and a cuddle beneath a bridge to block out the cold. After a few hours, we came across Bob and Billy, who were eating *tsampa* with a group of farmers in a field.

The sky was a bright cyan blue. We were so high that we hadn't seen a tree for days. Still, we climbed. Up and up, to the top of one of the highest roads in the world. At the crest, strings of prayer flags flapped in the relentless wind. Billy came up after us, dropped his bike and collapsed on the ground with a satisfied smile. Zach ran over, cupped his hands over Billy's chest and pretended to give him CPR.

"Please tell me that was the highest pass we'll climb," Billy moaned.

"Well," began Nathan, "it's the highest pass with tar-sealed tarmac we'll climb over."

"What?" Billy asked. Either the wind and flags were making a racket, or he didn't want to believe Nathan's fact.

"The highest pass on tar-sealed tarmac," Nathan repeated.

"Oh great," mumbled Billy. "Good!"

The rest of us laughed. I couldn't wipe the smile from my face. It was easy to feel a sense of accomplishment once we were at the top, even knowing there was a harder pass to come.

Two teenage Tibetans living in yak-wool tents laughed at Billy too. They made their living selling prayer flags, which Zach happily bought. One of the boys scurried up the ladder of previously hung flags. He checked to make sure we were ready and then a huge grin spread across his round face. With gusto, he hurled out the string of flags that represented our prayers, wishes and good thoughts. I hoped they would fly forever.

The joyful energy of the boys seemed boundless. They carried themselves as if nothing restrained them: no buildings, no trees. Himalayan peaks poked up over the horizon. The land was flat with rolling bumps, covered in short golden grass and dry stones. I marvelled at the horizon that seemed to go on forever. *It was like seeing the prairies at the top of the world*, I thought.

Thinking of the prairies made me think of home. I felt my heart lurch.

I walked alone, beyond the tent, and stared out into the distance. The wind blew at my jacket and I pulled the hood over my head. Suddenly, tears filled my eyes. It's not that I was sad. I was overwhelmed with happiness. And overwhelmed with a longing for home. Mike and I had grown up on the prairies, we'd fallen in love on the prairies and we had drifted apart on the prairies. When we needed to begin this trip, we did it by pedalling through golden wheat. The vast open space had guided us. I was surprised that, on this barren plateau, I felt a kinship to our home in Canada. The Tibetan landscape seemed representative of our families and of our future together.

Was part of me actually looking forward to going home?

Going home meant dealing with everything I had run away from. I knew now that this was what I had done. I had run away by pedalling as hard as I could. (As it turned out, it was the best thing ever.) But I couldn't pedal away from the emotions. They had followed me – *of course*. For so much of our trip, my demons were packed in my panniers.

I now understood it had been beneficial to run away from our negative situation. And it had been necessary to slash at the devils that travelled with me. After a year, I had unpacked my heartache and the disappointment I had in myself. Now I carried only the essentials for a successful marriage. *Am I ready to go back?*

I looked toward Mike. His hair and beard had grown long again, and both were blowing in the wind. He wore a red jacket and his eyes were lit up, laughing with Zach and Bob. I was totally in love with him. *Could we go home soon?*

From the pass, the road slipped away. Mike came out of my slipstream, soaring beside me with a grin on his face. Our eyes locked for a millisecond before we had to look back to the road. It was exhilarating to be in a tuck, my head hanging out in front of my handlebars, ready to tackle the world. I swerved just in time to avoid a yak that had leapt over the railing. We laughed the rest of the way.

Eventually, the road flattened, the wind picked up and we were working hard again. Kids rolled old tires into the road to play as we passed by. "*Tashi delek, tashi delek!*" they yelled. The braver ones asked us for candy.

Part of me never wanted to go home. Yes, I was still nervous about what awaited us. We had no jobs and our house had been rented. I also loved to travel. Everest, Kathmandu, Nepal? There was still a lot to experience.

A day later, we turned off the Friendship Highway onto a rutted road to start the climb to Pang La Pass. We knew there were 42 switchbacks up to 5205 metres. The pass was a beast and Mike and I often took up the entire road, navigating the best terrain between chunky washboard and loose gravel. Few vehicles passed and, when they did, it was Chinese tourists who stopped to take our photo.

At first, the switchbacks were long, but they became shorter as we rose toward the col. Late in the afternoon, we caught up to Zach. I noticed he had an armful of black slashes on his left arm.

"If my count is right, we're on switchback 28 of this monster!" Zach punched his fist up into the air and screamed, "Yahoo!"

"Hey Billy!" he yelled down. Zach had way more breath than I did. I started laughing until wheezing and coughing took over. From there, it was a struggle to talk at all, but we were so excited. The ride took hours, but each switchback brought a new view of the world's tallest peaks.

"There they are!" Mike said as we took the last corner. The Himalayas.

Vibrant strings of prayer flags framed the brilliant mountains. We dropped our bikes and Mike held me in a hug. I lifted my head to kiss him and we continued to hold each other until Kunchen walked over.

"That's Mount Lhotse," he pointed. "Mount Makalu and Cho Oyo." He moved his finger slightly and pointed to a massive mountain with a whiff of clouds hiding its top. Before he could say what it was, I knew.

"That's Mount Everest."

My heart fluttered and I took hold of Mike's hand. I was so proud of us. Not because we raced up the pass (we certainly didn't do that!), and not because we pushed ourselves beyond the pure enjoyment of the climb. I was proud because we had done it together. Mike and I: able to surmount anything, make it through and over the challenges we had created. Our relationship had beaten the odds. I knew that now.

We made noodles before we began the descent. The spices that came in the packages were intense and I was careful to only add a third of them to our bowl. I then handed the extra to Billy because he loved the spice. We all ate sitting on a rock ledge staring at the Himalayas. I leaned over, tilting my head to share another kiss with Mike. The moment was caught on video – unfortunate because my running nose covered Mike with snot. Everyone laughed. We bashfully wiped our faces with our sleeves.

From the pass, the view of the descent was as fantastic as the view of the Himalayas. It was a nearly 1000-metre elevation drop in 64 switchbacks to the village of Tasho Dzom, where we would spend the night. It would be two days of biking before we would arrive at Everest base camp. I was itching to begin.

We began as a group, sweeping around the first corner and then the second. A single-track trail came into view. It skipped off the road and wiggled its way steeply downward. Nathan noticed it too. I flashed a cheeky smile at Mike and he shook his head no. I smiled bigger. He knew I was going to go anyway. I couldn't *not* take the off-road trail.

"I'll meet you at the bottom!" I yelled, following Nathan.

Dust flew in my face. My fingers curled around the bars as I pretended I was on a downhill mountain bike, my racks, panniers and wheels bouncing up and down. I brought my bum back behind my seat, allowing me to have more speed and control of my bike. I chased after Nathan. My cheeks began to burn because of my huge smile. I was being true to myself. I knew Mike would be cringing that I treated the bike this hard, pushing it to its very limit, but I also knew he would be happy for me. It was the best downhill of my life.

A day later, Mike and I turned around the last bend in the road and majestic Mount Everest loomed. We stopped and stared. It really is that big. I grabbed Mike's arm and leaned my head on his shoulder. Never in my imagination was I going to be this tired by the time we reached the base of Mount Everest. But there I was. Completely wiped.

There was a dreamlike quality to everything we saw. Light brush strokes of clouds painted on a blue sky. The land beneath our tires was grey and brown. At the end of the valley, the colossal mountain blocked the trail; a massive rock encased in ice. The top half was covered in glistening snow. We were looking at the north face of the world's tallest peak. Steep, hard, but like all dreams worth fighting for, apparently not impossible.

With Rhongpu Monastery, the highest monastery in the world, appearing on our left, we knew we had three more kilometres and a military checkpoint to pass before we would arrive at base camp. The entire time I couldn't take my eyes off Mike or Mount Everest. Mike looked worn out but happy. Everest continued to look monumental.

Base camp consisted of a ring of yak-wool tents. Kunchen chose one for us and carried in a large potato sack filled with sheep dung for the fire, a sought-after gift in this harsh terrain. He told us the Chinese government owned the tents, but the Tibetan woman who managed ours made money from the food we bought. Over the next two days, as a group of hungry cyclists, we kept the woman managing our tent very busy. We couldn't stop eating.

That evening, I lay on one of the hard benches lining the edge of the room. I leaned my head back, propped up on all sorts of colourful pillows. My sleep-deprived body was wrapped in an orange and pink silk blanket. I could feel the immense energy of Mount Everest looming outside the fabric walls. The oxygen was thin and it felt as if someone was stomping on my chest. I tore at my clothes, trying to free the boot marks from my throat. My breath was frequent and shallow. Each time I lay down and shut my eyes, I stopped breathing and awoke with a start. We had been at altitude for a month. We were fit from a year of cycling. Even so, it wasn't to be a restful night. Struggling for breath, there was to be no sleep for me. I didn't mind. Bob also had sleep apnea, but we were both thrilled to be at Everest base camp. Lack of oxygen seemed to be a small sacrifice.

Mike's head was at my feet with his hands rested across my ankles. He, of course, could always sleep. I listened to his breath. His exhalations purred out in spurts. I knew his mouth opened slightly with every breath. I accepted the idea of no sleep and alternated between reading and getting up to stare into the abyss of stars outside. My heart had cracked open like a crevasse, filled with love, pride and happiness.

When the early morning light trickled in, our Tibetan woman pushed aside the heavy tapestry hanging over the door. I felt the chill sweep over my head. I heard the wind, pure, unfiltered. There were no trees for it to blow through, nothing for it to rustle except our tent. It moved unrestricted and strong.

I turned to watch her shadow walk to the middle of the room. She reached into the sack of dung patties and put more into the belly of the fire. On top of the stove, she lifted a pot and then ladled a scoop of water into it. Her hands dipped inside, her body swayed as she kneaded the dough. Her long hair, which was braided in plaits, swung back and forth. If I weren't so short of breath and energy, I would have salivated at the thought of warm fresh bread.

She took out the dough, slapping it against her hands. None of the boys woke up. Bob was now sleeping too.

I began to warm up and lowered some of my blankets. I reached my hands to my face; my eyes were so puffy, they drooped into my cheeks. I sat up and brushed Mike's hand to wake him.

"Will you take me outside?" I whispered.

"Mmm," he answered. Mike took hold of my hand and we shuffled outdoors.

The wind had calmed. The sky was clear and the summit of Everest was bathed in golden early morning light.

"This is amazing," Mike said. I couldn't agree more.

Everest base camp, for Mike and me, was our mountaintop. I thought about how the best relationships are the ones where you can ascend mountains together, cross fast-moving water, navigate crevasses and dig yourselves out of avalanches. This didn't mean holding hands to the very top. I knew that now. Sometimes we had to achieve our own milestones. But, together, we had navigated through countries without speaking the language, without being able to decipher the maps or understand the script writing. And just when we would begin to learn, we would start all over again in a new place.

"We made it," I replied.

I couldn't believe how perfect a day we were sharing. I looked up to find two young ravens soaring on an air current, flying with their wings tip to tip as if they were holding hands. Communicating in flutters. *Maybe they're starting off on a long journey*, I thought. *Or, perhaps like us, they're starting to think about going home.*

CHAPTER 32

NEPAL
It's Just around the Corner

A blanket of snow covered the ground outside our tent as we left Everest base camp. Icicles decorated my eyelashes like mascara. My cheeks were red from the wind and sore from smiling. We still had a few more days in Tibet before we would arrive in Nepal.

I had been thrown off course many times during this trip, but now I had a guide. Kunchen pointed us in the right direction. We followed him, and it was refreshing to have someone who knew which way we were headed. Even if all he said was "It's just around the corner." We had seen Mount Everest and were now on our way to Kathmandu, Nepal.

There were no plans after that. What would happen after was unknown. The group, our plans, *everything*, as far as I was concerned, ended in five days.

"Mike, what do you want to do after Kathmandu?" I asked.

"I don't know," Mike replied. "I know you want to go to India, but after riding through Tibet, India would be so busy. I'm not sure I'll have the energy, to be honest." We turned onto a faint track toward the Friendship Highway.

"At some point, we'll run out of money," he emphasized.

"But not yet. We still have enough to keep going," I said.

"We'll need time to find jobs and figure out where we're going to live."

I let out a big sigh before he finished talking. I respected what Mike was saying, but I could have happily biked, aimlessly for months more, if it weren't for the nagging feeling of *what's next?*

I knew eventually we would have to go back.

I wasn't tired of travelling, but I felt like going home would take *more* energy than continuing to ride. I didn't want to return there depleted. I knew I needed strength to navigate around Alex. I couldn't go back to the same job, because he was there. I couldn't go back to the same group of friends. They themselves had splintered, flung across the distant reaches of Canada.

I won't be going back to the same life, I mused silently.

"I'll plan us a route to ride around Nepal until we're ready," I said. I had my fingers crossed Mike would want to go to India by then.

In the meantime, we stopped a lot, and not just because we were tired. We didn't want to finish. Our days evolved around our desires and our sense of time lengthened because of it. We biked if we wanted to bike, stopped if we wanted to stop, and ate when we were hungry. We moved slower, did less, yet somehow experienced more. Our life consisted of minding the weather, oiling our chains and Mike and me. We weren't caught in a monotonous schedule. There was no drain on our creativity or a time limit for conversation. It was an easy and beautiful way to live. I wasn't ready for it to end.

I brought myself back to the present, to the Jeep track over Nam La pass on the western corner of Tibet, heading toward the village of Tingri. Sprawling yellow land, snow-kissed mountains, brooding skies and my favourite type of trail. The kind of trail that made us feel like we were in the middle of nowhere, which was precisely where I wanted to be.

"Want to take a break?" I asked Mike.

"Again?" he smirked, but I could tell he was impressed with the change in me and my slower pace of life. We stopped our bikes right there and lay down on the earth. Glacial rubble poked into our backs, but it hardly mattered; we were pretty used to sprawling out wherever. I squirmed over to rest my head on Mike's leg and stared up at the moving clouds. *I must remember everything,* I thought. The flapping sound of freedom within the tent. The self-sufficient hiss of the stove. The way Mike concentrated but didn't exert himself when he fixed a flat. The way he loved me unconditionally. *Let's go rogue,* I thought. *Let's never go back.*

But in the next breath of sanity, a longing for my family took over and I promised myself to never leave for so long again.

"C'mon, you two lovebirds," Billy called out half an hour later as he biked past, his camera swinging around his chest.

"Coming," Mike laughed, and pulled me up with him.

The next day, we were back on pavement and rode as a group. Bob and Billy were enjoying their first bike tour and I didn't think anyone was craving for it to end. Not yet. We still had the double Yarle Shung La pass to climb. Horse-drawn wagons passed us with bells clanging. Mike and Nathan grabbed onto anything going faster than us – tractors, trucks or carriages. I was too nervous to hitch a ride, but I did race after them to catch up. It seemed ridiculous that the road was paved since the majority of traffic was horses and tractors, but it did make cycling easier. Sometimes our voyage had been like this, smooth as asphalt. Other times it was jarring washboard, bumpy, rocky and full of holes. Or sand. Sand was tough too.

The relentless wind forced us to stop earlier than we expected. I was secretly happy because, internally, I was stalled. I didn't know where Mike and I were going after Kathmandu, so I didn't want to leave where we were. The headwind, I decided, was now my friend.

We set up camp, where Mike and I spent hours making french fries while Zach made a cucumber and tomato salad. The more towns we had passed, the more *chang* (beer) and luxury food (like potatoes) made it into the back of Kunchen's truck.

That night, the sky was big and the earth sank into the stars.

In the morning, I rolled over and looked at my watch. It was 8:30 a.m. *8:30?* It was time to get moving. I lay there listening but couldn't hear Nathan's stove. Mike was warm. I snuggled back into our zipped-together sleeping bags and fell asleep.

We all finally pulled ourselves out to start our last big climbing day. I don't think I could have biked slower. Mike and I spent different parts of the day riding beside Billy, Bob, Zach or Nathan. At one point, Zach zoomed up ahead. He loved to climb.

For hours, the end seemed like an illusion. The road looked flat but was not flat. It tilted uphill just enough that I couldn't turn my legs faster than eight kilometres an hour. It was a line advancing over the curvature of the earth, deceiving us, as if we might never arrive.

The vast, barren, windswept land ached with thirst, yet hundreds of sheep roamed boundlessly. Shepherds materialized at my shoulder, catching up to our wheels with only their feet.

"Those are your sheep," I said, motioning to the flock.

They nodded enthusiastically. I opened my handlebar bag for a snack and the young men pointed to the picture of my niece and nephew on the inner flap. I smiled. Mike gazed down too.

"I wonder what they're like now," he said.

They must be so much bigger, I thought. In the picture my niece was tiny, holding a pink daisy, with more brilliant flowers scattered at her feet. Her skirt was bright pink as well, a colour as foreign to Tibet as we were. My nephew sat in a basket, wearing a crisp, clean, button-up shirt. The shepherds wore browns and greys, camouflaged within the land they wished to tame. Clumps of raw wool hung from their pockets and they never ceased the revolution of their hand wool spinners. One shepherd stroked the photo and gave us a toothy-gapped smile. I inhaled lanolin, dust and sweat. My hands began to tremble. I immediately tucked them into my pants, suppressing my home-sickness. *Not yet*, I told myself.

When we reached the final peak on Yarle Shung La, flags flew wild in the wind. Breath hammering, I hugged Zach.

"Well, how does it feel?" I asked him.

"It's awesome! Though I'm a bit sad we're on our last 5000-metre pass." Zach shrugged his small shoulders and gave me a crooked smile. "I'll miss the climbing."

"I won't," Mike said. "Longest downhill in the world! Bring it on!" From the top, at 5240 metres, we would drop 4500 metres. We took a long break to eat before we began. There was a pile of yak horns beside us. Most were torn directly from the skull with the jagged edges left to dry. There was, however, one huge head still intact and with its buckteeth hanging out. Prayer flags and white scarves were woven between the bones. Kunchen explained that, for Buddhists, killing animals was terrible for karma. But sometimes they had to for food, so by bringing the head up to these high places one could ensure the yak's safe passage to the next life.

Standing on the pass, we could see for a long way. Uplifted ridges of rock encircled the edge of the horizon in endless peaks. Down in the valley, Nepal was landlocked, tucked in a little pocket of the Himalayas, bordered on one side by the high emptiness of Tibet and on the other by overcrowded India. The opportunities for us, in this part of the world, were running out. *Were we reaching the end of our road?*

I turned back to see how far we'd come. The road had shaped Mike and me. It pulled at us, gave us strength and fostered our determination. Sometimes it chomped on us, kilometre by kilometre. But mostly it fed us. Mike and I had found that, as a couple, we were worth fighting for. We had a future.

It had always been about the journey rather than the destination. I spun forward. There was running water, trees, our next life.

"Let's do it guys," I motioned, and got back on the bike.

I expected the downhill to be straightforward. (It was a *downhill* after all.) The wind had another plan. A storm of dirt, barley and dried yak dung flew in the air. I breathed through my neck scarf and squinted my eyes. I caught Mike giving me a cheesy grin as he placed his hand on my backside and tried to push me downhill. I loved that he was having fun even though it was an effort. I used to think our marriage would be a joyride too. But nope. There were bumps, friction and mechanical issues. And even when there was no resistance, I realized now we would always have to work on it. I was okay with that now.

"Longest, coldest, windiest downhill in the world!" I yelled.

"Hey!" cried Billy. "That's not how you sold it to me!" According to Billy, this downhill was the main selling point for him joining us. We had to laugh because of the bitter headwind. If we stopped pedalling, we were pushed backwards – uphill!

Kunchen swung in front of us and we all tucked in behind his windbreak. Sticking in this pocket of calm air, we made fantastic pedal strokes, grinning ear to ear with our jackets flapping, bikes bouncing and socks for mitts.

We stopped a few times to try to make camp, but the wind blew so hard our tents would've been damaged. We slipped behind the truck again until Kunchen found us a rock fence to hide behind. We pushed our bikes into the small hay pen. Dinner was a nightmare. The wind swirled hay and poo into our food as we cooked.

"What a lovely shit pen you have reserved for us tonight," Mike said jokingly. "Just the best for you babe," I replied. I couldn't stop laughing. The screen of our tent didn't stop the dust or hay from entering. We were a happy mess.

It took two days to descend. The wind calmed on the second day as the land went from vast to immediate. We were surrounded by dense jungle. Water fell from cliffs, spraying us as we biked along. I took a deep breath of refreshing moist air and filled my lungs to their breaking point. I let it out as a bird called, its grey head darting back and forth. Mist uncurled and the thick humidity had us stripping off our clothes.

The road narrowed, winding its way through the busy border town of Dram.

We spent one last night in Tibet. In the morning, we finished snaking through the town to the large white building signifying its end. Kunchen managed to park the truck among numerous bony cows.

"It's just around the corner, Kat!" he called out. His body convulsed in laughter as I tossed my bike on the ground beside him. "Kathmandu, that way! It's just there around the corner!"

I scooped him into a big hug and said goodbye.

Nepal was a million times busier and wetter than Tibet. Instantly, the roads were narrower. There were more buses, cars and people – even in the country. There were water buffalo and lush green terraces scrambling up the hillsides. Colours were vibrant with flowers thriving everywhere. I inhaled. At the lower altitude, each breath felt like a revelation, something I had nearly forgotten could be effortless.

We continued down the road until we arrived in a town called Dolalghat. The ride had taken most of the day and we were hungry. We found a bank and then a room with a rooftop terrace where I left Mike to watch the town bustle below. Street food was plentiful and I meandered among the distinctive smells of dhal bhat, garam masala, cumin and turmeric. My stomach did a flip when I saw chicken curries and spicy fried cauliflower. There was so much choice I didn't know what to choose. Then I saw a man making samosas.

"*Kati*?" (how much?), I asked, testing my Nepali for the first time. He told me the answer in rupees. I didn't know the numbers yet, so I handed him the equivalent of one dollar. He began to fill a bag with big, greasy samosas. My eyes bulged as I counted while he kept going. I ran back to our room.

"Mike! Mike! Boys!" I ran up the stairs yelling. "We can buy ten samosas for a dollar!" We split open the bag, shared the delicious snack and headed back outside for more.

After we rode into Kathmandu, the week consisted of eating, shopping and yoga. I bought an unlimited pass to a hot yoga studio and twice a day I sweated, purified and contemplated our life. We didn't move from the city. Before and after yoga, I stared at maps, willing the next road to present itself. None did. It was a strange feeling to not feel done with travelling but not to crave somewhere new. So we stayed put.

One by one, we said goodbye to our friends. Billy was off, back to work with Cirque du Soleil. Nathan headed to New Zealand, already ready for another adventure. And Bob went home to the Netherlands to dream up more wild trips. Elise had flown to Kathmandu to be with Zach and we hugged them both, knowing we'd see them again somewhere. We'd been so lucky to travel together.

One evening after yoga, Mike and I sat on the lumpy bed in our room, above the noisy streets of Kathmandu, and dialed my mom on Skype. When she appeared on the screen, we did our usual of letting tears flow down our cheeks and beaming ridiculously. My niece and nephew crawled up onto her lap. It was my niece Isabelle who spoke first. Her little voice shocked me. When we left, she hadn't been talking yet.

"Hi, Aunty Kat. Hi, Uncle Mike." My heart burst into a million pieces. Moments from our long trip flashed through my mind: the hike up Angels Landing, strolling through the ruins of Angkor Wat, throwing water at Songkran, biking in Ho Chi Minh City. But I had never felt further from home than I did sitting in that Kathmandu hostel.

I closed the laptop and ran my hand along its cover.

"It's Thanksgiving next week," Mike said. I looked up at him. His blue eyes fixed on mine. After a minute, he wrapped his arm over my shoulders and I leaned into his chest.

"Want to go home?"

I nodded yes. All my resistance to going home crumbled when my niece said those six little words: "Hi, Aunty Kat. Hi, Uncle Mike." It had tied us together, and tied us to home.

"Yes," I finally said. *"Yes, I do."*

Moonlight flooded through the small plane window. I felt like I was the only one still awake. My hand was tightly woven into Mike's as he slept. I, of course, couldn't stop thinking. I was excited about going home now. We had chosen to arrive when many of our family members were getting together for dinner, and I visualized us walking into the foyer, hugging everyone we missed so much.

I began to see our future. Mike taking care of me by plugging in my toothbrush before it died, changing over my vehicle and bikes to winter tires. I would pretend to not know how to fill up the salt and pepper shakers. I'd make him coffee, fold his clothes and map out more adventures.

What I couldn't visualize were the surprises. How our flirting would change. How our attraction to each other would adjust and adapt. How we'd grow older and redefine who we are, both individually and as a couple.

We walked off the airplane still holding hands. Nerves and excitement danced around us both. We hadn't told anyone we were coming home. We yanked our cardboard bike boxes across the floor and began putting the bikes together (somewhat expertly) in the corner. The panniers were holey and held together with duct tape. The frames of the bikes were chipped and battered but as reliable as ever. Our handlebar foam was compressed with palm prints and our seats were molded to the shape of our bottoms.

"Where are you from?" An elderly man came up to us, curious about our lives and our trip. I imagined he could smell the dust and sweat embedded in our clothes. "Where are you going?"

"Wolseley," Mike smirked. "Wolseley and Wolseley."

For the last few days, I'd been trying to think of a witty one-liner. A response for when someone asked me, "How was your trip?" I'd say, "Well, it was 13,000 kilometres in 13 months," or "It was 54 flat tires," or "It was a great way to eat as much as you want."

But it was so much more than that. I wanted to be able to explain that it was *everything.* "Welcome home," the man said. I caught the twinkle in his eye as if he totally understood what being home meant to us.

It was October and evening was upon us. We turned our lights on. It was a 30-minute pedal from the airport and we knew we had timed everything perfectly.

Our tires whirred past the shop where I had worked with Alex. It was dark inside. Closed for the night. Closed for good as far as I was concerned. I kept pedalling.

I thought about how Mike and I now had the resources to pull us back together whenever we'd feel our connection slipping. Perhaps, I grinned, we'd go on another big cycle tour.

This trip was not an epic bike ride. We didn't surpass major obstacles other than our own. We had not ridden where no one else had ridden before, or covered an obscene amount of kilometres. There were no firsts about this bike trip, actually, but it was ours. And it was awesome.

And then we were on Wolseley Avenue. Massive elm trees lined the way to our finish line. We stopped on the front grass outside the large window looking into my parents' dining room. My mom and dad, along with my grandparents, my sister's family, and my aunty, were in the middle of dinner. They all sat in the same spots as usual, still spaces for Mike and me. We watched them all in silence. In the morning we would go surprise Mike's parents. We had gone full circle. We had completed the trip and flourished. We did it together.

"Thank you for biking with me, Mike," I whispered. Mike reached in for a long hug and, when we pulled back, we both smiled. We smiled like fools, like we were on our first date.

"Ready, hon?" Mike asked me.

"Ready," I replied. I was so ready. Ready for the next part of the journey with my husband.

We opened the door.

ACKNOWLEDGEMENTS

Writing this book was more challenging than being lost for nights on end in the wild, without food or water, without a path. There were times when I wanted to toss its entirety into a bonfire, but invariably my support crew would come to the rescue and revive it from the ashes. Releasing this book has been the most daunting journey I've set out on. I'd never have been brave enough were it not for the encouragement and endless help from family and friends.

Mom and Dad, I was lucky to have you as incredible mentors who showed me what a great relationship looked like. You may have wished for an easier expedition for me and my marriage, and perhaps you would have preferred that I didn't write a book about it! But thank you for your support regardless and for loving me completely. To my sister, Michelle Brito, who let me read to her, over and over again, the truly crappiest first drafts. Who, over the years (too many years), never failed to exclaim, "Aren't you done yet?" Thank you for always listening to me, believing in this story and for being there even when I was spending so much time writing.

To Kathryn McDonald, oh those poor licking whales that got cut! Please forgive me for all the Oxford commas that snuck their way back into the manuscript. No amount of chocolate or champagne in the world can amount to the help you gave me. Heartfelt thanks to all those who read portions of this book and provided feedback: Eileen Rosen, Jenn Rowley, Wilma Wetluck, Michael Anderson, Gavin Harmacy, Tara Newbigging, Eleasha Sabourin, Leigh Woltman, Deborah Skelton, Reinira Lankhuijzen, Jennifer Laing and Jennifer Kitchen.

To my Monday night writing group: Sharon Wood, Wilma Rubens, Cori Brewster, Johanne Lortie, Barbara Parker and Erica Armstrong. Seriously. You made me better. At times, I even felt brilliant. Cheers for 15-minute free writes! To the gifted RMB authors who gave me advice: Ryan Correy, Helen Rolfe, Jocey Asnong, Jamey Glasnovic and Lynn Martel. Thank you.

Thank you to all the Warmshowers and Couchsurfers hosts and everyone who fed Mike and me, brought us home and showed that there is so much love and generosity in the world. There are a number of individuals who didn't make the final cut of the book; please know you are important to us and we were happy to have shared this journey with you.

Jack Burns and Cristi Frittaion, the first two to read the manuscript like a book: your comments gave me the strength I needed to press *send*. Thank you. This book is so much better (and funnier) with the expertise of Megan Dunn. Get ready, Megan! The next book will have lots of maps for you to draw. Melanie Birch and Tracy Laval, thank you for reading chapters and allowing me to always bring our conversations back to *With You by Bike*. I'm so lucky to have you in my life.

My first amazing editor, Tyler Pearce, knew and understood every word that needed to be pulled out of me. Tyler, you managed to make sure the story was complete and truthful, and that it read well. Don Gorman, Kirsten Craven and the Rocky Mountain Books team, thank you for taking me on and for making beautiful books. Any remaining mistakes are mine, of course.

To our son, Zion, I'll always cherish those early mornings when you cuddled in my lap, drawing pictures in my notebooks while I pecked away at the keyboard. Thank you for letting me read chapters to you as bedtime stories and thank you for being so amazing. I love you so much.

Finally, to my husband Mike. Thank you for encouraging me to tell our story and for inspiring me to be valiant, like you. It was only because you were with me 100 per cent that I was able to write. This is for us. "I do," and I'm all in. After 23 years, I look forward to many more adventures together.

ABOUT THE AUTHOR

Katrina Rosen loves the outdoors. She and her husband Mike have raised their son to believe it's entirely normal to sleep in huts and tents as often as your own bed, and to spend as much time as possible biking, skiing, hiking and playing. Eager to share her passions and inspire others, Katrina works as a guide in the Rocky Mountains, opening up her guests' minds to the forgotten possibilities in life. When she's not roaming through the wilderness or competing in ridiculously long races, she can be found curled up by a fire with a cup of coffee, staring over maps and dreaming up adventures. Katrina lives in Canmore, Alberta, with her family. Find out more at www.katrinatheexplorer.com or on Instagram (@katrinatheexplorer).